SOUTH AFRICA
THE SOLUTION

SOUTH AFRICA

THE
SOLUTION

LEON LOUW & FRANCES KENDALL

FOREWORD BY SAM MOTSUENYANE

AMAGI PUBLICATIONS

AMAGI PUBLICATIONS (PVT) LTD
P O Box 60, Bisho, Ciskei,
P O Box 92385 Norwood 2117 (S A Representative)

First published March 1986
2nd Impression June 1986
Revised edition November 1986
Cover concept by Gill Marshall
Cover illustration by Bernie DeHaas
Maps and Figures by Aubrey Lamour
Cartoons by Walter Pichler

© Frances Kendall Louw and Leon Louw, 1986

ISBN No 0-620-09371-4

Typeset, printed, and bound by The Natal Witness (Pty) Ltd.
Cover colour separations by Photoscan (Pty) Ltd., Johannesburg.

To the future of South Africa

Contents

Part three: The solution

Maps

Figures

Charts

Cartoons

Acknowledgements

This book is the culmination of many years of research, study, thought and debate, and reflects the influence of many great thinkers, the most important of whom are Ludwig von Mises, Friedrich A Hayek and Murray Rothbard.

Our first thanks go to Charles Koch, who persuaded Leon to embark on this book, and helped make it possible through his financial support; also to the Manhattan Institute (USA) for its generosity.

In our immediate circle of friends we are indebted to Eustace Davie, Libby Husemeyer, Graeme Levin, Terry Markman and Michael O'Dowd for comments, insights and ideas.

We thank Loraine Harris for her tireless efforts to produce a perfect manuscript, Joan Evans and Riana de Beer for their fortitude in the face of mountains of typing, and Roger van Niekerk for finding facts and figures at short notice.

Libby Husemeyer did the editing and proof-reading, and Graeme Levin ensured that the book was printed and distributed in double-quick time.

Our daughters, Justine, Camilla and Kate, cheerfully put up with very little attention for three and a half months.

Finally, we congratulate each other for managing to preserve our marriage and our sanity under conditions of extreme stress!

Foreword

At a time when SA is embroiled in a frantic search for an effective panacea to what the world has come to regard as one of the most vicious and morally indefensible political systems now in existence, the policy of apartheid, it is quite refreshing, hope-inspiring and stimulating to stumble across two young South Africans who, as husband and wife, could come forward to offer the country a solution.

It is indeed an extremely rare occurrence to find a husband and wife who are so happily married and so intellectually intimate as to attempt to write a book together. The fact that Leon and Frances have finally succeeded in completing their manuscript is a tremendous testimony of their dedication to the course of searching for a way towards a new South Africa of the future.

Reading through the 20 chapters of their book, *South Africa: the Solution*, was for me an absolute delight, not only because I agree with most of the positive ideas they have so clearly enunciated but more because they have unearthed a great amount of forgotten information about blacks and whites in our country that have for many years remained hidden in the pages of our history.

Despite the racial conflicts which have torn our country apart these days, it is heartening to get a positive picture about the past when the spirit of entrepreneurship, both amongst the black and the white people, persisted in a climate of greater freedom that made our country the great economic power it became on the southern tip of the African continent.

What is most important and encouraging in "The Solution" is how the couple speculates and dreams about the realisation of a united and prosperous South African nation of the future. They foresee that South Africa can achieve freedom for all its people in a federal system and under a constitution which contains a Bill of Rights securing the rights of all individuals.

The great problem which lies ahead of our country is surely not a lack of ideas and visions among the people of South Africa. Our most crucial challenge will remain the implementation of such bright ideas and visions. As for dreamers, we have galore, but it is the implementers who are few.

My fervent wish is that "The Solution" be read with interest, digested with enthusiasm and implemented with courage.

To Leon and Frances go my sincere congratulations. And I firmly hope that they shall make another effort at formulating a new strategy for determining how their "solution" can be put into effect in the corridors of power inside our troubled country.

SAMUEL MOKGETHI MOTSUENYANE.
President, National African Federated
Chambers of Commerce (NAFCOC)

Introduction

'We believe that the human dignity, life, liberty and property of all must be protected, regardless of colour, race, creed or religion.' These words were spoken by the State President, Mr P W Botha, at the opening of Parliament on 31 January 1986. He stressed that the government is committed to one citizenship for all South Africans within an undivided country, and to a democratic form of government in which all citizens will participate through their elected representatives. He emphasised that there will be equality before the law, and protection of individual and minority rights.

These words were welcomed by people far and wide, but the question remains in many minds — can they ever be translated into reality in this deeply divided country?

The answer to this question is yes. And the purpose of this book is not only to show that South Africans can have a free and just society, but also to provide an explicit and detailed blueprint of how it can be achieved.

Part One of the book examines some of the important historical factors which led to the present predicament, while Part Two analyses current political and economic circumstances which any viable solution must take into consideration. Part Three provides a comprehensive description of the political, economic and legal systems which are necessary to achieve individual freedom, the rule of law, maximum participation in government and protection for minorities.

We believe that South Africa will not be completely at peace until all references to ethnicity and race have been removed from the statute books. The system we propose is 'colour-blind', but it ensures that no one interest group can dominate another.

While we are fully committed to the free market ideology, the canton system advocated in this book allows almost the entire spectrum of economic systems to function side by side. Readers who disagree with our analysis of history and the status quo, and with our unconcealed libertarian persuasion, should still find our proposed constitutional model completely acceptable. Its strength lies precisely in its ability to accommodate a wide variety of apparently irreconcilable political, economic and social systems.

The time has come for us to work together to make South Africa the freest and most just nation on earth and to show the world that strength lies in diversity.

PART ONE
The history

History ought to judge the past and to instruct the contemporary world as to the future.

Leopold von Ranke

Part One is a brief survey of key aspects of South Africa's history. It aims on the one hand to dispel certain prevalent myths and on the other to reveal little-known facts which are critical in determining a solution for South Africa's problems. These chapters highlight the sequence of events which led to the current impasse. In doing so they focus primarily on South Africa's two most important groups, the blacks and the Afrikaners.

1 Black South Africans: Their rise and fall

But if the men of the future are ever to break the chains of the present they will have to understand the forces that forged them.

Barrington Moore Jr

When black South Africans first came into contact with the market economy of the nineteenth century, they responded so enthusiastically that within a few decades they were extremely successful farmers, transport riders, artisans and traders.

Today, few people are aware of these achievements and the general view is that blacks are naturally poor agriculturalists who lack enterprise. It is also commonly accepted that black tribal systems are fundamentally socialist. However, an examination of southern African tribes reveals political and economic systems based on individual freedom and private property rights, with considerable differences in levels of wealth and social status. Indeed, the political systems of most of the black tribes during South Africa's early history were similar in many respects to the canton system which we propose for South Africa, and which some might say is feasible only in a highly developed society.

The freedom which characterised tribal society in part explains why blacks responded so positively to the challenges of a free market that by the 1870s they were outcompeting whites — especially as farmers.

Their success had tragic consequences. White colonists feared black competition, and this fear, combined with their desire for cheap labour, resulted in a series of laws which systematically denied blacks all access to the market place and stripped them of any meaningful form of land ownership.

This appalling sequence of events set the tone for a century of racial socialism which led to the apparent deadlock we face today.

3

TRIBAL SOCIETY : A SYSTEM OF VOLUNTARY EXCHANGE AND PRIVATE OWNERSHIP

When the first white settlers arrived in the Cape in 1652, it was occupied by the yellow-skinned Khoikhoi (Hottentots) and the San (Bushmen), and further north and east by the Cape or Southern Nguni.

The Cape Nguni occupied a broad swath of territory between the Indian Ocean and the mountain ranges lying roughly parallel to the coast (the Winterberg, Stormberg and Drakensberg) bounded in the north by the Mzimkulu River and in the south by the Fish River. This is present-day Ciskei, Border Region and Transkei.

Nguni is a generic term for black-skinned people sharing a similar language structure. It includes a large number of groups and sub-groups. In the Cape there are the Xhosa, the Thembu and the Mbo and later immigrant groups such as the Mfengu. Notable among the Nguni further north are the Zulu and the Dlamini, who occupy KwaZulu and Swaziland respectively.

This chapter concentrates on the Cape Nguni because we have more detailed records of their history than of any of the other tribes. However, the political and economic systems of the other Nguni tribes and of the Sothos, Vendas and Tsongas — the peoples to the north of the Nguni with different languages and customs — although very different in detail, were similar in their fundamental structure.

Early economy

The Nguni people were hunters and cultivators as well as herders, but they were chiefly herdsmen, and in Nguni society cattle were wealth and a medium of exchange. The men and boys who cared for the cattle were experts, with a loving and detailed knowledge of animal husbandry.

Women cultivated the land and the traditional crops were sorghum, pumpkins, calabashes and melons, a type of bean and the coco yam.

All adult males were allotted a residential plot and land for cultivation, with a degree of security of tenure that surpasses that of the modern western freehold tradition. As long as land was not in short supply there was 'commonage' (common grazing land), but this also was subject to allotment or privately held grazing rights during times when land became a scarce resource. Land allotments were made by chiefs-in-council, or headmen-in-council. There were sophisticated procedures, traditions and laws relating to allocation, inheritance and transfer after initial allotment.

4

Political and social structure

The Nguni lived in scattered homesteads. Among commoners these were composed of two to forty huts. A chief's homestead was usually larger, with around fifty huts or more.

Each homestead was occupied by a man with his wives, his unmarried daughters, his sons and their families and poor people who attached themselves to the headman through voluntary vassalage. By serving him, they gained access to his cattle and grazing lands. They looked to him for advice and guidance and a homestead increased in size according to its headman's reputation as a man of judgement and equity, and his generosity to people poorer than himself.

The homestead of the chief inevitably attracted more unrelated men than those of the commoners.

The social structure, linked closely to the economic structure, was flexible and dynamic, with homesteads splitting from time to time, and near kinsmen building in the same neighbourhood to form a loose grouping with senior kinsmen.

A number of local homesteads or communities made up a village under the leadership of a headman. A group of villages in turn formed a chiefdom. Again the size of chiefdoms differed considerably, fluctuating and splitting to coalesce under popular leaders.

In any local area one clan (i.e. people all descended from a common ancestor) predominated. In any chiefdom, the chief's clan enjoyed the greatest prestige. But neither in local areas nor in chiefdoms was there any exclusivity regarding clans.

A chiefdom was a political unit occupying a defined area under an independent chief. These were sometimes subdivided under subordinate leaders. For example, in 1809 the Xhosa chief Hintsa had 10 000 followers and eleven sub-chiefs.

In addition to the poor people who attached themselves to headmen or chiefs, there was a system of clientship whereby a poor man would be loaned cattle by a wealthy community leader or chief. He herded these cattle and drank their milk, and received some of their offspring. In exchange, he assisted his benefactor in building or fencing, or attended him in a court case or in war.

The influence of each Nguni chief depended on the number of his followers and he was therefore constantly competing with his half-brothers and neighbouring chiefs for new supporters.

Van der Kemp, the first missionary to the Nguni, reported in 1800 of the Xhosa chief Ngqika:

'He has counsellors who inform him of the sentiments of his people, and his captains admonish him with great freedom and fidelity, when he abuses his authority to such a degree, that there is reason to fear that the nation will show him their displeasure. This is done if he treats the admonition with contempt, not by way of insurrection, or taking up arms against him, but most effectually, by gradual emigration. Some kraals break up, and march towards the borders of the country... they are successively followed by others, and this seldom fails to have the effect wished for...'[1]

Van der Kemp saw this process in action when Ngqika introduced two laws — one forbidding a man with an unfaithful wife to take the life of her seducer, and another making the chief heir to all his subjects who died without heirs in their direct line. Ngqika was forced to retract both these laws when his people demonstrated their disapproval by leaving. The law prohibiting revenge on a seducer was subsequently reinstated after thorough consideration. The other was not.

Followers were obliged to submit all disputes to their chief for judgement. If the chief felt that his own judgement was not competent in a given case, he would refer the parties concerned to an older and more experienced chief. People also had the right to appeal judgements in the court of a superior chief.

Hearings were usually held in open court. Proceedings were sophisticated, with ample opportunity for the arguments of all parties to be led. Tribal courts are based on these traditions to this day.

The followers of a chief attended his council, fought for him when called upon, and paid him death duties and fines. The wealthiest men in the chiefdom had the greatest influence at the councils, where all matters were subject to lengthy discussion (or Indaba) by all the adult men. Decisions were usually based on unanimity so government was by consensus. On the rare occasions when unanimity was not achieved, majority rule was invoked.

In the extended family there was a traditional voluntary welfare system whereby old and sick people were cared for by the clan.

Trade

Until the end of the eighteenth century few political and economic pressures were exerted on the Nguni by the Dutch people living in the Cape Colony. There were frequent skirmishes between the Nguni and the trekboers (Dutch farmers) on the eastern frontier of the Cape, and a fair amount of trading and social interaction took place, but the basic structure of the Nguni economy remained unchanged.

When the British took over the Cape Colony at the turn of the century, however, matters began to change. Where previous governments had tried to prevent interaction between colonists and Xhosas and had failed, the British sought to regulate it.

In 1817 they established a bi-annual trade fair at Grahamstown which the Xhosa were permitted to attend. By 1824 trade fairs were being held three times a week at Fort Willshire; this meant that Xhosas were entering the Cape Colony on a regular and legal basis.

In 1829, an ordinance (Ordinance 49) was passed which formally allowed the Xhosa to cross the frontier to seek employment or attend trade fairs. In order to do this, however, the Xhosas had to carry a pass. This system was introduced for two reasons: on the one hand, the Cape government didn't want to prevent the influx of blacks because Cape farmers badly needed labourers, but on the other hand they did want to control it because more and more black refugees were moving south as a result of conquests by the powerful Zulus.

While trade at Fort Willshire continued to grow, so did the number of Xhosa poaching raids into white farms. Homesteads were burned, stock stolen, and in retaliation white farmers led punitive expeditions into Xhosa territory.

Many different policies were adopted by successive British governments in an attempt to end the warfare on the Eastern Front. One of these proposed the establishment of a 'buffer zone' — an unoccupied strip of 'neutral territory' — between the colonists and the Xhosas. Another recommended the creation of a dense band of settlement along the frontier to discourage Xhosa raids. One of the settlements created for this purpose was that of the Mfengu.

The Mfengu — natural entrepreneurs

In 1835, 16 000 Mfengu with 22 000 head of cattle formally entered the Cape Colony at Governor D'Urban's bidding and were settled in the Peddie district. The Mfengu were Natal blacks who had been displaced by the rise of the Zulu Kingdom, and D'Urban was perfectly candid about his reasons for importing them:

'The "Fingo community" would supply military support against Mintza, the Xhosa paramount chief; the colony would gain the labour of "sober, industrious people, well skilled in the tasks of herding and agriculture"; the land in the Peddie district to which they were moved was "worse than useless", but, he confidently expected, would be turned into a "flourishing garden" by the newcomers'.[2]

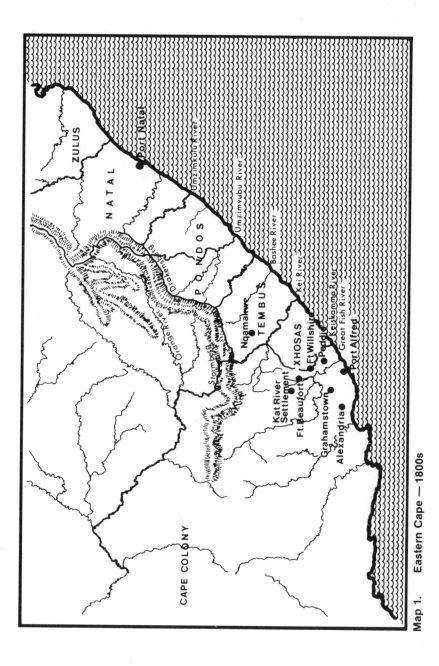

Map 1.   Eastern Cape — 1800s

8

The reason was, as mentioned, to provide a human buffer between the colonists and the Xhosa in the area which is now the Border Region.

The Mfengu responded spectacularly to the opportunities and incentives of the market economy. On arrival in Peddie, they entered agricultural service as cattle herders and shepherds, and were engaged in tilling, ploughing and reaping. But they very soon put their new-found skills to use on their own behalf.

They used their wages to invest in sheep, wagons and tools, and were rewarded with land for fighting in the Cape Army.

They also formed a close association with Methodist missionaries who keenly favoured the spread of black agriculture and who provided training and encouragement. The doyen of South African missionaries, the Reverend John Philip, argued that if the blacks were allowed to accumulate and develop land they would be peacefully integrated into the colonial economy. He called for a laissez faire policy toward the Khoikhoi and the Xhosa and Mfengu, saying that it would make them more productive farmers. He also maintained that the abolition of slavery would improve, not worsen, the labour market. He put the case (as this book does) for a work-force freed from government intervention and regulated only by market forces.

So the Mfengu could be found, not only farming their own land, but also working on smallholdings on mission stations, and before long they were engaged in trade and transport too. By the 1840s and '50s they were selling tobacco, firewood, cattle and milk, and disposing of surplus grain for cash or stock.

At this time the Mfengu, the Hottentots and coloureds who had settled at Kat River were making the most rapid advances in peasant agriculture. However, other very successful farming activities, also encouraged by the missionaries, were underway elsewhere in the Eastern Cape. By the end of the century, the Thembu in the Transkei rivalled the Mfengu as farmers and landowners.

In 1858, Governor George Grey issued a proclamation permitting blacks to buy grain land at £1 (R20 ±) per acre [3]. By 1864, 508 blacks had bought 16 200 acres, while a further 106 rented 6 000 acres from the government. A large number of blacks (squatters) also leased land from white farmers in exchange for labour, cash or produce. By the 1870s, black farmers in the Eastern Cape were extremely active and prosperous. The Mfengu competed against white farmers at agricultural shows and won many prizes.

A Wesleyan missionary, Mr Davis, told the 1865 Commission on Native Affairs: 'Even this year (after the drought) I think their exhibition far surpassed that of the Europeans. It was a universal remark in the district that the Fingo exhibition far excelled that of the Europeans both as to number and quality of the articles exhibited'.[4]

A Cape statistician noted: 'Taking everything into consideration, the native district of Peddie surpasses the European district of Albany in its productive powers'.[5]

In the Transkei, a black community raised £4 500 (R90 000 ±) in three years to build a school in Blythswood, and contributed £2 000 (R40 000 ±) towards roads and bridges through the territory. Headmen attended the opening of the bridge over the Kei to demonstrate their appreciation of improved transport facilities.

A feature of the 1870s was the increased use of ploughs and wagons and the development of a flourishing group of black transport riders. Many farmers turned to transport riding once their crops had been harvested.

There were also 'master tradesmen . . . in constant work (with) apprentices', artisans, contractors and builders. Commentators of the time described the blacks as 'very industrious', 'very thrifty', 'greatly progressing', with 'a desire to have their children educated'. It was observed that 'freedom from restraint is a ruling passion in them'.[6]

During this period, the purchasing power of blacks in the Eastern Cape exceeded £400 000 (R8 million) a year. Exports were many and varied, including angora hair, hides, horns, goat and sheep skins, tobacco, grain and cattle valued at £750 000 (R15 million) per annum.

A missionary in the Thembu area described the local shops:

'Now things are very different and every shop has some kind of European clothing . . . Yes, and not ordinary apparel such as *coats, trousers, boots,* stuff for making ordinary *dresses,* but often you will find a shop as well supplied in the heart of Kaffirland as in many a shop in the Colony . . . *soap, candles, tea, coffee, cocoa* and *sugar,* blue starch, ladies' kid boots, ready-made mantles, shawls, bonnets and hats (ready trimmed). All these sorts of things are to be purchased in the kaffir traders' shops. Also *scents, scented soaps, jewellery, etc.'*[7]

The black farmers were becoming extremely diversified in their produce: ' . . . at an agricultural show held in Nqamakwe, Fingoland, in 1880, prizes were awarded for wheat, barley, oats, potatoes, sweet potatoes, forage, maize, sorghum, tobacco, cabbages, turnips, beetroot, wool, bread, butter, dried fruit, cheese, bacon, ham and handicrafts'.[8]

By 1890 there were many progressive black commercial farmers who had purchased their farms outright. They invested much of their profits in fences, walls, irrigation and improved stock breeds, and adopted the most advanced farming methods of the time. They lived in brick houses (built by Europeans) and stocked them with furniture, crockery, cutlery, stationery and so on. They sent their children to multiracial boarding schools and employed labourers and leased portions of their land. They were the mainstay of agricultural societies and associations, owning farms of up to 1 710 morgen (±3 600 acres).

For example, there was Sol Kalipa who owned 120 cattle, 20 horses, 500 sheep and goats, two wagons and three ploughs.

By 1890 there were between one and two thousand of these affluent black commercial farmers. Now, one hundred years later, you will have difficulty finding even one.

What went wrong?

In the district of Herschel in the north-eastern corner of the Cape, as elsewhere, a healthy black farming community developed in the nineteenth century. In 1873, over and above their own requirements, they produced 1 000 bales of wool, 6 000 bags of wheat and 30 000 bags of 'kaffir corn' and mealies . In 1875, the blacks offered £2 000 (R40 000 ±) towards building a school.

Yet in the 1940s a Franciscan priest, Cosmas Desmond, touring the district described Herschel as follows: 'A lot of the area is mountainous and most of the rest is badly eroded, so there is not much left for cultivation... There is virtually no work in the whole area... All forms of malnutrition are obviously a problem throughout the Reserve.'[9]

In the Keiskama River valley, productivity is lower now, despite a R20 million government-funded irrigation scheme and heavy subsidies, than it was in the 1870s.

Where once black farmers took with alacrity to the market economy, western technology, literacy and the use of money, and competed as equals with immigrant farmers from Germany and England, there is now poverty, malnutrition and stagnation. Where whites were once dazzled by black entrepreneurship, they now look disparagingly at blacks, and pronounce them inherently bad farmers and poor entrepreneurs.

What went wrong? Why did blacks do so well in the Eastern Cape, and indeed throughout South Africa, in the nineteenth century and fail so badly in the twentieth century?

Have blacks retrogressed over the past 100 years? Have agricultural and climatic conditions deteriorated? No — the answer lies in changes which occurred in their economic and political conditions. Until the last two decades of the nineteenth century, blacks enjoyed a considerable degree of economic freedom; in this century they have been allowed almost none. How did this come about?

The truth was that white farmers felt threatened by blacks. Not only were the blacks better farmers but they were also competing with white farmers for land. Moreover, they were self-sufficient and hence not available to work on white farms or in industry — particularly in the Transvaal gold mines where their labour was badly needed. As a result, a series of laws was passed which robbed blacks of almost all economic freedom. The specific and stated purpose of these laws was to prevent blacks from competing with whites and to force them into the work-force. This was the beginning of the 'black socialism' which exists throughout South Africa today.

A people dispossessed

During the nineteenth century white expansion and black migration increased the demand for land and the eastern boundary of the Cape Colony moved further and further eastward. The areas allotted to blacks became smaller and smaller.

We have seen that by the 1870s blacks had purchased or been granted crown land as well as land in locations and in mission reserves. Many of them also leased land from white farmers in exchange for cash or labour.

During this period, white landowners were experiencing a severe shortage of labour. The blacks and Hottentots preferred self-employment, or working for higher wages in the towns, to being agricultural labourers.

In order to 'remedy the evil' the Cape Assembly passed a series of Location Acts in 1869, 1876, and 1884 to reduce the number of 'squatters' on white-owned lands. These 'idle squatters' were the black farmers we have mentioned, who rented land from white farmers and developed it for themselves. The purpose of the legislation was to prevent them from being self-sufficient so that they would be forced to become wage labourers.

However, many white farmers were perfectly happy to lease land to blacks in exchange for labour, so the anti-squatter legislation was largely evaded and the shortage of labour continued.

In 1893 the Cape Labour Commission was appointed to look into the matter. When the commissioners asked why there was a labour shortage they were told: 'The natives are independent. They have land and grow what they choose, and their wants are extremely small'; in Alice, a white farmer said that the blacks 'seem to be able to raise sheep here, the Europeans not'; in Alexandria and Stutterheim 'the native can live

12

by agriculture, but not the white man'; in Port Alfred they were told: 'Europeans cannot compete with natives. The labour kills them.'[10]

The rise of the gold and diamond mining, transport, construction and service industries throughout South Africa increased the need and competition for cheap labour.

Mine owners knew there would be no cheap labour as long as blacks had access to land. In 1911 the President of the Chamber of Mines in Johannesburg explained: 'He (the black) cares nothing if industries pine for want of labour when his crops and home-brewed drink are plentiful'. He called for a policy to force blacks into the labour force and urged the government to 'do everything to encourage the native to be a wage earner by extending the policy of splitting into family holdings land now held in the native reserves under tribal tenure'.[11]

Thus both white farmers and mine owners realised that the black man's independence had to be broken if he was to supply their labour requirements. The colonial government was ready and willing to help them and a series of laws was introduced to achieve their ends thoroughly and systematically.

Act 33 of 1892 put the onus on the white farmer to register blacks on his farm. The number of blacks living on his farm and not earning a wage (tenants) was limited. If that number was exceeded he had to pay a fine. As a direct consequence of this Act a number of black 'squatters' were turned off the land and suffered great losses of stock, homes, cultivated fields and other possessions. However, as in the case of the Location Acts, Act 33 was widely evaded.

In 1894, the Glen Grey Act drawn up by Cape Premier Cecil Rhodes became law. This Act was popular amongst socialists because it provided for individual land tenure in black reserves on the basis of equal distribution. It did this by splitting the reserves into agricultural holdings of ten acres each. No man was allowed to own more than one lot.

The aim of the Act was, on the one hand, to make the reserves self-supporting and, on the other, to boost the labour supply. The government was well aware that ten acres of poor land could not provide for the needs of one family, and that most of the men would be forced out of the reserves onto the labour market.

In addition, the ten-acre limitation prevented black farmers from competing with whites as it made it impossible for any black farmer to expand his holdings. Black commercial farmers were well aware of this, and strongly protested the violation of their property rights. Charles Pamla, one of the most influential black spokesmen, observed: 'No man is allowed to occupy more than *one* lot. This shuts out all improvements and industry of some individuals who may work and buy ... surely Mr

13

Rhodes can't expect that all natives will be equal. He himself is richer than others; even trees differ in height'.[12]

Further anti-squatting legislation was introduced. Act 30 of 1899 permitted whites to employ any number of blacks and made them buy licences costing £36 (R720±) per annum before they could lease land to blacks. The cost of the licences was passed on to the blacks in the form of prohibitively high rents.

Despite all these laws, many white farmers continued to rent land to blacks illegally, so Act 32 of 1909 was passed. This raised licence fees and tightened the definition of bona fide labourers.

Eventually all these laws achieved their ends. Share-croppers (blacks farming white land and sharing the produce) and lessees were evicted. Black farmers became wage labourers. Many of those forced off white land moved to the black reserves, where competition for the ten acre plots increased drastically.

When John X Merriman, head of the South African Party in the Cape, was asked if he would drive blacks onto white farms as labourers, he replied: 'I would not drive them, but they will drive themselves when they get congested in land held under individual tenure'.[13]

Finally came the notorious Native Land Act of 1913 which demarcated 8% of South Africa's surface area as 'Native Reserves'. Blacks were forbidden to buy land in white areas (the remaining 92%) and whites were prohibited from buying land in the reserves (where the blacks had the limited title described above). In addition, share-cropping and the renting of white farm land by blacks was forbidden. Only bona fide black farm labourers could live on white farms. (The 1913 Native Land Act is discussed in more detail in the next chapter.)

White farmers who had previously evaded anti-squatter legislation were eventually seduced into accepting the laws aimed at driving blacks into the reserves and into wage labour by a massive programme of subsidies, grants and other aid. This took the form of assistance for fencing, dams and houses, as well as generous rail rates, special credit facilities and bountiful tax relief.

In 1908 an economist, F.B. Smith, remarked: 'It is probable that during the last twenty years more money per head of the rural population has been devoted to the relief of farmers in South Africa than any country in the world'.[14]

A number of other factors penalised black farmers. Railways and good roads did not run into the black areas, so it was difficult and expensive to transport goods to markets. They had to sell their produce to licensed white traders in the reserves. Because these traders were granted a monopoly for an area of five miles radius, they were able to charge ±20% more than market prices whilst buying from the black farmers at well below market price.

After an epidemic of East Coast Fever (a cattle disease) black farmers were allowed to sell their cattle only to white traders with government concessions. Again, the traders' response to their monopoly was to offer well below market prices for the stock. Inevitably, this encouraged overstocking. Overcrowding on the small plots prevented rotational grazing and hastened soil erosion.

People soon forgot the impressive achievements of blacks prior to the turn of the century, and it became conventional wisdom that 'blacks are bad farmers', 'blacks lack motivation' and 'blacks are not entrepreneurs'. Throughout South Africa, the history of blacks followed a pattern depressingly similar to that of the Cape. We will deal with other areas only very briefly here.

Natal

The *Natal Witness* of 1 April 1870 reported: 'Perhaps the most striking feature in the Kaffir character is his energy and industry as a farmer. The thousands of acres that have been ploughed up by Kaffirs, and the hundreds of wagons they possess, are conclusive proof of their readiness and fitness to become agriculturists.'[15]

In 1880 regulations were passed allowing the sale of land to blacks and in the following decade blacks bought 67 077 acres for £36 412 (R720 800±). Between January 1890 and July 1891, they bought a further 56 000 acres for £34 000 (R680 000±).

But between 1890 and 1910, with the rising demand for agricultural products on the gold fields, railway lines were built to serve white farming areas. Also, white farmers were subsidised in many ways through the Agricultural Development Acts of 1904 and 1907.

With the help of these subsidies, the value of white farmland rose and it became less rewarding to let land to blacks who received no subsidies. White landowners no longer needed black tenants, so rents were pushed up. Marginal black tenants left the land spontaneously. Those blacks who had no binding contracts or title deeds were simply evicted. Even where this did not happen, blacks were afraid to make improvements because of the uncertainty of their tenure.

A number of levies and fees were imposed on blacks with the result that they paid a higher percentage of their income than whites in taxes. The 1913 Land Act brought all these pressures to a logical conclusion. Commercial tenants were reduced to wage labourers. Mr Nkantolo, giving evidence to the Natal Native Affairs Commission of 1906-7, summed up the situation:

'The money they paid was thrown into a big tank that never seemed to fill. What surprised them was that whilst on the one hand they were heavily taxed by government, on the other hand, they were called upon to pay high rentals by private land-owners. The Government had them by the head, and the farmers by the legs ... The Natives had no means of making wealth.'[16]

Transvaal and Orange Free State (OFS)
By 1904, 750 000 blacks in the Transvaal were hiring private land and crown land or farming their own land. Some 123 000 were in the reserves and only 50 000 were unemployed. This number of unemployed is so low that we may say the Transvaal had full employment with 77% of the black population owning or hiring land.

The 1904 Labour Commission commented that black farmers were competing with whites and causing labour to be withheld from industry.

By the 1890s there was a widely established practice of 'farming-on-the-halves' in the Free State. This was a form of share-cropping in which whites provided seed and land, blacks farmed the grain, and the returns were shared.

This caused many complaints amongst white landowners who didn't practise share-cropping and disliked the competition from blacks, who, as we have seen, tended to be more effective farmers.

In both states, a series of anti-squatting measures was passed, and finally the 1913 Land Act reduced the rent-payers and share-croppers to low-wage labourers, and did away with the system of 'farming-on-the-halves'.

A golden age forgotten
Thus ended a brief golden era for black South Africans. For a few short decades they were allowed to experience a relatively free market, unfettered land ownership, modern technology, equality at law, reasonable freedom of movement and unrestricted upward mobility for the enterprising. They responded magnificently.

One of the reasons they progressed with such alacrity is unquestionably the common ground between their traditional ways and the market economy — a fact which has eluded virtually every contemporary analyst. Pre-colonial African law and custom shared the following features with the free market system: assets such as stock, crops, huts, handicrafts and weapons were privately owned and land was privately allotted or subject to private grazing rights; there were no laws against free contract and voluntary exchange; there was no coercive redistribution of wealth and almost no taxes; chiefs and headmen had few autocratic powers and usually needed to obtain full consensus for decisions; central government was limited, with a high degree of devolution to village councils, and there was no central planning structure; there were no powers of arbitrary expropriation and land and huts could be dispossessed only under extreme conditions after a full public hearing.

Today it is said that black tradition and temperament call for African socialism. Many current political leaders maintain that blacks can be properly fed and housed only through massive state redistribution and welfare. In our view, such measures would be in direct conflict with black tradition and temperament and would lead to greater poverty and more misery than blacks currently endure.

History shows that socialism forged the chains which shackle South Africa's blacks. The only way to break the chains is to repeal all the laws which discriminate against blacks forthwith. If they are free to participate fully in a market economy, within a few years there will be an explosion of economic growth in South Africa that will astonish the world.

17

2 | The rise of Afrikanerdom

Seek in the past all that is fine and noble and build your future on it.

President Paul Kruger

The history of the Afrikaner is a history of a people's struggle to free themselves from government interference in their lives so that they might live according to their own values. But this heritage of individualism and the pursuit of freedom has been largely forgotten.

In the course of the twentieth century, the Afrikaner nation has become inextricably linked with the concept of the paternalistic state and powerful central government.

Now the Afrikaner has taken on the role of interventionist and it is the blacks who are fighting for their rights — and these rights represent, ironically, much the same freedoms for which the Afrikaners shed their blood.

The time has come for Afrikaners to rediscover the true principles of democracy and limited government which were held so dear by the Voortrekker and his forebears, because these are the only principles on which a system can be built which will offer freedom to all South Africans, regardless of race.

The Afrikaner nation

Since 1948, the Afrikaner has dominated the political scene in South Africa with formidable purpose. He has earned the world's condemnation but also, grudgingly, its respect. Whatever his faults, weakness has not been amongst them.

His beginnings were remarkably inauspicious — his earliest forebears no more than a handful of freed servants. Nonetheless, the desire for self-rule which created the powerful nation we see today was present from the start and has formed a dominant and recurring theme throughout South Africa's history.

A history of rugged individualism

On the 7th of April, 1652, an expedition of about ninety men, led by Jan van Riebeeck, went ashore at Table Bay near the southern tip of Africa. They had been sent by the Dutch East India Company (Vereenighde Oostindische g'octrooijeerde Compagnie — V.O.C.) of the Batavian Republic to 'provide that the ... East India ships, to and from Batavia ... may (procure) ... herbs, flesh, water, and other needful refreshments — and by this means restore the health of their sick — '.[1]

Van Riebeeck was instructed to establish a garrison (the Fort of Good Hope), to plant fruit trees, to create a vegetable garden and to breed livestock.

This was no easy task. The men who had been sent to the Cape with him were expected to work hard under rigid discipline and often on short rations. Many deserted and others worked unwillingly and carelessly.

Van Riebeeck decided that the solution to the problem was to turn over certain activities to private enterprise. As a consequence, some of the Company servants were freed and given land to grow vegetables and later to undertake tavern-keeping, milling, woodcutting, hunting, fishing, tailoring and even medical practices — usually under licensed monopolies granted by the V.O.C.

Van Riebeeck also suggested to the Company that families be imported from Batavia to grow corn and rear livestock.

The first nine freed servants (free burghers) were settled in the Liesbeeck Valley on Khoikhoi grazing land in 1657. The Khoikhoi (commonly known as Hottentots) were indigenous yellow-skinned, nomadic herders who grazed their cattle on the lush pastures of the Cape each spring. They objected strongly to the arrival of the farmers on their grazing land and the first of many skirmishes between whites and people of colour over land broke out.

During peace negotiations in 1660, Van Riebeeck informed the Khoikhoi that they had lost part of their grazing land as a consequence of war and he had a hedge of bitter almond trees planted across the Cape Flats to cut off 6 000 acres of the Cape Peninsula from the interior. The Khoikhoi and the whites were kept separate by this hedge and both were forbidden to cross it. This was the first apartheid measure in South Africa.

The seeds of Afrikanerdom

The number of settler farmers grew rapidly but the Company never had any intention of granting them real freedom and their activities were rigidly controlled. They were forbidden to trade with anyone other than the company. Laws against trading with the Khoikhoi were especially strict. The company bought their produce at fixed prices and told them what they may or may not farm. In 1658 they staged their first 'strike', declaring: 'It is too hard that they are compelled to plant... this or that, ... to refrain from following their own bent, and from bartering all sorts of things from the natives ... to sell ... to the ships' and 'we will not be slaves to the Company.'[2]

These men who were demanding freedom were the forebears of the Afrikaner. They were mainly Dutch and Low German, in a ratio of about 2 to 1, with a sprinkling of Scandinavians and Frenchmen. Most of them were adventurers who had been impressed into service with the V.O.C. by vague promises of eventual riches. Many had been displaced by wars in Europe and had experienced a long history of repression.

After 1688 they were joined by about 200 Huguenot refugees who came to the Cape assisted by the Company. To facilitate their rapid assimilation, the French were interspersed among the Dutch and German farmers and Dutch was the only language used in public schools.

By the end of the seventeenth century, there was a clear distinction between 'Afrikaners' — burghers who regarded the Cape as their permanent home, and 'Europeans' — Company servants who were temporary residents.

The Trekboers

Company government in the Cape was inefficient and corrupt. The Council of Policy (the legislative body) levied taxes on the burghers and fixed low prices for their produce which they could still sell only to the Company. The burghers had no representation in government.

Despite a V.O.C. ruling preventing company officials from farming and trading privately, they did so with impunity.

All distribution was undertaken by monopolies granted and controlled by the Governors, who used their powers to protect their own interests. Not surprisingly, they became extremely rich farmers.

In addition, the market for produce was virtually limited to Cape Town and visiting ships, and by the early eighteenth century, with both the burghers and the Company officials farming, there was a hopeless oversupply. As a consequence, more and more burghers turned to stock farming, and the stock-owners migrated further and further inland, away from Cape officialdom and taxes, and became known as 'trekboers'.

The government tried frantically to stop the trekboers and periodically proclaimed boundaries beyond which settlement was illegal under pain of confiscation of cattle and twelve months' hard labour, but the trekboers ignored them. These pioneering farmers were rugged and independent spirits who moved on if they were annoyed by wild animals, hostile tribes or tax collectors. They were isolated and self-reliant and became increasingly resentful and contemptuous of the feeble attempts made by Company officials to impose regulations on them.

The Cape Patriots

By the end of the eighteenth century there were almost 20 000 white colonists in the Cape, and highly placed officials in the Cape were once again threatening the livelihood of the free burghers.

During this period the burghers became influenced by the writings of various prominent European philosophers who espoused democratic ideals, such as Locke, Montesquieu and Rousseau. In particular they were influenced by John Locke, who believed that all men have the right to own property, to think and express themselves freely and to worship as they please. Political organisation can, at most, establish a limited authority whose power is justified only in terms of genuine common good. Thus, according to Locke, government is a trust which is forfeited when it exceeds those bounds and becomes oppressive.

These ideas, together with the success of the American Revolution, encouraged the burghers to make their first demands for the political rights which would guarantee their economic interests.

They called themselves the Patriots and attended secret meetings and distributed pamphlets suggesting that people are entitled to substitute a new regime for an oppressive one.

In 1779 they submitted a petition to the Directors of the Company demanding representation in government and on the Council of Justice, the right to export and import freely and sell on the open market, and the right to trade with the Company without intervention.

The Cape Patriots failed to attain their main aims, but the movement gave rise to the important and basic democratic idea among Afrikaners that people have the right to elect and dismiss their governments and that inviolable laws should protect people from official whims.

In the border districts of Swellendam and Graaff-Reinet the burghers had far more freedom to vent their dissatisfaction with the Company, and in 1795 the Graaff-Reinet burghers ordered the landdrost (the Company official) to leave and refused to obey Company laws or pay Company taxes. Swellendam followed Graaff-Reinet's example and the two districts declared their intention of governing themselves: 'We have been long enough under the Yoke of Slavery and are now resolved to venture the last drop of blood of our dear Fatherland and resort under a Free Republic.'[3]

British rule and policies leading to the Great Trek

The years between 1795 and 1806 were a period of political transition in which the Cape was governed first by the British, then by the Batavian Republic and finally by the British who occupied the Cape for the second time in 1806.

British colonial policy was heavily influenced by the French Revolution and the American War of Independence and the government was in no way ready to understand or sympathise with the aspirations of 'the people'. As a result, British policies over the next thirty years led inexorably to a mass exodus of Afrikaners from the Cape from 1834 onwards. This emigration, called the Great Trek, was an extremely significant milestone in South Africa's history.

One hundred and fifty years of weak Company rule had left the Cape Dutch and, more particularly, the trekboer in the interior, largely to their own devices. The trekboers had opened up the interior, protected themselves from cattle raids and attacks by indigenous peoples, made roads and educated their children on their own. They had also developed their own language — Afrikaans. They were obstinate and individualistic and their only requirement of any government was that it should leave them alone.

However, the colonial government had no intention of doing this. On the contrary, its primary aim was to import English immigrants and anglicise the Cape. It set out to achieve this by divers measures.

Under Company rule the burghers had experienced a certain amount of self-government. The various collegial institutions serving this purpose were now abolished. In 1813, the Governor, Cradock, announced that all future official appointments would depend on a knowledge of English. From 1814 onwards, and especially after the arrival of the English 1820 settlers, English-speaking officials were appointed in increasing numbers and favoured in many ways. In 1822, English became the sole official language of the Cape.

The Afrikaners' Dutch Reformed Church was brought under British rule, and the English Governor made head of the church. Cradock ordered prayers to be read at every service for the British royal family and for British victory at war. Vacancies in the Dutch Reformed Church were filled with English-speaking ministers and the church was opened to Hottentots and blacks, a measure which conflicted directly with the religious beliefs of the burghers.

Philanthropists in England put powerful pressure on the colonial office to stop practices which resulted in other races being subordinated to whites. One of the results of their pressure was the establishment of the Circuit Court of 1812, later known as the 'Black Circuit'. The purpose of the Black Circuit was to investigate allegations of cruel treatment and over a hundred alleged murders of Hottentots by colonists. Not a single murder charge was upheld and the trials proved that there was very little justification for the allegations, but the 'Black Circuit' caused a furore among the Cape Dutch.

It was the sincere conviction of the Afrikaners that the Bible forbade them to consort with heathens, that the children of Ham (ie people of colour) were condemned to perpetual servitude and that it was God's covenant that whites should be the guardians of blacks.

They considered it a gross affront that they should have been falsely accused by servants, and felt that even though most of the accused had been acquitted, their good name had been besmirched.

The activities of the 'Black Circuit' culminated in the Slagtersnek tragedy. When a frontier burgher named Frederik Bezuidenhout ignored repeated summonses to appear in court in connection with the alleged ill-treatment of his Hottentot servant, Hottentot soldiers were sent to arrest him and when he resisted, he was shot dead. His brother Johannes swore to avenge him and led a rebellion of about 60 men which was speedily crushed. Five of the ringleaders were hanged and four of them had to ascend the scaffold a second time because the rope broke.

To some frontier boers, Slagtersnek became a symbol of Afrikaner oppression.

In 1833, slaves in the Cape were emancipated. Compensation was offered on the same basis as for West Indian slaves, although Cape slaves were twice as valuable as West Indian slaves on the market. In addition, compensation in the form of government bonds had to be collected in person at the Bank of England in London. A commission of 12% had to be paid by those who wanted to receive their compensation in Cape Town. As a result, English speculators travelled into the interior buying up compensation claims at huge discounts. Many burghers were crippled by the financial losses they incurred. 'Nearly all the Trekkers who have left records mention this, as a rule carefully explaining that it was not emancipation as such but the way in which it was carried out that hurt them.'[4]

The Afrikaner farmers on the eastern frontier had suffered severe

losses as a result of a series of wars with the Xhosa from the late eighteenth century onwards. The boers received no help from the government and relied on the protective or punitive power of burgher com-
mandos to protect themselves from ruinous raids. Now the commando
system was banned and the farmer was bereft of any means of self-de-
fence.

It was a combination of these factors — the colonial Anglicisation
policy, the lack of representation in government, enforced equality between burghers and their servants in their homes and churches, lack of
compensation for their slaves, and lack of support in the border wars —
which finally brought about the massive revolt of Afrikanerdom against
British rule — the Great Trek.

The Great Trek 1834 — 1854

The Great Trek was an organised exodus of many thousands of Afrikaner frontier farmers from the British Cape Colony to the neighbouring territories to the north and north-east.

It was not a spontaneous folk-migration. It was the best solution a
group of Afrikaner frontier leaders could devise to enable a portion of
frontier society to withdraw from what they considered an intolerable
situation.

Most of the Voortrekkers came from the frontier districts because the
trekboers who lived there were accustomed to loading up their possessions and moving to new pastures. As we have seen, they had become
excellent and resilient pioneers but very impatient members of an organised state. The Great Trek was not, however, simply an acceler-
ation of the trekboer movement. Some of the trekboers remained in a
tenuous sense loyalists, whereas the Voortrekker was a rebel looking for
a permanent home in an independent republic. The leaders of the
Great Trek were Louis Trichardt and Hans van Rensburg, who opened
the way to the Transvaal Lowveld and Portuguese East Africa; Andries
Hendrik Potgieter, who founded a settlement in the far north; and Gert
Maritz and Piet Retief.

These leaders made the other boers aware that once they crossed the
Cape frontier, they would be free of British control and could pursue
their own material and spiritual values in their own republics. They
would be able to fulfil the ideals of self-government and personal freedom which had been advocated by the old Cape Patriots and which
were being implemented in North America. 'The idea of an Afrikaner
state acted as a clarion-call to the frontiersman, and aroused the imag-
ination of the idealist. It transformed the Trek from a reckless rebellion

25

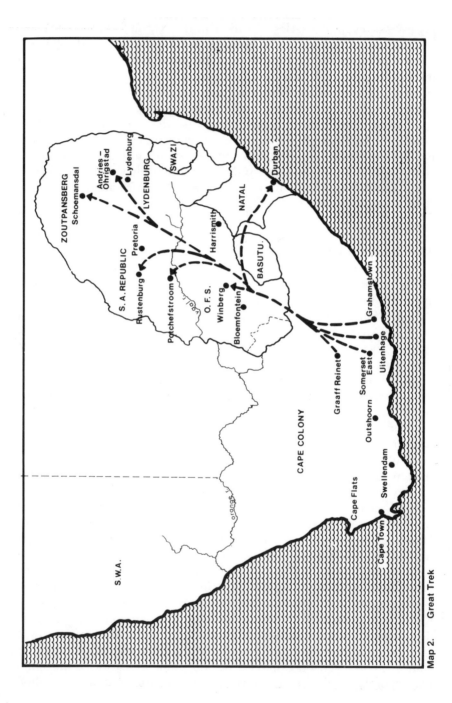

Map 2.   Great Trek

26

into a divinely inspired mission in Africa.'[5]

In 1837, an historic document appeared in the *Grahamstown Journal* explaining the main causes of the great emigration. This was Retief's Manifesto and it is regarded as the authentic voice of the Great Trek: 'We are resolved, wherever we go, that we will uphold the just principles of liberty . . . no-one shall be held in a state of slavery [but we will] preserve proper relations between master and servant . . . We will not molest any people, nor deprive them of the smallest property, but if attacked, we shall consider ourselves fully justified in defending our persons and effects . . . We make known that when we shall have framed a code of laws for our future guidance, copies shall be forwarded to the colony for general information . . . We purpose in the course of our journey, and on arriving at the country in which we shall permanently reside, to make known to the native tribes our intentions, and our desire to live in peace and friendly intercourse with them . . . We are now quitting the fruitful land of our birth, in which we have suffered enormous losses and continued vexation, and are entering a wild and dangerous territory; but we go with firm reliance on an all-seeing, just, and merciful Being, Whom it will be our endeavour to fear and humbly to obey.'[6]

Voortrekker republics
A dozen or more voortrekker republics were established outside of the Cape Colony, and all were characterised by a high degree of individual autonomy and very limited central government. One of the first was De Vrye Provincie van Nieuw Holland in Zuid Oost Afrika, popularly known as Natalia. A constitution was drawn up in 1838 and a Volksraad of 24 members elected. However, the Volksraad had little stability and basically every man acted according to his own values. Natalia's independence was shortlived. The republic was annexed by the British in 1843 and many of the Voortrekkers left again on a second trek.

The Transvaal
Several republics were established in what was to become the Transvaal*. Some were never formally proclaimed, others had no written constitution. Often they were nothing more than spontaneous settlements with ad hoc administration. The boers prided themselves on

The most extreme example of this independence was Klein Vrystaat (1886-91), a miniature republic established in the Eastern Transvaal. It was a constitutional anarchy having no formal government. There could not be a more unambiguous statement of boer anti-government sentiment!

having acquired their land by agreement with local chiefs. However, as the chiefs did not always understand fully what was involved, there were often serious misunderstandings. These various trekker communities were all fiercely independent and none of them was willing to be ruled by another. However, Andries Pretorius persuaded them to meet in 1849 and form the 'Verenigde Bond'. This was a 'United Bond of the entire community on this side of the Vaal River'.

In 1852, at the Sand River Convention, the British recognised the right of Afrikaners north of the Vaal River to 'manage their own affairs and govern themselves according to their own laws'. The Zuid Afrikaansche Republiek was formed — popularly known as the Transvaal.

In 1857 a constitution based in part on the United States constitution was drawn up by the Transvalers. There was an elected Volksraad with legislative power and the republic was divided into six field-cornetcies, each consisting of 60 — 100 households. There was a land tax on farms and a tax on ammunition sales. Only the Dutch Reformed Church was officially recognised; foreigners and people of colour were not accepted as citizens; and Englishmen, Germans and especially missionaries were discouraged from settling in the territory.

The freedom the Afrikaner believed in and was prepared to fight for was, first of all, the freedom of the family to do what it wanted to on its own property; secondly, the freedom of the group to regulate common affairs; and thirdly and rather tenuously, the freedom of the entire community to control its own affairs.

As a consequence, the Transvaal remained a happy minarchy for many years. The Volksraad met here and there but had no money to do anything, and the people were guided by their own dictates and by what was socially acceptable.

In 1877, the Transvaal was annexed by the British who charged that there was chaos, the government was not functioning properly and annexation was for the good of the boers. In truth, the boers simply had a healthy disrespect for government per se. Regulations and taxes were anathema to them, and they were happy with their 'sketchy administrative system'.[7]

The Transvaal fought for independence under the triumvirate of Paul Kruger, Piet Joubert and M W Pretorius, and the republic was restored under Paul Kruger in 1881.

Orange Free State
The area between the Orange and the Vaal rivers was occupied by the boers in much the same way as the Transvaal. In 1848 it was annexed

by the British and called the Orange River Sovereignty, but six years later England granted it freedom at the Bloemfontein Convention.

A provisional government and 29 representatives drafted a constitution based on the French Constitution of 1848 and including clauses from the American Constitution. The legislative body was a Volksraad elected to a four-year term. The Volksraad was not allowed to pass any laws which interfered with the rights of the inhabitants to peaceful assembly. Private property rights and press freedom were guaranteed. Citizens had the right to petition the government to introduce, revise or revoke a law. Essentially there was only one statute, the Wetboek, which could be amended. Like the Transvaal, the Free State did not grant citizenship to white uitlanders (foreigners) or to people of colour. Justice was administered according to the liberal principles of Roman-Dutch Common Law. Sir John Henry Brand became President of the Free State in 1864, and during his twenty-five year presidency, it came to be regarded as a model republic.

Conclusion
The traditions of blacks and Afrikaners living in southern Africa in the nineteenth century differed in many ways, but they shared certain important key elements.

In both, if people didn't like the rules governing their local community, they could freely move off and join another. Both were characterised by minimum central government and numerous small autonomous communities in which people were intimately involved in decisions regarding their own lives.

3 The rise of apartheid

The past thirty years have seen the greatest number of laws restricting our rights and progress, until today we have reached a stage where we have almost no rights at all.

Chief Albert Luthuli, 1952

In South Africa and internationally the concept of apartheid is firmly linked with Afrikaner nationalism. Most people believe that the Afrikaner both invented and implemented apartheid, and is entirely to blame for it. This is completely untrue.

The first apartheid law was passed in 1660, only a few years after whites arrived in the Cape, when Van Riebeeck planted his hedge of bitter almonds to keep the Hottentots and free burghers apart. The first separate school for blacks was established in 1663 and in 1678 the VOC forbade all inter-racial 'concubinage' on pain of up to three years' imprisonment with hard labour on Robben Island. In 1681 the VOC issued prohibitions forbidding whites to attend parties with slave (black) women, and when there was an inland expedition, it issued a special regulation forbidding sex between whites and Khoikhoi (hottentots).[1] The first law prohibiting marriage between whites and blacks was introduced in 1685. In Chapter 1 we discussed some of the subsequent measures aimed at preventing blacks from competing with whites and keeping blacks out of white areas.

This chapter will briefly consider the most important developments in the twentieth century which contributed to the structure of apartheid so that by the time the Nationalists came into power in 1948, it was already thoroughly integrated into the South African political and socio-economic system. The present government inherited a legacy of race laws which it subsequently enhanced and refined.

Prior to 1948, no one ever pretended that racist laws in any way served the interests of blacks. The various governments openly spelt

31

out their aim to protect whites, mainly from economic competition, and to maintain a supply of cheap black labour. Only gradually did the fear of political domination become a factor, and social segregation an end in itself. It was not until the 1940s when Hendrik Verwoerd refined and systematised the policy of apartheid, that the attempt was made to justify race legislation on an ideological basis and to maintain that it served the interests of blacks as well as whites.

Lord Milner's contribution to racial conflict

Time began to run out rapidly for the hard-won freedom of the boer republics when the British cabinet decided in 1899 to establish firm control over the whole of southern Africa. The main thrust of imperialism came from Sir Alfred Milner, British High Commissioner from 1897. He engineered a petition from the Transvaal Uitlanders (foreigners who were not granted Transvaal citizenship) to the Queen, listing their grievances, especially concerning the franchise, and then used it to provoke a crisis, insisting that 'the case for intervention is overwhelming'.[2]

Despite the efforts of the Cape Government and President Steyn of the Orange Free State to achieve a peaceful settlement, Milner finally had his way. Negotiations broke down and in October 1899 both sides resorted to force to settle their disagreements. The Orange Free State was automatically drawn into the conflict by a mutual assistance treaty with the Transvaal republic.

The combined republican armies comprised around 60 000 men, of whom never more than 30 000 were in the field at a given time. They were pitted against a British force which eventually numbered almost half a million. Approximately 7 000 British and nearly 4 000 Boers died in the field. A further 30 000 Afrikaners died, mostly in concentration camps, and mostly under sixteen years of age.[3]

Both the war and the Boer republics came to an end with the Peace of Vereeniging in 1902, and Lord Milner became High Commissioner of British South Africa, and Governor of the Transvaal and Orange River Colonies.

Milner called himself 'an imperialist out and out' and a 'British race patriot'. His main aims were to increase the British population by immigration until the majority of South Africans were English-speaking, and to anglicise South Africa by force, primarily through education.

In his Education Ordinance of 1903, he made English the sole medium of instruction in state schools. He imported English teachers and made primary education free but voluntary.

The Dutch Reformed Church was hostile to Milner's plans and set up the 'Christelike Nasionale Onderwys' which gave primacy to the Dutch language. Over 200 of these schools were established with no state aid.

Milner was vehemently against granting political power to blacks. He said: 'One of the strongest arguments why the white man must rule is because that is the only possible means of raising the black man, not to our level of civilisation — which it is doubtful whether he would ever attain — but to a much higher level than that which he at present occupies'.[4]

Joseph Chamberlain, head of the colonial office in England, was in favour of enfranchising the blacks so that they might become self-governing. Milner persuaded him that they should rather be represented in the legislature by whites nominated for this purpose. Article 8 of the Treaty of Vereeniging made the enfranchisement of non-whites (including Asians and Coloureds) dependent on the consent of a white majority.

A South African Native Affairs Commission appointed by Milner in 1903 to make recommendations to the Transvaal, Orange River and Cape colonies formalised the idea of racial segregation in a new way. It envisaged the territorial separation of blacks and whites for the purpose of residence and ownership, and approved the establishment of segregated 'locations' for urban blacks in various centres. It urged that blacks be represented only by whites in government, and argued for the separation of blacks and whites in political life.

In 1905, Milner was recalled to England and the colonies were granted 'self-government'. The parties in power at this stage were Het Volk in the Transvaal, Oranje Unie in the Orange River Colony, the South African Party in the Cape and the Labour Party in Natal.

A National Convention was called in 1908 to decide whether the colonies should form a union or a federation. The government and opposition white parties of the four colonies were represented in almost equal proportions. No blacks, coloureds or Indians were present.

In the ensuing debate, Jan Smuts, one of the leaders of Het Volk, argued in favour of a union with uniform race and economic policies. The Natal delegates wanted a federation, believing that this was the only way to protect the rights of the English-speaking minority. The Unionists won the day, but certain policies remained specific to the provinces, for example, the question of franchise for blacks, coloureds and Indians. In the Transvaal and Orange River Colony they had no vote, whereas in the Cape and Natal, qualified franchise was retained.

The Union was formed in 1910 and in the first election, which took

33

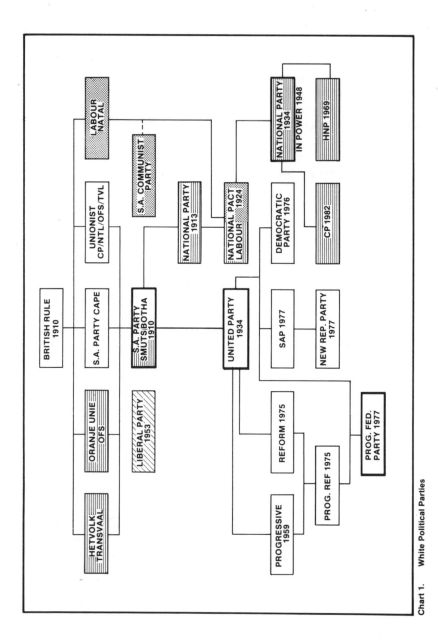

Chart 1. White Political Parties

34

place that same year, Het Volk, the Oranje Unie and the South African Party joined forces and won a firm majority of seats. The three then united to become the South African Party and Louis Botha, who had been leader of Het Volk, was elected Prime Minister. However, Botha's desire to unite Afrikaans and English-speaking South Africans soon led to a rift between him and the leader of the former Oranje Unie, J B M Hertzog. Hertzog, an Afrikaner nationalist who wanted Afrikaners to run the country, was finally expelled from the cabinet and formed the National Party.

The Native Land Act (No. 27 of 1913)

This legislation was introduced during the first term of the South African Party government and has been briefly discussed in Chapter 1. It forms such an important part of the foundation of apartheid that it must be considered in more detail here.

The bill was in response to numerous complaints which the government had received about blacks living in white areas, either on land which they owned or rented, or as tenants on white farms. It demarcated part of South Africa as black territory, and prohibited the sale of land in the remaining (white) area to blacks. The area granted to the blacks — 10,4 million morgen — comprised only the reserves and locations and was only slightly more than half the area the blacks already inhabited. Though intended as a preliminary delimitation, to be reconsidered and increased to more realistic proportions, this was not done until 1936.

Although theoretically the bill applied to all of South Africa, in practice it was relevant only to the Transvaal and Natal. The Free State already had legislation prohibiting the sale of land to blacks (Ordinance 5, 1876) and in the Cape, property ownership was a qualification for black franchise which was entrenched in the constitution of the Union, so the Act did not apply.

All the black leaders objected to the Act. The African National Congress sent two deputations to the South African government and one to the British government protesting the bill, but the British were not prepared to intervene.

Interestingly the blacks did not object to the principle of territorial segregation but to the provisions preventing them from buying land, and giving white farmers the right to eject them from land on which they had lived for generations.

35

The Indians

Indians were brought into Natal from 1859 onwards as indentured labourers to assist with the sugar industry. After three years, they could either buy their freedom for £5 (R100 ±) or be indentured for another two years. After five years, they were free to live and work as they chose, and after ten years, they were entitled to passage back to India or crown land to the value of the passage.

In addition to indentured labourers, Indian traders came in increasing numbers and the Indian population began to create serious competition for whites in trade and agriculture. By 1902, Indians in Natal outnumbered whites. Considerable pressure was exerted to slow down the influx of Indians and in 1913 an Immigration Act was passed which, while not referring specifically to Indians, made further Indian immigration impossible. M K Gandhi led a protest against the Immigration Act and various other laws mitigating against Indians, and as a consequence the Indian Relief Act, which granted some concessions to Indians, was passed.

In 1919, Botha died and Smuts became Prime Minister of the Union. He lacked Botha's personal following, however, and the South African Party began to lose ground to the Nationalists under Hertzog in the rural (Afrikaans) areas and the Labour Party in the urban (English) areas.

Militant white trade unionism

The beginnings of militant unionism date from the 1880s and 1890s when branches of British labour unions were opened in South Africa. One of the leading lights of the labour union movement was an Englishman, W M (Bill) Andrews, who later became first secretary of the Communist Party.

The main problem facing white trade unionists was competition from black unskilled and skilled labour. The general secretary of the white workers' labour union blamed 'the capitalist class' for this. He explained that while he was 'a Socialist as far as all the workers in the globe are concerned', he believed that his union had the right to fight against and to oust blacks if they were 'used [by capitalists] as semi-slaves for the purpose of keeping others down'.

What he was really objecting to, of course, was the beginning of the end of what he called the 'semi-slavery... of... dirty, evil-smelling Kaffirs'[5], because they were threatening the jobs of white miners. These fears came to a head when an economic slump between 1920 and 1923 resulted in the Chamber of Mines proposing a wage cut for whites, and an adjustment of the ratios of black and white wages and the number of black and white workers, in favour of blacks.

If the proposals had been accepted, many black workers would have been able to enter the mining industry and, in some cases, replace whites because blacks were prepared to work for £1 per week as opposed to the £1 per day which the whites demanded.

The white miners found themselves in the somewhat confusing position of fighting on two fronts — on the one hand, against the capitalists and, on the other hand, against black workers. Thus, when they marched through Johannesburg waving red flags, they chanted: 'Workers of the World fight and unite for a white South Africa'!

In December 1921, the coal-mine owners announced a wage cut and on January 1 1922, the coal miners went on strike, followed ten days later by the other white miners.

Feelings ran high against the government, which the striking miners regarded as being hand-in-glove with the mine owners and in February they resolved to overthrow the government and declare a republic.

Gangs of white miners roamed the streets committing robbery and arson and attacking blacks. Smuts finally declared martial law and, after fierce street fighting, aircraft bombed the strikers' headquarters.

The rebellion resulted in great loss of support for Smuts and paved the way for co-operation between the Nationalists and Labour, who agreed to join forces at the next election. Their alliance was based on resentment at the government's alleged disregard for the Afrikaans farmer and for the English-speaking white worker and on the mutual esteem of Hertzog and Creswell, leaders of the two parties.

In June 1924 the socialist Labour and Afrikaner National Party Alliance easily unseated the South African Party, and the Pact Government (1924-1933) took over the running of the Union.

An unholy alliance — apartheid and socialism

The Labour Party members of the Pact Government were in favour of further measures to protect white workers from black competition; the National Party members wanted farmer support programmes and job creation to alleviate the poor white problem.

General Hertzog, the new Prime Minister, formulated his 'Civilised Labour' policy which spelt out the direction of future labour legislation.

Civilised labour was defined as 'all work done by people whose standard of living conforms to the standard of living generally recognised as decent from a white person's point of view'. Uncivilised labour he defined as 'work performed by persons whose goal is restricted to the mere necessities of life in accordance with the ideas of undeveloped and savage people'.[6]

Government departments were instructed to give preference to civilised (white) workers. The fact that blacks were prepared to work for lower wages was to be ignored. One result of this was that the percentage of whites working for the South African Railways and Harbours (nationalised under Milner) grew from 9,5% in 1924 to 28,7% in 1929.

In his capacity as Minister of Labour, Creswell incorporated the civilised labour policy into the Wages Act of 1925, which introduced a 'rate for the job' and minimum wage rates with the specific intention of keeping blacks, Indians and coloureds out of certain jobs. No rate was fixed for work that did not interest whites. The Mines and Works Amendment Act of 1926 tightened job reservation on the basis of colour (first introduced with the Mines and Works Act of 1911) in the mining industry. This latter bill, though strongly opposed and rejected in the Senate, was passed by a joint session of the Houses of Parliament.

Creswell was so intent upon white worker exclusivity on the mines that he tried an experiment at Village Main mine of having only poor white workers — it was a 'deplorable failure'.[7]

The civilised labour policy also aimed to reinforce the powers of discrimination which were latent in a number of former Acts.

The Factories Act of 1918 enabled the Minister of Labour to withdraw exemptions from customs duties on raw materials if labour conditions were not 'satisfactory' — in other words, if non-whites were being employed when whites were available. The Act also required separate facilities such as toilets, restrooms and canteens for whites and non-whites in order to increase the cost of employing non-whites. The Apprenticeship Act of 1922 made attendance at technical college compulsory for apprentices. Administered in the spirit of the 'civilised labour policy', it ensured that all better-paid jobs were open only to whites.

The Industrial Conciliation Act of 1924, which was ostensibly intended to prevent a recurrence of the violence of the 1922 strike, established industrial councils through which employers and labour unions could negotiate terms of employment. With the approval of the Minister of Labour, such agreements would then acquire the force of law. Whites, coloureds and Indians were covered by the Act, but not blacks. Thus blacks were unable to negotiate at all.

The Labour Party hoped that through these various measures, black labour would be permanently excluded from the industrial system. However, 'the force of profit-seeking incentives proved more powerful than legislation, and ... the attempt to segregate the Africans from the modern world and confine them to primitive tribalism in the reserves, or to labouring work on the farms and mines, was far from successful. It barred them only from semi-skilled and skilled employments and not from work classed as unskilled'.[8]

The Labour Party also pushed for the nationalisation of the iron and steel industry. The more industries the government controlled, the more power it would have to ensure white workers were protected.

Again, there was very strong opposition to this bill. It was blocked twice by the Senate but passed by a joint sitting.

The United Party

In 1933, the National Party under Hertzog and the South African Party under Smuts formed a coalition which won a resounding victory, capturing 136 of 150 seats in the House of Assembly. The following year the two parties fused to form the United Party and a number of National Party supporters broke away under Dr D F Malan to form the Herenigde Nasionale Party or Volksparty (Reunited National Party).

In 1936, the Representation of Natives Bill was passed by a majority of 168 to 11 in a joint sitting of the two houses, thus abolishing the Cape franchise for blacks. The bill provided for three whites to represent Cape blacks in the House of Assembly.

The Native Trust and Land Act (No 18 of 1936) added 7,2 million morgen to the land allotted to blacks by the Native Land Act of 1913, increasing it to 13% of South Africa's total land area. The Act also exerted further pressure on labour tenants, rent tenants and share-croppers on white farms to become wage labourers. It created Labour Tenant Control Boards with the power to terminate voluntary contracts between farmers (mostly Afrikaners) and tenants (mostly blacks).

The Apprenticeship Act (No 37 of 1944) ensured that standards required for acceptance into an apprenticeship were such that no black would qualify. This Act prevented blacks from entering over 100 trades, and was so effective that by 1974, according to the Minister of Statistics, J J Loots, there were 19 259 white, 331 coloured and 426 Indian motor mechanics — but not one black.

The 'Swart Gevaar' (Black Threat)

During the years following World War II colonialism became unfashionable, as did the concept of white rule over other races. India and Pakistan gained independence and, in Africa, blacks started demanding self-rule. In South Africa, the Native Representative Council, the African National Congress and the South African Indian Congress began to press for a greater share in government and for the abolition of discriminatory laws.

Whites in South Africa felt increasingly insecure and United Party policy (of racial groups living side by side with administration and legislation taking their differences into account) did nothing to alleviate their fears. The Herenigde National Party under Malan, on the other hand, offered them the continuation of white domination through the concept of separate development. In addition, the Herenigde National Party appealed strongly to Afrikaner nationalism, and Afrikaners constituted approximately 60% of the white population. Thus it was that in the election of May 1948 the Afrikaner came to power.

The fruition of apartheid

When the National Party came into power in 1948 its apartheid policy was certainly not new. Nonetheless, it contained elements which made apartheid before 1948 and apartheid after 1948 somewhat different.

Dr Malan and his associate, Dr Verwoerd, decided that the only way to prevent whites, and particularly Afrikaners, from being submerged by blacks and losing their cultural identity was to separate the two races completely. Legislation was, therefore, aimed at consolidating social, residential, cultural, economic and political apartheid, with the ultimate goal of ending all interaction between racial groups except on a superficial level in the work place.

For the first time, an attempt was made to prove that separateness was also in the interest of blacks. It was argued that blacks would be happier and better off governing themselves in their own areas and maintaining racial purity in their ethnic groups.

The new government implemented apartheid with a ruthless consistency which coincided with increasing world opposition to white supremacy.

The Nationalists added the following Acts to the already impressive body of race laws:

Social apartheid

The Prohibition of Mixed Marriages Act (No 55 of 1949) and the Immorality Amendment Act (No 21 of 1950, Section 16) forbade marriage and extramarital sexual intercourse between whites and blacks, asiatics and coloureds.

The Reservation of Separate Amenities Act (No 49 of 1953) was the primary source of 'petty apartheid'. It enforced the segregation of lifts, toilets, parks, beaches, hotels, cinemas, restaurants and so on.

The Population Registration Act (No 30 of 1950) made provision for a central population register in which all people were classified as whites, coloureds or blacks.

Residential apartheid

The Group Areas Act (No 41 of 1950) augmented the various laws providing for racially segregated areas. It provided for areas to be proclaimed as belonging to a particular racial group, in which case no other racial group could live, trade or own land there, and any members of other racial groups living there already were moved out.

This was supplemented by the Natives Resettlement Act (No 19 of 1954) which was intended to eliminate 'black spots' (i.e. black townships) from white areas. Blacks were moved from white areas and no longer permitted to own their homes. Since the Act, over three million blacks have been forcibly relocated in an extreme exercise in social engineering.

The Natives (Urban Areas) Amendment Act (No 16 of 1955) aimed at moving blacks out of servants' accommodation in apartment blocks by stipulating that no more than five non-white servants could be accommodated in a block of flats. Subsequent amendments further restricted the movement of urban blacks; these are now known collectively as 'influx control'.

Cultural apartheid

In order to keep black and white cultures separate, the Bantu Education Act (No 47 of 1953) and the Extension of University Education Act (No 45 of 1959) both allowed for segregated education. Prior to this, there was virtually no government education for blacks but a very effective system of mission schools.

Economic apartheid

Existing laws promoting economic apartheid were supplemented by the Native Labour Act (No 48 of 1953) and the Industrial Conciliation Act (No 28 of 1956) which segregated trade unions and forbade blacks to strike.

The Native Trust and Land Act (No 18 of 1936), now called the Development Trust and Land Act, was supplemented by various amendments and proclamations which enabled the government to control every aspect of the black economy including business, farming, building, townships, land tenure and tribal authorities. Some indication of the extent of this Act may be gained from the fact that it stipulates how

41

many times a year buildings must be white-washed.

The Natives (Urban Areas) Amendment Act, now called the Black (Urban Areas) Consolidation Act, governs all aspects of black urban living including business rights, housing and land allocation.

Over the years, numerous ordinances, by-laws, regulations and proclamations were introduced to control licensing. Many of these, while not openly discriminating against blacks, achieve 'covert apartheid' by setting such high safety, health and educational standards that blacks are unable to meet them.

The Physical Planning Act (No 88 of 1967) forced industry to 'decentralise' to 'growth points', 'border industry' areas and homelands. Industries in white areas were not allowed to employ more than three blacks to every one white. This created the current anomaly whereby South Africa has a skilled labour shortage and unemployment simultaneously.

Political apartheid

Black representation in white government was abolished and replaced by local boards with a degree of control over local affairs.

The Asiatic Laws Amendment Act (No 47 of 1948) abolished Indian representation and replaced it with nothing, since the government regarded Indians as visitors who should return home. In 1964, this policy was reviewed and the South African Indian Council was formed to give Indians a measure of representation.

The Separate Representation of Voters Act (No 46 of 1951) removed Cape coloureds from the white voters' roll and placed them on a separate voters' roll with a Coloured Affairs Council.

The Bantu Authorities Act (No 68 of 1951) abolished the Native Representative Council of 1936 and expanded black self-government in the black homelands. The Promotion of Bantu Self-Government Act (No 46 of 1959) abolished black representation in the House of Assembly and laid down guidelines for government systems in the homelands.

In the elections of 1953, 1958 and 1961, support for the National Party steadily increased. This was largely because the voters were satisfied that apartheid would protect them from economic competition and from black political aspirations. The party became firmly identified with the Afrikaner nation, and could count on Afrikaner support —especially after South Africa became a republic in 1961.

Comment

In this brief history of South Africa we have attempted to highlight certain factors which are not commonly known and to dispel some myths, as well as to trace the history which has led to the current impasse.

It is commonly accepted that the Afrikaner is entirely responsible for apartheid and for the current state of massive economic intervention which will be considered in more detail in the next chapter.

However, it is clear from the foregoing pages that prior to the Boer War and Union at the turn of the century, the Afrikaner was in favour of limited government and wanted nothing more than a part of the country in which he could live as he wished.

In addition, when the National Party came to power in 1948, the structure of apartheid was already there, almost in its totality. All the NP had to do was systematise it. This is not to say that the Afrikaner had not been party to racist legislation introduced before that time, but that all such legislation (apart from laws inherited from the Dutch) was developed jointly with the British colonial government and English-speaking South Africans.

We have also demonstrated the fallacy of the idea that the black tribal system is fundamentally socialist. On the contrary, it too is based on individual freedom and private property, which in part explains why blacks responded with such alacrity to market opportunities in the nineteenth century. With new knowledge and the freedom to use it, they became highly successful and enthusiastic entrepreneurs and artisans.

It is primarily these two groups, the Afrikaners and the blacks, who must resolve South Africa's future. Many Afrikaners have moved away from their roots, away from their early love of freedom, and now espouse racial socialism or fascism. Similarly, many blacks have moved away from their original belief in individual freedom towards socialism, marxism or communism. Both have largely forgotten that decentralisation and limited central power were the distinguishing features of their traditional political institutions.

Fortunately, there are many Afrikaners and blacks who are still strongly individualistic, and the future of this country lies in their hands. It is only by returning to their origins, to a system which maximises individual freedom, that blacks, Afrikaners and all of South Africa's other groups of people can live together in peace and prosperity.

PART TWO
The status quo

But man, proud man,
Drest in a little brief authority, ...
Plays such fantastic tricks
before high heaven
As make the angels weep.

Shakespeare
Measure for Measure

Part Two considers the relative degree of government intervention in the lives of black and white South Africans and the causes of the current political unrest. It also provides a description of the policies and positions of all the main political parties and pressure groups and a discussion of the problems created by redistribution and affirmative action.

White capitalism

*That government is best which governs the least,
because its people discipline themselves.*

Thomas Jefferson

South Africa is a country of immense, wasted potential. It has the
richest endowment of mineral resources per capita in the world; it
is extremely well-located geographically with natural harbours,
fertile agricultural land, low population density and easy access to
western markets, capital and technology.

This country started industrialising in the late nineteenth century, at
the same time as Japan. Japan is an economic miracle and South Africa
is one of the less developed countries of the world. Why?

Economists posit many different and contradictory preconditions for
prosperity: a country needs to be small; it should be big; it needs a homogeneous population; it must have natural resources; it needs to be
near western markets — and so on and so on. But none of these conditions correlate with what is actually happening around the world.

Most countries that are well-endowed with natural resources are
economic failures. Successful countries, on the other hand, are often
conspicuously devoid of natural endowment; many are land-locked,
small and mountainous, some have no mineral resources, and they are
often heterogeneous. Consider, for example, Switzerland, Singapore,
Hong Kong, Britain during the Industrial Revolution, Lichtenstein,
Luxembourg, Taiwan, Sri Lanka, South Korea, Japan and Iceland. All
of these are economic success stories, while richly endowed countries
such as Angola, Zaire, Zambia, Mexico, Nigeria, the USSR, North Korea, China and India are dismal performers.

The reason for this apparent anomaly is strikingly simple. Countries
with free or relatively free markets do well, countries with unfree or
controlled economies do badly. Hong Kong, originally little more than
a rock in the sea, even has to import water, but it has a free economy.
Mexico has vast oil reserves, but the oil industry is nationalised and the
country is impoverished.

47

South Africa should be out-performing Japan. In this chapter, we will attempt to show that the reason we are lagging so far behind is that our economy has been throttled by policies which would have prevented any country in the world from being a great economic success story; and that these policies have not only prevented blacks, Indians and coloureds from realising their potential, but have also shackled whites.

Are white South Africans free?

It is generally agreed by South Africans of all races, as well as the international community — critics and sympathisers alike — that, in this country, whites are free and blacks are not. The assumption is that if one simply extends whatever whites have to blacks, blacks will be free. This is not true.

Certainly blacks enjoy far, far less freedom than whites and, equally certainly, they would be very much better off than they are now if they had the same rights as whites. But the economic activity of whites in South Africa is extremely heavily regulated and controlled, and if all racially discriminatory legislation were repealed tomorrow, the people of this country would still be far from free, and South Africa's problems would still be a long way from a satisfactory solution.

Economic factors — the root cause

Economic factors have a more powerful effect on the course of events than any other consideration. Almost everything else — politics, law, education, unemployment, poverty, unrest and so on — tends to be a consequence of economic processes. The real issues behind virtually every piece of legislation are economic: the motives are economic, the means are economic and the consequences are economic.

When a chain store gives evidence to the government in favour of shop-hour legislation; when a manufacturer is in favour of minimum standards; when a trade union is for a certain labour policy; when a bank supports a particular monetary policy or an industrialist favours certain tariffs — the measures which they propose always and inevitably coincide precisely with their self-interest.

But none of those who call for legislation will ever admit that they act in their own self-interest. Not one will say, I believe you should introduce the following law because it is good for my company, or my business, or the members of my union, or because it gives me a competitive advantage over others in my field. Instead, they conceal their real motives under a pretence of concern for the 'public interest', or the 'national interest', or the 'common good'.

Cabinet Ministers often observe, legitimately, that it is not the government that wants a particular intervention but the private sector. 'We were asked by the estate agents to pass the Estate Agents Act,' they say, 'so don't blame us. The private sector wanted these laws.'

Behind every single intervention there is a vested interest which benefits from that intervention at the expense of competitors and the general public. We will now examine some of the major categories of regulations in South Africa and assess who stands to gain from them, and who to lose.

Guild socialism

Members of most professions and occupations in South Africa are protected from competition by means of professional and occupational licensure. In the name of the 'public interest', established members of an occupation or profession ask the government to empower them to stipulate minimum entry qualifications, to introduce regulations and to rule that only they may provide certain services for a fee. These measures enable them to set artificially high fees for their services with no fear of competition.

At the behest of law societies new lawyers will soon have to have an LL.B degree despite the fact that some of the lawyers on the Councils do not themselves have an LL.B. They are protected by a 'grandfather clause' ensuring that those already in the profession do not need the qualifications they prescribe for their competitors. They get in and slam the door behind them, just as their counterparts in other professions do.

Lawyers argue persuasively that touting or advertising or discounting of legal fees should not be allowed. A lawyer may not say to a poor person, 'I will handle your case and charge you only if I win.' He may not let it be generally known that he wins 80% of his cases and is, therefore, worth consulting. Nor may he advertise that he specialises in consumer or labour protection.

Most lawyers will explain, at great length, the need for the strictest regulations and for a lawyers' monopoly regarding deeds and company registration; they will offer many reasons why only they should be paid for drawing up agreements or wills, although anyone else may do so free of charge. Eminently qualified people such as accountants, bankers, legal advisers and conveyancers employed by building societies or stockbrokers may not sell or use their legal expertise freely.

49

In large law firms, conveyancing, debt collecting and the administration of deceased estates are often handled by 'unqualified' paraprofessionals. These individuals have to work for lawyers and may not open specialist practices even though they are manifestly competent to do so. The result is that there is no effective competition in the legal profession, and only a rich man can afford legal advice and services.

Occupational and professional licensing protects not only the competent but also the professionally incompetent. There is a presumption on the part of the public, for example, that someone with a law degree is both competent and qualified. A law student might complete his training without ever having read the Black Urban Areas Act, yet he is entitled to open up offices and offer professional advice to employers and blacks on the Act, and he will not be guilty of fraud or misrepresentation of his professional competence.

Thus the public loses twice over. Firstly, it is led to believe that every member of a profession or occupation is competent, and secondly, it accepts without question that anyone who purports to have a qualification does in fact have it — there is an assumption that big brother is policing this. We have chosen the legal profession for our example, but the same principles apply in many other closed shop professions, although some, such as engineering, are policed by criteria of competence rather than formal qualification.

By preventing competition, licensure also discourages innovation and improved technology. Because there is no competition, insiders have no incentive to develop more efficient and productive sales methods.

In addition to all the professions, there are over 200 licensed occupations in South Africa. A look at this list unearths some examples of really rich creative thinking. For instance, the sugar industry has special sugar industry radio communications servicemen; and hypertrichologists who remove unsightly hair need certain scientific and aesthetic qualifications in order to do so.

The reason why there are so many licensed occupations is that any small, motivated group — window-cleaners, for example — can ask the government to pass a law to protect the public from incompetent window-cleaners (in other words, to protect them from competition). The effect is precisely the same as that caused by the occupational guilds of Europe in the Middle Ages: services are kept in short supply, prices are kept high, and innovation is discouraged.

All that is needed to protect the public from being exploited by charlatans is an effective application of the law against fraud. It is fraudulent and, therefore, illegal, to purport to have competence and skills which one does not in fact have. If occupational licensure were abolished, people would not employ anyone's services without a thorough check or a referral. If they did make a mistake, they could sue for fraud.

Minimum standards regulations
In the same way that professional and occupational licensure is promoted in the name of the public interest, so are minimum standards regulations.

Standards regulations in South Africa tend to be modelled on first world examples. For instance, when new electrical standards are introduced by the Federal Trade Commission in the USA, our bureaucracy in Pretoria hears about them, embellishes them, and then introduces them with the proud announcement that we have the highest standards in the world. Because our electrification standards are so high, our electricity is unnecessarily expensive. Consequently, poor people cannot afford it and every winter old people in low-income areas die because they have no heating.

In the USA, earthing is not required. Investigations showed that if earthing were introduced to save lives (a supposition which is unproven) it would cost in the region of $10 million per possible life saved. Many states in the USA do not require that expensive switches be fitted on wall plugs or that wiring be set into walls. But in South Africa, where cheap electricity is so much more important than in the USA, these standards still apply.

Health and safety regulations are sacred cows, but according to Ancher Packer of the SWA-Namibia Health Department, health regulations should be repealed *in toto*. For various reasons health laws have not been enforced in the Operational Area in SWA-Namibia for ten years. The benefits for the people living there have been spectacular. Protein-rich foods are much cheaper and more readily available than elsewhere. Fewer children go hungry, malnutrition has decreased and life expectancy has risen. Small business is booming. There has not been a single recorded incident of illness or disease which health inspectors and health laws would have prevented.

In Ciskei health regulations are not enforced and 'unsafe' foodstuffs are freely available: unpasteurised milk from unchecked cows and goats, meat and fish which are not shielded from flies, and bread baked in dirty tins, are all being sold with impunity. Slaughtering is not regulated and there isn't a single approved abattoir in the country.

What are the consequences? A former Secretary for Health revealed in evidence to the *Louw Commission of Enquiry into the Ciskei Economy* that

51

in fifteen years there had not been one reported incident of disease or food poisoning resulting from unhygienic conditions.

If health laws were applied strictly, the effect would be to double or treble the cost of food. Animals would have to be slaughtered in abattoirs costing millions of rands, and regulation butcheries, dairies and bakeries would cost hundreds of thousands of rands to build and run. The result would be starvation for thousands of Ciskeians who are presently struggling to sustain life.

Health officials enforce regulations because they will be blamed if one child dies from food poisoning or an epidemic. If thousands of children die from malnutrition, however, 'rural poverty' is cited as the cause.

There is an open-and-shut case for repealing health and safety regulations in low-income areas, but what about rich areas? The rich can afford to patronise expensive shops which maintain high standards through choice to attract a wealthy clientele. An alternative to legislated minimum standards could be provided by a voluntary organisation which would check standards and award health and quality ratings to shops and manufacturers, in the same way that star ratings are applied to hotels. There are organisations of this nature in several other countries where standards are not controlled by statutory law.

Apart from health and safety regulations which have tragic consequences, there are many thousands of petty rules and regulations which price goods out of the reach of the poor. For example, someone has taken it upon himself to conduct hazardous research to discover precisely what the optimum toilet paper specifications are, so that none of us will make any mistakes in this respect. The provisions of item 130 in paragraph 2 of regulation 10, schedule 6 to the *Trade Metrology Act* (No. 77 of 1973) govern the 'sheet count, ply and sheet size' of toilet paper. In particular the reader will be pleased to know that, for his protection, suppliers and retailers 'shall sell toilet paper in rolls only when wound around a core having a maximum inner diameter of 40mm ...'.

Who gains from these regulations? Certainly not the public, many of whom cannot afford regulated toilet paper and are forced to use torn-up newspaper collected from refuse dumps; and certainly not those manufacturers who are willing to enter the market with cheap, 'substandard' paper.

Standards regulations produce a multitude of ill-effects. They discriminate against small businessmen who cannot afford to enter the market if they have to comply with them. They raise the costs of established businesses so that they have less money for wages, which results in lower pay for workers and in unemployment. Consumers are robbed of their freedom to choose from a wide variety of standards and prices and, as we have mentioned, most products which comply with standards are priced out of the range of poor people. Minimum standards also discourage innovation because nobody wants to put effort and energy into developing a new product only to be told it does not comply with the standards laid down ten years ago.

Radical though this may sound, we do not need any compulsory standards regulations. It is unlawful under common law to endanger people's health or safety or to commit fraud, and that is all the protection anyone needs. The new small claims courts are a first step in bringing common law protection within the reach of ordinary people. Over and above that, people should be free to decide for themselves on the quality of the products they buy.

Agricultural interventions

There are about 25 agricultural control boards in South Africa, including quasi-boards such as the Ko-operatiewe Wijnbouwers Vereniging (KWV). All of them grant insiders the statutory power to regulate the market to their own advantage. In addition, there are many more agricultural regulations which do not involve control boards. For example, there are extensive controls regarding the planting and selling of timber, even though there is no timber control board. A permit is required to plant trees, to cut them, to process, to transport, to sell, export and so on. It is not clear how all these permits protect the public, but it is very clear how they protect some of the existing plantation and mill owners.

Not only are efficient farmers penalised by a labyrinth of controls but inefficient farmers are supported by a network of subsidies at the expense of good farmers and consumers. Farmers who make losses don't go out of business, they receive state subsidies. And they are encouraged to overcapitalise because they can write off 100% of expenditure on capital equipment against tax in the first year.

Rent control

Those in favour of rent control argue that it protects people who rent accommodation from being exploited by landlords. A few people do benefit by paying low rents, but many more suffer through the shortage of accommodation which rent control causes. Investors will not put money into apartment blocks or townhouses if rent control will prevent them from receiving a competitive return. Also, landlords are not all wealthy 'exploiters', but often ordinary people whose flats or cottages represent all their savings. Rent control prevents them from receiving a fair financial return on their assets. These facts are well known, and there has been a net reduction in rent controls. In fact, but for a pre-election vote-catching ploy by the opposition, Rent Boards would now be a thing of the past.

Price control

The South African government has performed heroically in the area of price controls. In 1976, there were something like 200 000 controlled prices in South Africa; even the Price Controller's Office was unable to keep an accurate count. Now fewer than 20 prices remain under the jurisdiction of the Price Control Act. (There are still many price controls under transport regulations, control boards and so on.) During the early 1970s people became very creative at finding ways to escape the price controller. In the sweet industry,for example, if a Whoozy Bar was controlled at 5c, they would change the shape and package and call it a Woggy Bar, and when a price control was slapped on that, they would bring out a Wiggy Bar. Prices behaved like frogs: as soon as one reached out to catch them, they jumped out of the way, and the Price Controller never caught up.

Naturally, this was all very wasteful and the real cost of the products was forced up, to the detriment of the consumer whom the controls were supposedly intended to protect. Price controls interfere with the laws of supply and demand so that controls which fix a maximum price always result in shortages and those that fix a minimum price inevitably create surpluses. This has been amply demonstrated by the agricultural control boards.

All of the regulations which we have discussed interfere with private economic transactions between individuals of all races in South Africa. Thus they are not apartheid laws in the overt sense, but they create a kind of 'hidden apartheid' of which most people are unaware. Wherever regulations prevent less qualified people from getting jobs or starting businesses, or prevent poor people from buying and selling, the least qualified and the poorest people suffer most. In South Africa, primarily as a result of 'black socialism' which is discussed in the next chapter, the poorest, least qualified people are usually blacks. If the government were to delegislate in these areas, blacks, and to a lesser extent Indians and coloureds, would be the first to benefit.

In addition to regulations which interfere with private enterprise, the government controls many other aspects of the economy to the detriment of us all.

54

State monopolies

There are both state-owned and state-protected monopolies in South Africa.

Amongst the state-owned monopolies, there are the Electricity Supply Commission (ESCOM), the Iron and Steel Corporation (ISCOR), S A Transport Services (SATS), Posts and Telecommunications (telephones) and the South African Broadcasting Corporation (SABC). The tentacles of SATS and ISCOR, in particular, reach out to encompass a tremendously wide area of activities. SATS controls railways, airlines, harbours, road haulage and pipelines. These controls are very far-reaching so that, for example, no railway line may be built without the consent of parliament.

South Africans have become so accustomed to government control in these areas that the state monopolies have become sacred cows. For example, the idea that harbours should be run by private enterprise seems shocking and inconceivable. People trot out the old argument that the private sector cannot afford such big capital projects. But this argument has no basis in reality. Gold mines are more costly than harbours and have longer lead times before becoming profitable, yet they are run very efficiently by private enterprise. Britain has both private and government harbours. The private ports are efficient, have high growth rates, and without any subsidies outperform the government ones. They are profit-making business ventures. The biggest container harbour in the world is currently being built in Hong Kong entirely privately, and Hong Kong is a smaller economy in every sense than South Africa.

The provision of water by the state is another sacred cow. Of course water must be controlled by the state, people say; it is a public good, a natural monopoly. However, water on the Witwatersrand used to be supplied very efficiently by private enterprise. The water supply system in Johannesburg's northern suburbs was installed by a property developer named Frederick Cohen. He bought water from the Rand Mines Water Supply Company and ran a profitable and efficient operation which was, after tremendous resistance on his part, expropriated. The water rates went up, and profits turned to losses, as always seems to happen when governments supply services. At the turn of the century the Rand Mines Water Supply Company was providing water for much of the Witwatersrand. It was nationalised by Lord Milner in 1903 to create the Rand Water Board.

In addition to the state corporations, there are many other parastatals in this country such as the Small Business Development Corporation, the Development Bank of Southern Africa and the Industrial Development Corporation. Each homeland has one or more development corporations, and the Development Trust owns most of the homeland 'consolidation' land and the bus operations in black areas.

The agricultural control boards are essentially state marketing and processing corporations with varying degrees of monopoly power.

Labour

In 1984, amendments to the Labour Relations Act of 1956 created a situation in which agreements between employers and trade unions are not enforceable in court unless both the union and the employer organisation meet requirements laid down in the original Act. These requirements involve details of constitutions, accounting, office-bearers and so on. A further amendment extended the Minister's discretion to suspend the operation of agreements, orders or awards made by arbitrators 'in the interests of employers or employees, or in the public or national interest'.

Labour relations in South Africa are already a source of major conflict. Greater government involvement simply results in greater politicisation and more interracial ill-feeling and violence. The government should withdraw from labour matters and allow contracts between employers and employees to be subject to the jurisdiction of the courts only. Non-consenting parties should not be bound by labour agreements or forced to join employer bodies or unions.

Education

In this country, there is 'free' and compulsory education for whites but not for blacks. Most people think it is an important priority to provide the blacks with the same education as whites. However, since our white education system is one of the least cost-effective in the world, we would question that assumption. Private enterprise can do an excellent job of providing education at all different levels, catering for different income groups, different ages, and for a wide variety of needs — ranging from basic literacy to professional training and the teaching of technical skills.

At present, the cost of private schools is loaded because all taxpayers must pay for government education whether their children are in government schools or not. The chapter on socio-economic solutions suggests an alternative to this inefficient system.

Conclusion

There are some 500 Acts and numerous ordinances, by-laws, regulations and policies which inhibit free enterprise in South Africa. Of these, nearly all apply to whites, blacks, Indians and coloureds alike. Six Acts apply only to Indians, five to coloureds and 28 to blacks. Some, like the Group Areas Act, have different effects on each group but apply to all.

If the Acts which apply to blacks, Indians and coloureds were repealed, the economy would still be severely restricted by the other 450 + Acts. However, whites, and to a lesser extent Indians and coloureds, still enjoy a degree of free enterprise, whereas the laws which specifically inhibit blacks strike right at the heart of their economic freedom. This is why the South African economy is sometimes described as 'white capitalism/black socialism', and for this reason the next chapter argues that the repeal of laws which prevent blacks from participating in the economy is of the utmost urgency.

5 | **Black socialism**

*Force, violence, pressure, or compulsion with a view
to conformity, is both uncivilized and undemocratic.*

Mahatma Gandhi

If someone from Mars was told that in South Africa there is a law
which decrees that blacks must live in one part of the country and
whites in another, he would have no reason on the face of it to think
that one group was worse off than the other. The Group Areas Act discriminates against blacks, not because it creates separate areas, but
because the laws in white and black areas differ. The areas allocated to
blacks are much smaller than those allowed to whites, but many places
with much higher population densities than our current black areas are
extremely prosperous.

If apartheid did no more than separate blacks and whites, Soweto
would be a flourishing city with a CBD, high-rise buildings, banks, department stores, supermarkets, prosperous business people and numerous entrepreneurs. But it is not. The reason for this is that blacks
live in a socialist world — a world in which almost everything is owned
and controlled by the state. This has changed somewhat since certain
regulations were relaxed in the 1970s, but essentially, right up to the
present time, we have black socialism in South Africa.

There is no genuine private ownership of land or free exchange of
land rights in black areas. Government controls the trade unions and
the distribution, allocation and movement of labour. Virtually every
aspect of life is provided or controlled by government, from houses,
hospitals and creches to schools and transport. It is this which prevents
Sowetans from progressing, acquiring capital and becoming entrepreneurs, industrialists, artisans and professionals.

One of the results of black socialism has been an unholy alliance in
South Africa between white nationalists and radical socialists, both

59

black and white. Both are in favour of state subsidisation and control of blacks; indeed, there is very little difference between their policies for blacks — they just label them differently. Radical white nationalists say they want to preserve white identity, while socialists say they want to protect blacks from exploitation by whites. But both want the state to provide black housing, jobs, medical services, education, staple foods, transport and so on. If marxists took over the government tomorrow, they could simply maintain all the current regulations pertaining to blacks and extend them to whites, Indians and coloureds as well.

Before 1970

Until the early 1970s, all the land in black areas was owned by the state. The Development Trust and Land Act of 1936 made the government by far the biggest landowner in South Africa. The Act is a draconian piece of legislation, and it is probably still the single greatest source of control over blacks.

Land cannot be used efficiently unless people are free to sell it, mortgage it, let it and develop it: to be productive, it must be privately owned. And the efficient use of land is a necessary condition of progress.

Prior to the late '70s, no black could open a business in a black urban area unless he had 'Section 10' rights. Section 10 of the Black Urban Areas (Consolidation) Act prevented blacks from living in urban areas unless they were born there, had lived there lawfully for fifteen years or had served with a permit under the same employer in the area for ten years. For those lucky enough to obtain Section Ten rights, there were up to thirty further regulations to contend with before they could start a business. The process of obtaining permission to start a new business could take up to two years and cost thousands of rands. And when all these obstacles were overcome, the applicant would be granted one small site which he could not sell or mortgage, and which he had to occupy personally.

One of the few businesses blacks were allowed to run was a general dealer's store. No one was allowed to own more than one store, and this could not be bigger than 400 square metres. Such trading stores were granted monopolies under a so-called radius restriction: no two were allowed within three or four kilometres of each other, sometimes eight. Thus even if the monopoly ensured a measure of success, no expansion was allowed. No black could have partners or form a company. Trading was severely curtailed, but industry was banned outright.

There was a handful of successful black businessmen, but so few you could count them on your fingers. Three or four of them made their money on filling station franchises with exclusive monopolies granted prior to the clampdown on such licences. That is why Ephraim Tshabalala's filling station in Soweto is said to have had the biggest turnover of any in South Africa — no one could get a filling station licence nearby.

Other businessmen, like the now famous industrialist Habakuk Shakwane, worked illegally in their backyards, making furniture, fixing cars and so on, and selling their products as underground black market operators. When various development corporations were established in the '70s, they sought out these underground entrepreneurs to offer them help. Black businessmen describe how one day, government inspectors were trying to close them down by confiscating their goods and equipment and fining them, while on the following day, other government officials were offering them subsidies and financial assistance to build factories in black development areas.

These few early success stories are important because they testify to the ability of real entrepreneurs to overcome the most extraordinary obstacles. Prior to the 1980s, the black reserves, locations and national states probably had less private enterprise than any East European country. There was more economic freedom in Poland, Yugoslavia, Bulgaria and East Germany than in black South Africa.

After 1970

In the course of the 1970s, many restrictions on blacks were lifted. In 1979, the 99-year leasehold was introduced in black townships. Land could still not be sub-let, mortgaged or sold freely but leasehold did offer some security of tenure. The Section 10 requirements for businesses were lifted, as were other regulations, and blacks were allowed to register companies and own industries. These reforms resulted in the creation of a substantial black business sector, but they did not put an end to the single greatest source of frustration for blacks — discretionary law.

Discretionary law

If a white person wants to open a fish and chip shop in a white area, all he has to do is fill in a form, find a zoned business site and sign a lease with the landlord. If he complies with objectively-established health regulations, he is entitled, as of right, to sell fish and chips. No one must approve of him as a person; no questions are asked about his nationality, competence, resources or language. No bureaucrat decides if there is adequate 'need and desirability' for such a shop. Simply because he is a white in a white area, he is entitled as a right, according to objective criteria, to run a fish and chip shop — or almost any other business or industry.

For a black, the situation is very different. Before he can open a fish and chip shop in Soweto, he has to ask an official for a site. The official may or may not grant his request, for reasons which he need not disclose. He may say 'yes' because he likes the applicant, or is related to him, or because he has received a sufficiently generous bribe. He may say no for equally subjective reasons. Once the site has been granted, the potential entrepreneur has to apply to another official for a licence. This may or may not be issued, for similar reasons. Then on to the health officials. And the building inspectors . . . until, many months and hundreds of rands later, he might be turned down for unspecified reasons.

South African blacks today have no experience of law which is equally applicable to all regardless of sex, creed or colour. What they experience now, from day to day, is arbitrary rule by men, a system which by its nature is rife with both real and suspected corruption. No self-respecting human being can be subjected to such a system without feeling frustrated or angry.

This frustration and anger is vented on apartheid and on free enterprise, which is mistakenly viewed as part and parcel of separate development. This is particularly ironic because, as we have shown, the source of the frustration is not free enterprise but its opposite — socialism.

Whites say there has been change and reform in South Africa which they can see and feel. Blacks are allowed in places where they were prohibited before; there is black advancement in jobs; blacks share restaurants and theatres and play sport with whites. Opinion polls show a dramatic change in white attitudes. To whites, these changes are substantial, and they cannot understand why blacks keep saying there has been no real change and that all reform to this point has been mere tokenism.

The reason for these divergent perceptions is obvious. Most of the changes which have occurred affect only the ability of blacks to interact socially with whites, which is relatively unimportant. Blacks, in their areas, are still subjected to all the same administrative discretions and controls as before. Although they now have freehold title, they still suffer from the bureaucracy, the red tape, the insults; their frustrations remain. There are more opportunities than before, but these too are subject to arbitrary discretion. Where black officials have replaced whites nothing has improved, because the discretionary powers remain the same.

The frustration has little to do with 'separateness', which, strictly speaking, is the meaning of apartheid. When the notorious 1913 Natives Land Act was introduced, it was not the separate areas to which black leaders objected: it was the violation of their economic rights that concerned them so deeply. They could see very clearly where the real problem lay.

If the requests of the deputation of black leaders which approached the Minister of Native Affairs and the British government in 1913 had been granted, and territorial separation had gone ahead, but within their own areas blacks had the same rights as whites, South Africa would be very different today.

In addition to scrapping influx control in July this year, the government should completely deregulate small business and introduce racial 'equivalence' by summarily repealing all laws affecting blacks in black areas which differ from those affecting whites in white areas. Over the years, a massive 'informal sector' has developed in black areas. Some estimates suggest that by 1980 there were over 800 000 underground businesses, comprising 30-40% of all economic activity. These will all surge ahead when government gets out of their way.

By removing influx control, deregulating small business and introducing equivalence, the government would, almost overnight, defuse the present critical situation, thus giving itself time in which to find an enduring political solution.

Does apartheid benefit whites?

There is a world-wide assumption that apartheid benefits whites. However, it can be easily shown that laws which interfere with voluntary exchange are bad for all the people involved.

Whites do not benefit when they may not develop townships for blacks, rent accommodation to blacks or trade with blacks. Whites in general do not benefit when blacks are prevented from providing services in white areas; most would favour black bus operators, taxi drivers, traders, shopkeepers and hoteliers if this meant lower costs and better service. Whites have never benefited from influx control limiting the number of people in black townships. It penalises whites not only because there is less labour available, but also because influx control pushes up the cost of labour, which in turn increases the cost of production and the price of goods to white consumers. And whites do not benefit when they pay for the decentralisation and small business development policy which establishes jobs for blacks in areas where they would not otherwise go.

Any two human beings who choose to deal with each other both benefit in their own view. Any two people who engage in a voluntary exchange are better off than they would be if they were prevented from making that exchange (see Chapter 8).

Whites who seek political security have been deluded into thinking they are also gaining economic advantages. We have seen in the historical analysis that almost every apartheid law passed prior to 1948 was aimed at protecting whites from competition. In the short term, these laws did keep some whites employed who would otherwise not have been, and they did prevent some inefficient white farmers and businessmen from going under. But in the long term they benefited no one, and they stopped South Africa from becoming one of the richest countries on earth.

Ethnicity and achievement

Many people believe that, by nature, blacks are not achievement-oriented. There are even studies which 'prove' that blacks have low motivational and aspirational levels. Whites in South Africa frequently remark that blacks live for the day — they are not interested in saving, investing or creating wealth.

There is considerable evidence to the contrary. The 1985 World Bank figures place Botswana and Malawi among the top ten countries in the world with regard to growth rates. The Ivory Coast has a prosperous economy and an enterprising, successful and wealthy black business community. Kenya under Kenyatta achieved consistently high growth rates. Why do these countries succeed whereas Ethiopia, Zaire and Tanzania do not? The reason is that the former countries enjoy economic freedom, and it seems that motivation is directly linked to the opportunities that arise in free markets.

We predict that if the aspirational levels of the Chinese in Hong Kong were studied, they would be found to be very high, while those of the Chinese in the People's Republic of China would be very low. Similarly, the aspirations of West Germans would be high, and those of East Germans low. People's aspirations relate to their economic environment and the opportunities it offers them, not to their genetic make-up or cultural background.

Most of the homelands in South Africa suffer from the same degree of socialism as the black locations and townships. Consequently, they are notoriously poor and dependent on South African government support.

In Ciskei, and to a lesser extent, Bophuthatswana, moves have been made to deregulate the economy. Within one year the Ciskeian economy turned around and Ciskei is now achieving a much higher growth rate than the rest of South Africa.

In Soweto and other townships, the relaxations in the 1970s led to a dramatic increase in the number of successful black entrepreneurs. NAFCOC, the black Chamber of Commerce federation, now has ten thousand paid-up members, which makes it the second-largest business organisation in South Africa. There has been an explosion of black entrepreneurs onto the business scene despite the vast array of laws which continue to inhibit black business.

Black African countries are not impoverished because blacks run them, but because their economic policies are wrong. Most black South Africans are not frustrated simply because whites rule them, but because they suffer under bureaucracy, red tape, over-regulation and officialdom. The real problem is not the colour of the people who control the machine, but the nature of the machine. If people have entrenched property rights, freedom of movement, exchange and association; if they are equal before the law and not subject to the whims of officialdom, then racial differences will cease to be so crucial.

This is not to imply that a solution for South Africa should maintain ethnic separation, but to emphasise that separation per se is not what has prevented blacks from advancing. In the course of the last century they have suffered a series of such devastating blows that one can only marvel at the extent to which they *have* progressed. First they were driven off the land; then when they sought employment in the cities they were denied access to the job market by labour legislation. When they tried to enter business they were stopped by licensing laws, costly minimum standards regulations and group areas laws. Back in the black reserves and locations they received the final blow — the Black Urban Areas Act and the Development, Trust and Land Act prevented them from starting businesses or entering industry there too.

The time has come for all this to change, and for black South Africans to show the world how much they can achieve if free to do so.

6

Political unrest: Causes and cures

Non violence is the answer to the crucial political and moral questions of our time; the need for man to overcome oppression and violence without resorting to oppression and violence.

Martin Luther King, Jr

Since August 1984, South Africa has experienced the most pro-longed and widespread black civil unrest in its history. Unlike the riots in Sharpeville and Soweto in 1960 and 1976, the current un-rest is not confined to major townships but has spread throughout the country, to small locations and townships as well as big ones. It is an expression of widespread black frustration and anger.

Unrest has taken the form of violence and rioting, stay-aways from work and schools, and boycotts of white shops. Individuals who are seen to be connected with 'the system' have been targets of violence, mainly in the form of petrol bomb attacks on their homes.

The trouble began in 1984 when several disturbances preceding the coloured and Indian parliamentary elections in August culminated in a serious outbreak on the day of the Indian election. In September, rent increases in the Vaal Triangle led to rioting which claimed many lives. Similar waves of violence continued throughout 1985. Since the decla-ration of a state of emergency in the middle of 1985, the unrest seems to have been only partially contained.

This chapter will consider the underlying causes of the unrest, what can be done to bring it to an end, and why reforms already undertaken have had so little positive effect.

Causes
The economic recession
The South African economy entered a major recession late in 1981, experienced two consecutive years of declining gross domestic product (GDP) in 1982 and 1983, and enjoyed only a brief upswing from mid 1983 to mid 1984 before resuming the downward trend. The revival which seems to be occurring now, towards the end of 1986, has not yet been sufficient to reduce unemployment.

67

The poor economic performance we have experienced in the 1980s has been largely a consequence of the deteriorating ratio of export prices to import prices and the prolonged drought, but it is perhaps even more a result of rising taxes and an increase in government spending as a proportion of total spending in the economy.

During the past fifteen years total public sector spending rose alarmingly from 20 % of GNP in 1970 to 30 % in 1985. The ratio of public sector employment to total employment, which had also risen sharply in the 1970s, continued upwards from 27 % to 30 % between 1980 and March 1986.

The failure of financial policy was and is the main proximate cause of unrest. There are many other causes too, but there is a powerful correlation between unrest and economic decline. Riots and boycotts tend to occur when people are unemployed and are struggling to make ends meet. People are inclined to accept almost any political order as long as there is prosperity, growth and job opportunity. In Hong Kong, the Chinese do not have the vote, but they are too busy improving their standard of living in a booming economy to care much about it. In many Swiss cantons, women received the vote only recently, but it was relatively unimportant to them because they were free and prosperous.

Over-regulation

When blacks are asked in surveys what upsets them most about the current system, the factors which rank highest are red tape, queues, bureaucracy, corruption, harassment and intimidation. The frustration caused by over-regulation, which was discussed in the preceding chapter, is an extremely important contributing factor to the current unrest, as is the hardship and deprivation caused by minimum standards regulations (see Chapter 4).

Another very important aspect of over-regulation is politicisation. As soon as something is regulated it becomes a political issue. Housing is regulated, so when rents rise, the government is blamed and rioting results, as occurred in Sebokeng. Transport is regulated, so when fares rise, the government is blamed and buses are stoned and burned, as happened in Mdantsane. Labour is regulated, so labour relations are strained. The political cost to the government of granting the Putco Bus Company a monopoly is immense — and the government gets no compensating benefits. Education is regulated, so when students are unhappy with some aspect of their schooling, the government is blamed and rioting ensues.

The following analogy illustrates why over-regulation provokes conflict. The production of trousers is an entirely non-political issue at the moment. One never reads in the newspaper that the price of trousers has gone up. Politicians have nothing to say about trousers. Trousers provoke absolutely no political conflict and yet they are very important!

We are told that transport, housing and education are important and that, therefore, government has to control them. But surely people would rather have trousers than transport! Let us assume that the government, because of the importance of trousers, establishes a Trouser Control Board, and a Trouser Development Corporation, and there is a Minister of Trouser Affairs. Trouser prices would become a source of political conflict and embarrassment for the government. Every time the price of trousers increased, it would result in boycotts, unrest and unpopularity for the government.

It is especially ironic that every major wave of unrest in this country has resulted from government controls regarding bus fares, rents, transport, education and wage rates, none of which were necessary for the maintenance of apartheid.

Unfulfilled expectations

The government's declared policy of change and the announcement of the Minister of Foreign Affairs, Pik Botha, to the United Nations that 'apartheid is dead', along with promises of political representation for blacks outside the homelands, have raised black expectations. These expectations have not been met for various reasons which are considered below.

To most blacks, it seems that only violence produces change. During times of peace and prosperity, reform efforts subside. Then there are the Sharpeville riots, the Soweto riots, the Sebokeng riots, and as a direct consequence, it seems, comes reform. This is not always the case. The regulation enforcing Afrikaans as a medium of instruction in black schools was the proximate cause of the Soweto riots. The regulation was withdrawn soon after, and apparently as a consequence of, the riots. But the government had decided several months prior to the riots that Afrikaans should not be compulsory. The decision had not yet been implemented by the bureaucracy.

The failure of reform

We have seen that the political cost to the government of controlling and subsidising the black economy is immense. The government seems to be aware of this and to understand the advantages of deregulation and privatisation. A process of reform was set in motion in the 1970s, with the introduction of 99-year leasehold, the relaxation of restrictions on black trading rights, relaxations on influx control, the scrapping of job reservation, the legalisation of black unions and the decision to privatise all government houses in the black townships. More recently, the Mixed Marriages Act, the Political Interference Act, the Immorality Act (Section 16) and influx control were repealed, the policy of progressively opening central business districts to all races was introduced, and segregation regarding amenities such as cinemas was relaxed.

If government intervention is indeed the main cause of unrest, why have these reforms had so little effect? Why are they regarded by so many blacks as irrelevant? One reason, which was discussed in the previous chapter, is that the repeal of laws preventing blacks and whites from integrating socially does nothing to ameliorate the real frustrations and grievances which result from economic interventions and discretionary law in black areas. But many reforms have involved potentially meaningful and important economic changes, and even these have had little effect. The reason for this is the bureaucracy.

Bureaucratic sabotage
Bureaucratic sabotage is one of the most serious problems facing South Africa. Many politicians would make a considerable contribution to solving problems if their wishes were actually carried out. They accept their portfolios with grand schemes to deregulate, to get rid of bureaucracy and red tape. They make repeated pronouncements to this effect but nothing gets done. Every year, for three years in a row, we have heard the Minister of Co-operation and Development announce that there will be open trading areas — but only now have the first few been declared.

When 99-year leasehold was announced, it was politically quite popular amongst blacks. That was in 1978. Not until 1985 were leases registered in any significant quantity. Civil servants simply did not implement the change expeditiously. Why not? Perhaps they were opposed to black home ownership, regardless of what the politicians said, so they dragged their heels; or perhaps they were just hopelessly inefficient.

Whatever the reason, when the law was finally implemented, blacks discovered that the leasehold title was a sham. The leases could not be freely traded or mortgaged. The bureaucracy continues to regulate the development, letting and exchange of land between blacks and therefore there are still virtually no estate agencies, no newspaper property columns — and, indeed, no property markets — in the townships.

When Dr Piet Koornhof was Minister of Co-operation and Development in 1980, he asked his officials to draw up three bills to get rid of all 'hurtful and unnecessary discrimination'. The bills were duly drafted and tabled in parliament, where, during the second reading, it was realised that the draft bills would have made the situation worse rather than better. Was this a mistake, or was it done deliberately by civil servants who wished to sabotage reform?

The Soweto riots might not have occurred if the government's decision to scrap compulsory Afrikaans had been speedily implemented. The current unrest might similarly have been averted if other political decisions had proceeded expeditiously. The bureaucracy simply will not — either because it is inefficient or because it is a law unto itself — expedite politically determined reforms.

How are these problems to be overcome?

How can we effectively deregulate and depoliticise society so as to satisfy black expectations?

Firstly, civil servants who disobey orders should be fired, as they would be in the private sector. Secondly, the government should consider putting deregulation and privatisation in the hands of competent and willing private sector agencies which will serve politicians directly, such as the Free Market Foundation, the Law Review Project, and the Privatisation and Local Government Centre.

Power must be devolved from central to local government. Social, racial, ethnic and economic decisions must be returned to the people they concern, and central government must be limited to aspects of administration which are not conflict-provoking. Part 3 of this book will attempt to provide a detailed blueprint of how all this might be done.

7 | The political status quo

The difference between politics and statesmanship is philosophy.

Will and Ariel Durant

What are the major political groupings in South Africa? Where do they fit into the scheme of things? What are their various positions and how do they differ from each other? How representative are they? And how, ultimately, would they fit into a solution to South Africa's problems? These are the questions addressed in this chapter.

The false left-right dichotomy
The political distinction between 'left' and 'right' is always dangerous and misleading. Firstly, it implies that there are only two political and economic options whereas in reality there are many. (See Fig. 1)

Secondly, it is based on the assumption that 'left' and 'right' positions are at opposite ends of the political spectrum, whereas in truth the groups which the terms popularly describe have a great deal in common with each other.

Left-right analysis suggests that there are two distinct classes engaged in a struggle: the working class on the 'left' and the dominant or ruling class on the 'right'.

Typically, the 'left' is identified with an economic order in which the state owns and controls everything, supposedly on behalf of 'the people'. The 'right' indicates an elitist group who, with or without the assistance of the state, acquire wealth by 'exploiting' employees and consumers.

This inadequate and misleading dualistic analysis is rendered even more confusing in South Africa than elsewhere by the fact that 'left' and 'right' usually refer specifically to one's position regarding race policy.

If you are opposed to apartheid, even if you are a radical laissez faire

73

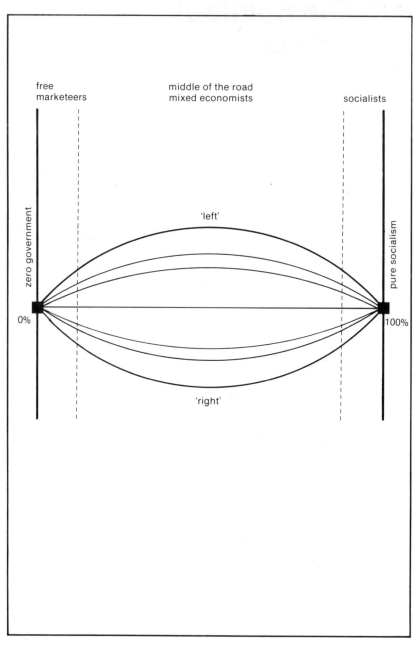

Fig. 1   False left — right dichotomy

capitalist, you are considered left by all but a handful of intellectuals. If you are in favour of apartheid, even if you are in favour of fully-fledged nationalisation, welfare statism, unbridled state control, central planning and all the other trappings of socialism, you will be called right-wing. The advocates of apartheid and socialism regard the two dogmas as opposites even though 'social engineering' is central to both.

'Left' and 'right', in South Africa, have little to do with one's position on nuclear energy, civil liberties, economic policy, foreign policy, environmental policy, welfare, trade unions, education and so on. In fact, such matters scarcely feature in the South African debate; only active members of a recognised political group, who read its literature and attend its congresses, will have some idea of the party's policy on these issues.

If you were to ask well-informed South Africans — political journalists or academics, for example — about NP constitutional policy, NRP policy on control boards, PFP policy on pollution or environmentalism or ANC policy on trading-hours, the chances are they would not know. But they would have a good idea of every party's position on race. Enquiries reveal that in truth none of the political groups except the National Party has established positions on most issues. Racial politics is all-absorbing.

Since left-right analysis in no way contributes to an understanding of South Africa's political groupings, we will avoid it.

The political groups discussed in this chapter include political parties, politicised labour and other pressure groups. They are dealt with in alphabetical order rather than by size or prominence because, on the one hand, size in terms of following is impossible to determine for many groups and, on the other hand, there is almost no correlation between the prominence a group achieves and the number of people it represents.

The actual membership of each of the major groupings is surprisingly small — and that includes even the prominent white political parties as a percentage of the white electorate. People are no longer blindly committed to particular groupings and there is a large floating vote in South Africa at present.

During the 1950s and '60s, there was a much clearer delineation between the United Party and the National Party, the PAC and the ANC and so on. Now numerous splinter groups have cropped up in between the major parties and it is difficult to establish the precise position of any group regarding South Africa's future.

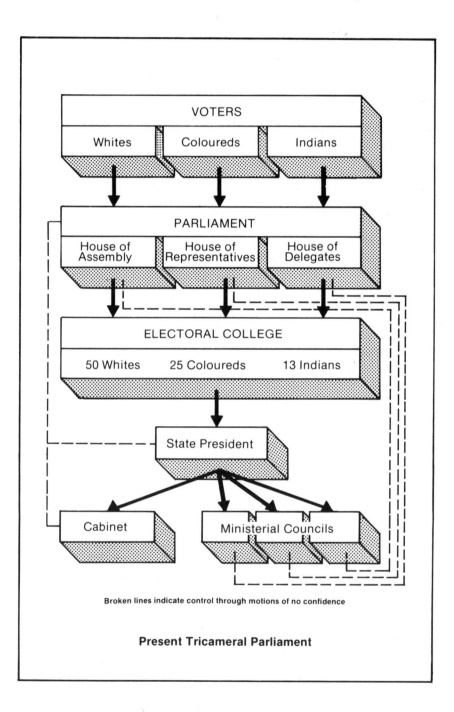

VOTERS

| Whites | Coloureds | Indians |

PARLIAMENT

| House of Assembly | House of Representatives | House of Delegates |

ELECTORAL COLLEGE

50 Whites   25 Coloureds   13 Indians

State President

Cabinet   Ministerial Councils

Broken lines indicate control through motions of no confidence

Present Tricameral Parliament

Tricameral parliament

Prior to 3 September 1984, only white South Africans were represented in parliament. Then a new constitution came into effect with the formation of two additional houses of parliament: the House of Representatives for coloureds, and the House of Delegates for Indians. Whites continue to be represented in the House of Assembly.

Five coloured and four Indian political parties participated in the elections. The UDF, NF, ANC and Inkatha called for potential voters to boycott the elections. Low polls were recorded and the election period was characterised by violence, intimidation and the detention of members of organisations opposed to the new constitution.

POLITICAL PARTIES AND PRESSURE GROUPS

African National Congress (ANC)

The ANC is a largely black political grouping which was formed in 1912 and banned in 1960. Its leader, Nelson Mandela, was convicted of sabotage and conspiring to commit treason and imprisoned on Robben Island under a life sentence. The ANC re-formed itself in South Africa's neighbouring states under the leadership of Oliver Tambo.

At the Morogoro Conference in 1969, the ANC confirmed a policy of violence against the South African government. During the 1970s, it went through a period of political and military consolidation accelerated by the arrival of some 9 000 black refugees from South Africa after the Soweto riots in 1976.

It is difficult to assess the number of ANC sympathisers with any accuracy but it is safe to say that the organisation has one of the biggest followings.

In a sense, the ANC has internal apartheid. It is multiracial rather than non-racial and has associated members from non-black groups who are represented in the Coloured People's Congress, the regional Indian Congresses, the Congress of Democrats for whites and the South African Congress of Trade Unions (SACTU), which comprises 'working class' people from all racial groups. All these are united under the Congress Alliance.

The ANC's aim is to turn South Africa into a social democracy as described in the *Freedom Charter* which was formulated at the Congress of the People in 1955.

The charter is important as it represents the first formal expression of the aspirations of a group possibly representing the majority in South Africa. However, it means different things to different people and contains sweeping generalisations which are highly ambiguous and open to widely varying interpretations. This may prove to be a good thing.

The charter includes the following aims: all 'national (race) groups' should have equal rights; land should be shared among those who work it; there will be work and security for all, houses and comfort for all, and peace and friendship. There will be private land ownership and most of commerce and industry will be private. The charter would nationalise mineral wealth, banks and monopoly industry.

Some political groups would like to push the ANC towards a more radical socialist position. One of these is the Communist Party. After the party was banned in the 1950s, South African communists decided to support the Congress Alliance — but they regard the ANC goal of a democratic capitalist state as Stage One only. The Communist Party envisages a second stage in which there would be a socialist revolution and the working class would come to power. The state would then confiscate and control all the means of production and distribution.

It should be noted that the ANC was willing to talk to the Government prior to its banning in 1960. Only then did it embark on military action. The government should lift the ban and release Nelson Mandela if it seriously seeks dialogue with all representative groups.

Azanian People's Organisation (Azapo)
AZAPO was formed in 1978 out of the ashes of various black consciousness groups after a clamp-down in 1977.

By early 1984 the organisation had 93 branches in 12 regions and 1 547 delegates and observers attended its annual congress.

AZAPO is fundamentally a black group. Some members would like to exclude whites from its ranks completely while others are prepared to accept some on an individual basis on the understanding that they work in white communities preparing their fellow whites for change. AZAPO is anti-capitalist, anti-liberal and anti-foreign interference. It is not interested in talking to the government or in co-operating in any way. It sees the government's desire for dialogue as a move to compromise liberation movements.

Its aim is to achieve black majority rule in a socialist state and to nationalise all means of production, all productive land, all means of communication, and all banks and insurance companies. It is affiliated to the National Forum and its members experience considerable harrassment by the security police.

Afrikanerweerstandsbeweging (AWB)
(Afrikaner Resistance Movement)
The AWB was formed in 1973. Its members are Afrikaner nationalists operating outside the political party system who advocate rigid ethnic separation in South Africa.

The AWB maintains that its leader, Eugene Terreblanche, speaks to at least 1 000 people a week and that cassettes of his speeches have been borrowed 100 000 times. It is not prepared to give membership numbers for 'strategic reasons'. Amongst its sympathisers are supporters of a cross-section of Afrikaner nationalist political parties.

The AWB advocates a Boer Republic for the Boerevolk. The area it wants for this is rather large, comprising a good third of the country and including the entire Transvaal and Free State. It would like to see South Africa divided into 'vrye volkstate' based not on colour but on history, tradition, language and culture. In other words, it would split both whites and blacks into separate cultural groups. Each 'volk' would have its own leaders within its own geographical area. The electorate of the boerevolkstaat would consist only of Afrikaners.

Conservative Party (CP)
The Conservative Party was formed in 1982 by a group which broke away from the ruling National Party in protest against its policy of 'change'. The party leader is Dr Andries Treurnicht, and its official newsletter *Patriot* has 17 000 subscribers.

The CP would retain all current apartheid legislation and restore separate development where it has been partially eroded. It advocates a policy of partition whereby each nation (race) would have its own area of jurisdiction: Indians would have part of Natal, the coloureds an area in the Western Cape and the various black nations their present territories. The states would be politically independent but economically interdependent.

The CP advocates a relatively free economy, but in white South Africa white workers would be protected and there would be anti-monopoly legislation.

Herstigte Nasionale Party (HNP)
(Reformed National Party)
The HNP, led by Mr Jaap Marais, was formed in 1969 and won its first seat in parliament in 1985. Its policy is very similar to that of the CP and the two parties have jointly contested seats in by-elections. Some members are in favour of a merger between the two.

The HNP maintains that the task of the authorities should be to ensure full freedom for every citizen (burgervryheid), including religious freedom and freedom of speech, and to ensure that no one group or organisation obtains coercive power in society.

Like the CP, it advocates separate development with no integration between groups of different race, culture, language and religion. It is in favour of redistribution of wealth to farmers and white couples with four or more children.

Inkatha Yenkululeko Yesizwe (INKATHA)
(Organisation for Freedom of the People)
Inkatha, under the leadership of Zulu Chief Mangosuthu Gatsha Buthelezi, has approximately one million members, nearly all of whom are black. While about 85% are Zulus, the non-Zulu membership is growing: there are many Sothos in the Inkatha hierarchy and the leader of the Youth Brigade, which has more than 480 000 members, is Sotho. The organisation has over 2 000 branches and the 10th general conference in 1984 was attended by 8 000 members and observers.

Inkatha's political position is moderate, and similar to that of the Progressive Federal Party. In the past both organisations have called for a national convention of representatives from all political and pressure groups to map out South Africa's political future.

Inkatha is committed to achieving radical change through non-violent means, including the total eradication of apartheid. Buthelezi is firmly committed to free enterprise as the economic system which will best serve the interests of the masses. He has said that the future holds the prospect of either a unitary state with universal suffrage as 'the end product of an armed revolt', or a federal system of government as the 'end product of the politics of negotiation'. He has denounced the ANC's commitment to violence on the basis that it retards the process of black liberation.

Inkatha has never made any major effort to recruit members outside the Zulu constituencies and this is perhaps a pity as there may well be many moderate blacks who would feel comfortable with the Inkatha philosophy but who do not wish to belong to a group which is overwhelmingly Zulu.

Labour Party (LP)

The first general election to the *House of Representatives* — the coloured chamber of the new tricameral parliament — was held on 22 August 1984.

The Labour Party, led by Rev Allen Hendrickse, won 76 of the 80 elected seats. As a consequence, it was accused by various black, Indian and coloured groups of 'selling out' and was suspended from the SA Black Alliance.

The Labour Party agreed to participate in the new system on the basis that it was a step toward the dismantling of apartheid. The LP is committed to eradicating apartheid, opposes communism vigorously, and subscribes to democracy and the rule of law. It is in favour of a mixed economy with a 'happy medium' between capitalism and socialism.

The LP has a non-racial constitution and, in addition to its coloured members, has about 200 black members, up to 1 000 white members and a few hundred Indian members.

At the LP's annual congress in Kimberley in December 1984, Mr Hendrickse proposed a federal system in which 'racist' and 'non-racist' states could co-exist. A special committee was set up to research the whole question of a federal structure based on one-man-one-vote in a non-racial state.

National Forum (NF)

The National Forum is a loose grouping of black nationalist individuals and 200 organisations which was launched at Hammanskraal in June 1983 by AZAPO and various black consciousness luminaries.

Saths Cooper, convener of the National Forum and the former leader of Azapo, declines to estimate how many people support the organisation but it is apparently not yet strong enough to form a national movement.

The NF was set up primarily as a think-tank to discuss and formulate policy for member organisations and its position is unequivocally socialist. It envisages a future for Azania (South Africa) in which the black working classes will be acknowledged as the true leaders. Whites who want to contribute to the struggle should do so in their own constituencies.

The NF sees apartheid as a socio-political expression of 'racial capitalism', or, in other words, as a system whereby the white state main-

81

ORGANIGRAM OF BLACK POLITICAL/LABOUR MOVEMENTS - AUGUST 1986

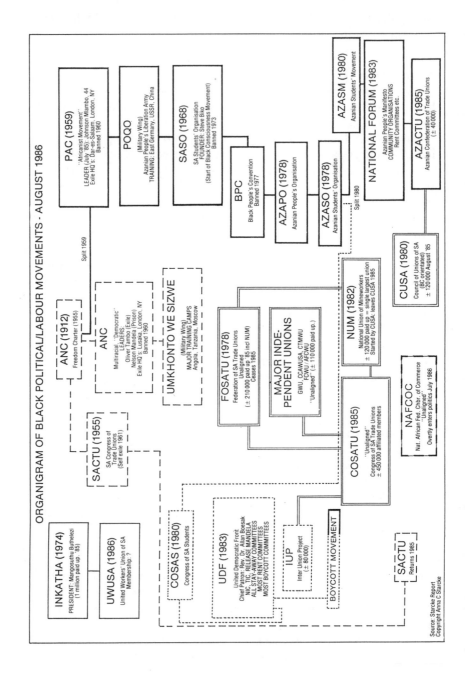

INKATHA (1974)
PRESIDENT: Mangosuthu Buthelezi
(1 million paid up ' 85)

UWUSA (1986)
United Workers' Union of SA
Membership: ?

SACTU (1955)
SA Congress of
Trade Unions
(Self exile 1961)

ANC (1912)
Freedom Charter (1955)

ANC
Multiracial "Democratic"
LEADERS:
Oliver Tambo (Exile)
Nelson Mandela (Prison)
Exile HQ's Lusaka, London, NY
Banned 1960

UMKHONTO WE SIZWE
(Military Wing)
MAJOR TRAINING CAMPS
Angola, Tanzania, Moscow

Split 1959

PAC (1959)
"Africanist Movement"
LEADER (July '85): Johnson Mlambo, 44
Exile HQ's: Dar-es-Salaam, London, NY
Banned 1960

POQO
(Military Wing)
Azanian People's Liberation Army
TRAINING: East Germany, USSR, China

SASO (1968)
SA Students Organisation
FOUNDER: Steve Biko
(Start of Black Consciousness Movement)
Banned 1973

BPC
Black People's Convention
Banned 1977

AZAPO (1978)
Azanian People's Organisation

AZASO (1978)
Azanian Students Organisation

Split 1980

AZASM (1980)
Azanian Students Movement

NATIONAL FORUM (1983)
Azanian People's Manifesto
COMMUNITY ORGANISATIONS
Rent Committees etc.

AZACTU (1985)
Azanian Confederation of Trade Unions
(± 40 000)

FOSATU (1978)
Federation of SA Trade Unions
Unaligned
(± 210 000 paid up ' 85 incl NUM)
Ceases 1985

**MAJOR INDE-
PENDENT UNIONS**
GWU, CCAWUSA, CTMWU
FCWU / AFCWU
"Unaligned" (± 110 000 up.)

NUM (1982)
National Union of Mineworkers
± 120 000 paid up = single largest union
Started by CUSA: leaves CUSA 1985

CUSA (1980)
Council of Unions of SA
(BC orientated)
± 120 000 August '85

COSATU (1985)
"Unaligned"
Congress of SA Trade Unions
± 450 000 affiliated members

NAFCOC
Nat. African Fed. Chbr. of Commerce
"Unaligned"
Overtly enters politics July 1986

COSAS (1980)
Congress of SA Students

UDF (1983)
United Democratic Front
Chief Patron: Rev. Dr. Allan Boesak
NIC, TIC, RELEASE MANDELA
ALL STAY-AWAY COMMITTEES
MOST RENT COMMITTEES
MOST BOYCOTT COMMITTEES

IUP
Inter Union Project
(± 80 000)

BOYCOTT MOVEMENT

SACTU
Returns 1985

Source: Starcke Report
Copyright Anna C Starcke

tains economic hegemony by means of racial oppression.

The concept of 'racial capitalism', now called 'racialism and capitalism', was introduced to the black consciousness movement by Dr Neville Alexander, who spent ten years on Robben Island followed by a five-year banning order which expired in 1979. He then reappeared to lend impetus and coherence to the Marxist aspect of the black consciousness movement. He gave the keynote address at the NF launch.

The NF disagrees with the UDF's acceptance of the concept of different national groups which coincides with the government position. It rejects the Freedom Charter and the Charter's recognition of the 'rights' of different 'national groups and races' to 'use their own languages and develop their own folk culture and customs'. It views the UDF and the ANC as anti-apartheid and reformist, but not revolutionary. It believes that the government recognises this and, as a result, may legitimise the ANC.

The NF would have an Azania peopled only by Azanians, all speaking English and all paying allegiance to the nation rather than to any minority interests. Its manifesto pledges the movement 'to struggle tirelessly for . . . the development of one national culture inspired by socialist values'.

Several of its constituent organisations are more interested in promoting a black Azania than a workers' Azania.

Natal Indian Congress (NIC)

The Natal Indian Congress is affiliated to the UDF and subscribes to the Freedom Charter. It is strongly opposed to the new constitution, which it sees as a means of entrenching racial oppression in South Africa.

It campaigned vociferously for a boycott of the 1984 elections and clashed publicly with the security police. Several of its leaders have been charged with high treason, and others have been detained without trial.

National Party (NP)

The National Party was formed in 1915 and has been the ruling party in South Africa since 1948.

In 1959 Dr Verwoerd, then leader of the National Party, formulated a master plan for separate development in South Africa, based on the concept that different racial groups should be divided into homelands or national states with political autonomy. This plan was put into action and homeland states were formed which were intended to satisfy black political aspirations. However, as the NP did not consider it possible to identify and establish separate states for Indians and coloureds, these groups had no representation in central government until the new constitution of 1983 was approved. As mentioned earlier, this created a tricameral parliament with a House of Representatives for the coloureds and a House of Delegates for the Indians.

This new system represented many different things to South Africans and met with a wide variety of reactions. White nationalist groups saw it as a step in the direction of racial integration, which they rejected. There was a negative reaction on the part of many blacks, Indians, coloureds and whites who saw it to be a further entrenchment of racial separation and a reiteration of the refusal to grant blacks any kind of real political power. There was a positive response amongst many whites, coloureds and Indians who saw in it the thin edge of the wedge, a first move towards a multiracial or non-racial society, which they welcomed; and a positive reaction amongst some who saw it to be a final solution to South Africa's problems.

The government has emphasised that it was a step in the process of constitutional development and President P W Botha is openly committed to constitutional, social and economic reform which will involve blacks in political decision-making.

There are major differences of opinion amongst party members as to what is meant by reform and change. President Botha is not prepared to offer any kind of blueprint for the future. But for the first time, groups outside the ruling party are able to make significant contributions towards policy formation through formal and informal channels.

National People's Party (NPP)
The National People's Party, which is led by Mr Amichand Rajbansi, is an Indian party which won 18 of the 40 elected seats in the House of Delegates.

It stands for the elimination of racial, cultural and sexual discrimination by non-violent means. Its following is estimated at around 29% of Indians.

New Republic Party (NRP)
The NRP was formed in 1977 and is generally regarded as the successor of the previous official opposition, the United Party. It has been

weakened over the past few years by internal friction, financial problems, the loss of several by-elections and the defection of three MPs to the NP. The party now has only five MPs, but remains strong in local government structures in Natal. Led by Mr Bill Sutton, the party has a white membership but is prepared to accept Indians and coloureds.

The NRP advocates a federal-confederal plan for South Africa in which there would be a 'Common Area' occupied by whites, coloureds, Indians and urban blacks. Each racial group would have its own local authorities running community affairs. A federal council would provide co-operation between the groups in the common area. 'Open areas' would be provided for those who did not wish to identify with any specific group.

The common area and the independent homelands would form a confederation. A confederal assembly would administer matters of common concern delegated to it by agreement of the confederal states.

Pan-Africanist Congress (PAC)

The Pan-Africanist Congress, formed in 1959, has been prevented by serious internal conflicts from being very effective inside or outside South Africa in the past few years. The PAC's central committee suffered a three-way split in 1984, and the Congress has been plagued by questions as to what its role should be, given the visible support for the ANC whose platform is very similar to its own. Nevertheless, the PAC maintains that it 'continues to lead the people in the struggle'.

Progressive Federal Party (PFP)

The Progressive Federal Party was formed in 1977 and is the official opposition to the ruling National Party. The PFP was a white party but when legislation prohibiting multiracial parties was repealed recently it opened its membership and is now actively recruiting all races.

The PFP is in favour of equal citizenship rights for all South Africans; shared political rights; religious freedom and the right of people to maintain their own language and culture; equality of opportunity and the protection of property rights. It advocates a fairly free economy combined, at least initially, with considerable state welfare, and it is against group domination and statutory apartheid. It has called for the release of Nelson Mandela and other political detainees, the unbanning of political organisations and an end to the state of emergency.

The PFP has been the most vociferous of the groups calling for a national convention at which representatives of all South Africa's major groups would draw up a new constitution. Inkatha and the Labour Party have also expressed themselves in favour of a national convention, while the NP, CP, and AZAPO are against it.

SABRA

SABRA is a white nationalist organisation which was formed in 1948. Its 4 000 paid-up members do not see themselves as a political group but as an Afrikaner scientific/educational society organised to provide scientific information regarding relations between races and nations.

SABRA advocates the development of free, democratic nation states with free enterprise economies which would co-operate on matters of common interest. These states would be based on racial segregation and the primary aim would be to secure the future of whites.

Sofasonke Party

The Sofasonke Party is a black moderate party which functions primarily in the Vaal Triangle. It claims a registered membership of 180 000 people spread among 33 branches. The party has a majority in the Soweto City Council and plans to establish itself nationally.

It concerns itself mainly with local politics and its membership is open to coloureds . It believes that peaceful, constructive participation is the route to reform. There are similar parties in other urban areas.

Solidarity

Solidarity is an Indian party which was formed in January 1984 to contest the election to the House of Delegates. Led by Mr J N Reddy, Solidarity won 17 of the 40 elected seats. It is in favour of free enterprise, a unitary education system and a bill of rights guaranteeing individual freedoms. Like the NPP, its main objective is to promote a non-racial society through consultation rather than confrontation. It does not see any marked differences between its policies and those of the NPP.

United Democratic Front (UDF)

The United Democratic Front was launched by Rev Allan Boesak and others in Cape Town in 1983. It claims the support of two million people belonging to its 648 affiliate organisations, which range from small insignificant groups to important and influential organisations. The figure of two million is reached by counting all the members of all the affiliates and does not allow for overlapping memberships.

Most of the groups under the UDF umbrella are racially defined, such as the Transvaal Indian Congress, and they include trade unions and civic associations.

The UDF's sole formal manifesto is the Declaration of the United Democratic Front which calls for 'a united, democratic South Africa based on the will of the people'. It provides no details which expand on this. Many UDF affiliates support the Freedom Charter, which they regard as the embodiment of the liberation movement. The Charter envisages a future for South Africa in which the rights of different national groups are protected, but in which all have equal status. Some kind of power sharing is envisaged, and certainly a degree of wealth redistribution — especially regarding land. It is against violence.

The UDF is regarded by many as the legitimate front of the ANC. This may or may not be true. But both subscribe to the Freedom Charter, and Zinzi Mandela, daughter of the ANC's Nelson Mandela, has given the UDF her public blessing.

Some UDF affiliates have joined the call for a national convention, while others, amongst them Mr Cassim Saloojee, UDF treasurer, have argued that a national convention cannot be held 'when our true leaders are still in detention, banned, or in exile'.

There is no love lost between the National Forum and the UDF. Ideological differences have recently resulted in open warfare, especially amongst students, and campuses and hostels have become the settings for knife battles, stabbings and persecutions.

Trade Unions

Trade unions in South Africa are highly politicised. Various unions reflect the political positions of all the major parties and pressure groups which have been discussed.

Congress of South African Trade Unions (COSATU)

COSATU is the most recent federation of trade unions to appear on the South African scene, and possibly the biggest. Launched in November 1985, it has 33 affiliates representing 'nearly 450 000' workers. It is non-racial but predominantly black; it is not aligned to any political party but has a position similar to that of the UDF.

Council of Unions of South Africa (CUSA)

CUSA has twelve affiliates and approximately 120 000 paid up members. It is open to workers of all races but reserves leadership posts for blacks. Its position is similar to that of the National Forum.

South African Confederation of Labour (SACLA)

SACLA has twelve affiliates and about 124 400 members. Its membership is exclusively white and about 40% are state employees. The two main affiliates are the Mine Workers' Union and the South African Iron, Steel and Allied Industries Union, both of which favour apartheid.

General

COSATU and CUSA, along with about thirty-five unaffiliated unions — notably the African Food and Canning Workers' Union, the Commercial, Catering and Allied Workers' Union of SA, the General Workers' Union, the National Union of Mineworkers and the SA Allied Workers' Union — are sometimes collectively known as the emerging union movement, which is racially mixed in composition but predominantly black. They have been responsible for increased strike action, boycotts and stay-aways and some unionists see them as the only legal outlets for black political aspirations.

The established union movement consists of SACLA and more than 100 unaffiliated registered unions.

The number of whites-only registered unions has dropped dramatically — from seventy-one in 1982 to forty-three in 1983.

The total membership of all unions in South Africa is about 12,4% of the economically active population (including the ten homelands). This is far lower than the percentages in most European democracies, where 50 to 80% of the workforce is unionised. It is closer to unionisation rates in the USA and Far East capitalist countries.

Homeland political parties

In the homelands there are many black political parties, some with large followings.

They are ethnically homogenous and all oppose apartheid in that they are against laws which discriminate on racial rounds. Most, but not all, favour some kind of homeland policy, and ultimately a Southern African federation or confederation. Homeland parties generally rely on tribal loyalties, and traditional chiefs are prominent in most of them.

Other pressure groups

The nature of the problems which confront South Africa has resulted in a high degree of political consciousness. As a result, organisations formed for entirely different reasons have become political pressure-groups. There are many examples — too many to mention — but they fall into the following main categories.

Black, white and mixed students' organisations represent all the main positions from white to black nationalism, marxism to free enterprise and violent confrontation to peaceful dialogue.

The Civic Associations movement, started by the Committee of Ten in Soweto in the 1970s under the chairmanship of Dr Ntato Motlana, concerns itself primarily with local government issues in black and coloured townships. Unlike Sofasonke, it is firmly opposed to participation in urban council elections.

The church is involved in the debate in varying degrees. The S A Council of Churches rose to prominence under Bishop Desmond Tutu's leadership in the 1970s. It supports the UDF and is the South African counterpart of the World Council of Churches.

The two major Afrikaans churches, the Nederduits Gereformeerde Kerk (NGK) and the Nederduits Hervormde Kerk van Afrika (NHK) have made a material contribution in the past to the conviction amongst Afrikaners that apartheid is consistent with the scriptures. The NGK has now renounced racism and this should have a significant impact on Afrikaner thinking.

Organised business groups are playing an increasingly overt political role, as are institutes, welfare and service groups, public policy and cultural groups. In Natal representatives from a wide variety of interest groups have formed the Natal-KwaZulu Indaba in an attempt to agree on economic and constitutional proposals for a post-apartheid Natal. Delegates from the farming community, business, industry, women's groups and mainstream political groups meet together for two days every week to consider various proposals. The Indaba has agreed on a Bill of Rights and the Chairman, Professor Desmond Clarence, told the *Cape Argus* in August 1986: "Although there is no real framework, it looks as if the plan could be influenced by the Swiss Canton system. Authors of the book *South Africa — The Solution*, Leon Louw and Frances Kendall, are among the few people who have been asked to give evidence to the Indaba."

In addition, there are numerous international anti-apartheid and 'Friends of South Africa' organisations.

Relative to its size, South Africa must have one of the greatest proliferations of political and pressure groups in the world. Many of them make a significant contribution to the course of events.

Conclusion
Almost all of these political groups are characterised primarily by op-

position politics. It is clear what they are *against*; it is not at all clear what they are *for*. None of them, except for the classical marxists and the Afrikaner nationalists, have offered concrete proposals for reform.

Moreover, no single group is representative of anything approaching a majority of the population. The UDF and Inkatha claim memberships of around two million and one million respectively, but even these numbers are small in relation to a South African adult population of approximately fifteen million. So we have many small divergent groups, few of which have any clear direction, policy or constituency.

The extreme black nationalists (AZAPO and the National Forum) and the extreme white nationalists (the AWB, HNP and CP) reject each other equally, yet share a lot of common ground in terms of racial exclusion. Both aim to take control of the country and to impose their systems on everyone else.

The more moderate groupings — the ANC, UDF, NP, NRP, PFP, Inkatha and so on — all talk about equal rights, recognition for national groups, devolution and power sharing, but none of them articulate clearly what these concepts imply.

What *is* clear is that most white South Africans and many Indians and coloureds will strongly resist the formation of a unitary state with a heavily centrally controlled economy and massive wealth redistribution. Afrikaner nationalists in particular would fight to the bitter end against any system which would rob them of their cultural identity. At the same time, blacks, coloureds and Indians will not settle for anything less than full South African citizenship, and equality with white South Africans.

In a recent television news programme South African businessmen who met with ANC representatives in Lusaka reported that they had been unable to agree with the ANC 'on economic policy'. The question one must ask is, why were they trying to agree? Why were they not considering an option in which each group could pursue its own economic policy? The answer is that they were locked into a debate based on the collectivist assumptions that the 'winner takes all' and 'unity is strength'.

As long as these remain the underlying assumptions, South African political life will be characterised by escalating conflict and bloodshed.

The current impasse in South Africa exists because all the various options under debate lead to a dead end. If you ask supporters of any of the political parties or alliances whether they think their organisation could bring peace and prosperity to the country, most would say no. Very few people think that their own group really has a solution; most anticipate continued and escalating conflict, and desire only that their group should preside over it.

But there is another option, and that is to replace opposition politics with 'pro' politics; to become aware that we can choose a multi-option situation in which there is strength in diversity.

There is only one way in which the wide diversity of social, cultural, ethnic and political aspirations of South Africans can be accommodated: the country must be divided into states or cantons, each governing itself according to the dictates of its citizens. Central government must be constitutionally limited to a few general areas of jurisdiction which are agreed upon by all the cantons and which do not provoke conflict.

Under such a system, every person born in greater South Africa, regardless of race or nationality, would be a South African citizen with the same rights as every other citizen. Every adult would have the vote and all political parties would be free to contest elections in any or all of the autonomous districts. All major groups would govern sizeable areas and run them in their own way.

Freedom of movement would be entrenched in the constitution so that if an HNP supporter found himself in an AZAPO area, he would be free to move to an HNP or CP canton, and vice versa.

The only political group that stands to lose power under this system is the NP. But the NP has already accepted the principles of power sharing and devolution. It would continue to control certain areas in a canton system for many years: the alternatives it now faces are that it might find itself out of government altogether or that it may soon be presiding over a bloodbath.

8 The redistribution of wealth

The inherent vice of capitalism is the unequal sharing of blessings; the inherent virtue of socialism is the equal sharing of miseries.

Winston Churchill

Many blacks believe that because they have suffered severe historical disadvantages, any solution to South Africa's problems must begin with massive wealth redistribution.

In the previous chapter, we saw that the ANC, AZAPO, the National Forum and the UDF all favour some degree of wealth redistribution.

The analogy of a race helps to explain their perception. In this race, blacks have been held at the starting line and whites are halfway around the track. Now blacks are being told that they can join the race, and understandably they feel that this is unjust. Whites should rather come back to the beginning, and then blacks and whites can all start again together.

It is easy to sympathise with this view. Blacks have been subjected to gross injustices. If these could be redressed simply by redistributing wealth, we would have a quick and easy solution to our problems. But all the evidence at our disposal shows that redistribution doesn't help the people it is intended to help. The poor are not helped by the destruction of the rich.

In this chapter, we will attempt to expose the economic myths which have given rise to the mistaken view that by taking wealth from the rich and giving it to the poor, the poor will benefit. We will discuss the negative consequences of redistribution, as well as the practical difficulties involved in implementing it. And we will offer a suggestion as to how compensation could be made to blacks in a way which would benefit the economy.

93

ECONOMIC MYTHS

The zero sum fallacy

According to the zero sum theory of exchange, one person's gain is another person's loss. In the words of John Ruskin, 'Whenever material gain follows exchange, for every plus there is a precisely equal minus.'

The argument is, then, that whenever a profit is made, it is made at the expense of another person. In other words, if Pick 'n Pay makes profits, then consumers are being exploited.

This is clearly nonsense. On the contrary, both parties gain from voluntary exchange. Professor Carl Bauer, head of the Economics Department at Fort Hare University, uses a simple analogy to demonstrate this:

Two boys meet in the street. One plays rugby and the other soccer. The rugby player has a soccer ball and the soccer player has a rugby ball, and they agree to exchange balls. Everyone will agree that now they are both better off, yet neither has incurred a loss. There is still only one soccer ball and one rugby ball, but there has been a gain. Similarly, when Pick 'n Pay stores sell goods at lower prices than other supermarkets, their customers benefit and more people want to buy from them. If their turnover increases, they make bigger profits and are able to open more stores so that even more people may benefit from their low prices. When an employer offers someone a job and the job is accepted, both the employee and the employer gain: they are both better off than they were.

This is true of every free exchange ever made, because people would not agree to an exchange if, in their own view, they did not gain from it. Sometimes they make a mistake, but this doesn't alter the principle. The only time mutual gain does not occur is when laws are passed which interfere with free exchange.

The zero sum theory implies that if blacks suffer disadvantages, whites automatically benefit and conversely, if blacks benefit, whites inevitably lose. In truth, in a free society, every exchange between blacks and whites would be to their mutual gain. Clearly, a white landlord is better off if he is allowed to lease or sell property to blacks, and a black restaurateur benefits if he can serve whites.

In South Africa, as we have seen, many laws have been passed which interfere with free exchange, especially with black freedom of exchange. It is these laws which have held blacks back, not white advantages.

The rich get richer and the poor get poorer

One corollary of the zero sum fallacy is the view that as the rich get richer, the poor get poorer.

Apart from the theoretical weakness of this view, various studies undertaken in South Africa, and in particular a research project on white and black incomes undertaken by the Department of Economics at the University of Natal, present incontrovertible evidence to the contrary.[1]

Between 1917 and 1970, black and white shares of national income remained remarkably constant. White income averaged 73,5% of the total while blacks, Indians and coloureds shared the remaining 26,5%, with blacks averaging 17% of the total.

After 1970 a dramatic change occurred. In five years, the black, Indian and coloured share of income grew from 26% to 32% and the white share dropped from 74% to 68%. By 1980, the black, Indian and coloured share rose to approximately 40% of the total.

Gains made by blacks, Indians and coloureds were not made at the expense of whites. South Africa experienced very high growth rates during the early '70s. In other words, while the black share of the cake was increasing, the cake itself was increasing at an impressive rate, so that blacks were getting a bigger share of a bigger cake. Whites were getting a smaller share of a bigger cake, but their slice was nonetheless significantly bigger than before. A study by the Bureau of Market Research of the University of South Africa showed that between 1960 and 1980, the real personal income of all South Africans (excluding the independent homelands) rose by 115,2%. White incomes rose by 112,1%, black incomes by 220,8%, coloured incomes by 246,6% and Indian incomes by 332,5%.

What brought about this sudden change? Prior to 1970, there was massive wealth redistribution from whites to blacks and, simultaneously, severe restrictions on black economic activity. After 1970, there was a net relaxation of restrictions on blacks which resulted in a rapid increase in black upward mobility.

Redistribution failed to improve the lot of blacks, whereas a very small measure of black participation in the market achieved remarkable results.

The rise in black incomes was linked to large wage increases in the mining industry when the price of gold rose rapidly in the early 1970s, but perhaps had even more to do with a substantial growth in the numbers of black professionals, technicians, managers, administrators, clerks and salespeople. The annual growth rates for the six-year period 1969-1975 were:

	Whites	Coloureds	Asians	Africans
Professional and Technical	7,7%	8,9%	10,6%	15,4%
Managerial and Administrative	9,8%	28,8%	17,6%	44,7%
Clerical	4,9%	14,1%	16,9%	15,1%
Sales	5,7%	20,7%	12,1%	6,8%

During the 1980s, for reasons which have been mentioned, the general economic growth rate has declined to an average of 2% per year. The economy is now performing badly and everyone is worse off.

The onerous cost of black socialism

In the course of this country's history, a staggering amount of wealth has been transferred from whites to blacks.

South Africa has one of the most severe progressive tax systems in the world. Sweden is generally regarded as redistributing more wealth than any other country, but we are not far behind. Maximum personal income tax in Sweden is 57%, in South Africa 50% +. Maximum company tax in Sweden is 40% of profits, in South Africa 50%.

While it is difficult to assess precisely who carries the final tax burden, the bulk of direct tax is paid by whites. Taking all forms of taxation into account, it is estimated that at least 75% of national tax is paid by whites and probably more. Whites pay about 90% of income tax and an even higher percentage of company tax. Much of this money pays for black socialism and apartheid. Whites pay for black housing, transport and schools as well as decentralisation, homeland development, influx control, food subsidies, separate amenities and necessary incidentals such as international propaganda and ideological censorship.

Dr Frederik van Zyl Slabbert, until recently leader of the PFP, observed in parliament that the government has paid R1,6 billion per annum directly to the homelands in addition to the R627 million which they receive indirectly. This expenditure has only succeeded in increasing the real per capita gross domestic product (GDP) in the homelands from R40 to R46 between 1970 and 1980. In the tax year 1984/85, the homelands were paid a combined total of R2,2 billion. This constituted 8,8% of the budget.

We have talked about the rape of black land which has occurred throughout South Africa's history, but many whites have been driven from their land too. Thousands of white farms have been expropriated for incorporation into homelands, locations or the Development Trust. Many more thousands have lost their homes, along with blacks, Indians and coloureds, as various residential areas have been re-allocated from one group to another. A classic case of 'musical townships' occurred when whites were moved out of parts of Mayfair in Johannesburg so that it could become an Indian area, while simultaneously Indians in Pageview/Vrededorp, just down the road, were evicted so that their area could become white.

Both government and homeland officials have made the disastrous mistake of confusing ownership and jurisdiction. In other words, they have assumed that if a boundary is moved, all the land affected must be expropriated. As a consequence, entire white towns such as Port St Johns and Seymour have been expropriated for incorporation in black areas, when boundaries could simply have been moved so that the towns would fall under a new jurisdiction. When farms, shops, hotels, and businesses are expropriated, all the goodwill, expertise, energy and capital invested by their erstwhile owners are lost. None of this waste need have occurred.

Income gradients

Mathematicians and econometricians have made some interesting discoveries about income gradients which directly contradict the view that if all incomes are roughly equal, most people will benefit.

In grossly simplified terms, an income gradient is the measurement of the ratio of high income to low income earners in a society. The greater the difference between high and low incomes in a country, corporation or business, the higher the income gradient.

An examination of the income gradients in various countries shows that gradients exceeding 0,6 correlate with times of prosperity. In fact, the higher the gradient, the greater the prosperity of the country as experienced by the average citizen (see Fig 2).

During the nineteenth century, when income tax rates were negligible, gradients were usually between 0,58 and 0,78. In the twentieth century, as taxation increased, income gradients began to fall. A few years ago South Africa had the lowest gradient in the world, at 0,33. It has now risen to 0,4, more or less the same as the UK.

South Africa's heavy progressive tax system, combined with black socialism, is the primary reason for this inordinately low income gradient.

Income gradients vary in different sectors of the economy. In sectors with high gradients, there is high upward mobility. People are motivated to work by the potential for advancement. This upward mobility affects the entire sector so that ultimately, the lowest incomes are higher than those in sectors with low gradients.

Sectors with low gradients lose personnel regularly as people migrate to greener pastures where income gradients are higher.

K A H Adams, one of the world's experts on income gradients, concludes that if steps are taken to improve conditions by equalising incomes, conditions will in fact worsen.

Diagrammatic representation of high and low income gradients
On the base line of the triangles are the lowest income earners, at
the apex are those who earn the most.

A illustrates an economy with a high income gradient: relatively
few poor people; lots of upward mobility; high expectations.
Dotted △ shows potential income distribution.

B illustrates an economy with a low income gradient: many poor
people; little upward mobility; low expectations.

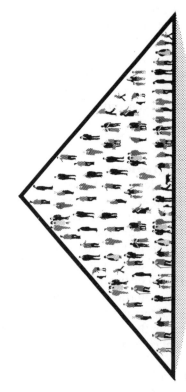

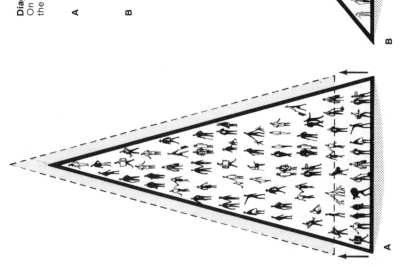

Fig. 2

98

Instead, marginal tax rates should be reduced to a maximum of $33\frac{1}{3}\%$, which will result in steeper gradients and rapidly increased growth rates. The fiscal loss would be quickly made up by increased productivity.[2]

Practical difficulties with redistribution

It is very easy to talk about redistributing wealth, and superficially the idea has obvious attractions. In reality, a host of problems arise.

It is virtually impossible to determine which blacks should be compensated and to what extent — and which whites should pay the cost. There is no way of knowing who has suffered most and who is most to blame.

Neither is it easy to decide what should be redistributed. We have mentioned that our tax system is already so severely progressive that it retards economic growth and penalises whites and blacks alike.

If white property is to be shared out, the question is how? If all white cars, homes and farms were dumped on the market, their prices would drop precipitously and revenues would be much lower than anticipated. Everyone would be a net loser. Alternatively, if cars and houses belonging to whites were given to a few black families, as happened in Transkei and other countries, the vast majority of blacks would be no better off. In the process, most whites with skills, qualifications and productive potential would leave the country; many would go out of business; and there would be massive distortions and malinvestments throughout the country.

If white farmland were divided into small plots and parcelled out to blacks there would be the same disastrous results throughout the country that this policy caused in the homelands, and which we discussed in Chapter 1 as a major cause of the downfall of blacks. If the new land-owners were free to lease or sell the land it would rapidly find its way back into the hands of the best farmers, who for the present are mostly whites. If they were allowed to dispose of the land only to other blacks it would gravitate into the hands of the best black farmers, of whom there are presently only a handful with the same proven competence as whites. This would lead to an even greater concentration of land in the hands of a small elite than at present.

If the intention is to redistribute wealth by transferring assets to the government on behalf of 'the people', we must repeat that massive redistributions have already occurred. Billions of rands have been transferred to black homeland governments from whites. Most of this money supports bureaucratic structures. 'The people' do not benefit. In addition, all the assets presently owned by the South African government — state corporations, black townships, vast expanses of land, beaches, harbours, roads, buildings — belong to 'the people'. If the government consisted of black instead of white people, it would not make an iota of difference.

If wealth is to be redistributed in the form of welfare, an observation made by American economist Thomas Sowell should be kept in mind: 'The poor are a gold mine. By the time they have been studied, advised, experimented with and administered, the poor have helped many a middle-class liberal to achieve affluence with government money.' Statistics for the USA, which is presumably more efficient than most countries, show that while welfare spending is calculated at around $48 000 per poor family of four, each poor family receives only between $6 500 and $8 000 worth of welfare. The rest is swallowed up by the administration.[3]

The frustrating truth is that redistribution is very difficult to achieve. In the past, attempts to redistribute wealth have invariably resulted in a redistribution of poverty.

In Africa, this has been true of every attempt to transfer wealth from the rich to the poor. In Zaire, President Mobuto Sese Seko nationalized all private assets so that white wealth could be enjoyed by blacks. When the economy collapsed, he invited the dispossessed businessmen, farmers and industrialists back, but his invitation was declined.

In Zimbabwe, the Mugabe government promised redistribution but soon found that the consequences of any move in that direction were disastrous. As a result, whites' assets have by and large been left alone, and black disadvantages are being offset by greater access to opportunities previously reserved for whites. Zimbabwe's economy is performing fairly well, while Zaire is virtually bankrupt.

Compensation is possible

We have argued that the economic theory behind redistribution is fundamentally flawed and that, in practice, wealth transfers from rich to poor result in a net loss for everyone.

Nonetheless, for three hundred years South African blacks, and to a lesser degree Indians and coloureds, have suffered gross violations of their rights. Their anger is entirely justified.

The damage which has been done cannot be accurately calculated, nor can it be adequately redressed. But it is possible for white South Africans to offer some compensation as a gesture of contrition.

The government's share of the country's wealth has grown throughout this century so that now, directly or indirectly, it accounts for almost half of new capital formation and one-third of all economic activity. If government assets were privatised, vast amounts of money would be mobilised for compensation and at the same time the economy would receive a tremendous boost.

If government assets were put on the market, most of the buyers would be white because whites own most of the wealth. The money raised in this way could be used to establish a fund from which compensation could be made to blacks. Everyone would gain: new investment opportunities would be created; the economy would benefit enormously because private enterprise is so much more efficient than government enterprise; and blacks would receive a capital sum to invest or to use to satisfy short-term needs.

This method of redistribution would entail little or no economic disruption, and would significantly reduce malinvestment. It would be popular among whites, and the wealthiest whites would foot the bill. It would also attract much needed foreign investment.

Who should qualify for compensation?

Some may believe that only adult blacks should be compensated. Others will argue that present disadvantages will affect future generations. A practical compromise might be that all blacks born before the year in which apartheid is abolished, say 1987, will be entitled to compensation; monies owing to children would be held in trust by their guardians until they have reached the age of majority. Whether Indians and coloureds should receive the same or less compensation than blacks would have to be considered.

How much compensation should be paid?

The amount of compensation would again have to be based on practical considerations. A starting point would be the potential income from privatisation of government assets, divided by the number of people qualifying.

Administration of compensation

This should be done through established financial institutions such as banks and building societies in order to prevent the kind of bureaucratic waste and obstruction mentioned earlier. Financial institutions have the machinery and expertise to handle the issuing, cashing and transfer of redistribution payments; they also have branches throughout the country which are accessible to most people. Interest would automatically accrue on unclaimed amounts.

That the market is able to mobilise enough capital to privatise vast state assets was demonstrated unambiguously by the public flotation of Sasol's shares, which were over-subscribed something like 20 times. Presumably privatisation would occur over a number of years. The proceeds would go into a fund out of which fixed amounts could be paid at regular intervals, or dividends could be declared from time to time as resources become available.

Conclusion

We have suggested a method whereby compensation might be made without undue disruption of the economy.

In the long run, though, the unrestricted mobility of people and resources is much more important to blacks than compensation. Throughout the world, over and over again, we have seen that free markets lift people out of poverty far more rapidly than any other economic system known to man.

Underlying all the arguments for the equal distribution of wealth and income is the implication that all people should be the same, that no one should have more or less than the next man. The Glen Grey Act of 1894, which was discussed in the first chapter of this book, was based on this principle. It decreed that no black man could buy more than one piece of land, so that no man could become richer than another.

The response of Charles Pamla, spokesman for the black commercial farmers, to this law bears repeating:

> 'This shuts out all improvements and industry of some individuals who may work and buy ... surely Mr Rhodes can't expect that all natives will be equal. He himself is richer than others; even trees differ in height.'

Black South Africans have been manacled by socialism for over a century; now is the time to break those chains, not to strengthen them.

9 Affirmative action: Fashionable racism

My race needs no special defence, for the past history of them in this country proves them to be the equal of any people anywhere.
All they need is an equal chance in the battle of life.

Robert Smalls (Black Congressman, USA. 1874 – 1886)

I f you ask the average person whether people should be free to mix with one another or not, as they choose, the answer will nearly always be yes.

Yet many of those who strongly oppose apartheid are now calling for a new kind of racial intervention — affirmative action.

The argument for affirmative action goes something like this: it is wrong to keep people apart, so it must be right for them to mix. Since it is right for them to mix, the government should pass laws to ensure that they do so.

Affirmative action takes many forms. Anti-discrimination laws make it illegal to refuse on the grounds of gender, nationality or skin colour to employ someone; to serve them in a shop or restaurant; to rent them accommodation or to deny them membership of a club or organisation. Under such laws there could be no black housewives' league, no Christian men's club, no restaurant serving Chinese people only. Quota laws ensure that all organisations employ a fixed percentage of black or female staff, and equal pay and minimum wage laws are intended to save them from exploitation. Bussing regulations take children from one school district to another to ensure that schools are integrated.

Affirmative action laws violate property rights and freedom of disassociation, increase racial prejudice and have extremely deleterious economic effects on those they are intended to help.

103

Negative economic effects

In the USA, black incomes are substantially lower on average than white incomes. During the 1950s and 1960s, the gap between the two began to close, and the black share of the GNP increased. If these gains had continued at the same rate, it was calculated, young educated blacks entering the labour force in the year 2000 would have been earning as much as whites. But the growth of the 1960s was slowed almost to a standstill by the affirmative action laws of the civil rights era. Anti-discrimination laws were introduced to help blacks; instead they hindered them.

For both objective and subjective reasons certain categories of people are less preferred in the labour market than others. Amongst these are people who lack skills or education, teenagers, the aged, blacks, women and immigrants. Skilled white men find jobs most easily.

Blacks, women and other less preferred groups can compete with white men only by offering to work for less. Once they have jobs they can prove their worth and demand higher wages. But equal pay laws and minimum wage laws prevent less preferred people from undercutting their competitors in this way. When an employer has to choose between a white man and a white woman with equal qualifications and apparently equal ability, if there is an equal pay law he will probably choose the man because the woman could get married or have a baby and leave. Often, the people who lobby for laws 'to protect workers from exploitation' are the insiders who don't want competition.

It is well known that equal pay laws and minimum wage laws discourage employers from hiring less preferred people, so quota laws and wrongful dismissal laws are introduced to counteract this effect. These laws force employers to hire a given number of blacks and women, and prevent them from dismissing anyone without 'good reason'.

Quota laws and wrongful dismissal laws aggravate prejudices and make employers less inclined than ever to employ 'protected' people. This attitude is typified by the joke that the worst person to employ in Britain or the USA is a pregnant black Moonie, because you'll never get rid of her!

Unskilled workers suffer most under affirmative action. In 1948, black teenagers aged 16 and 17 had an unemployment rate of 9,4%, while the rate for whites in the same age group was 10,2%. Now white teenage unemployment is around 17%, but black teenage unemployment has soared to 40% and, in some cities, as high as 70%.[1] This is a direct result of civil rights laws combined with minimum wage laws, occupational licensing laws and apprenticeship laws which block entry into the market.

Freedom to disassociate

The freedom to disassociate is just as important a part of individual liberty as the freedom to associate.

In South Africa, children are *prevented*, solely on account of their skin colour, from sitting next to each other in school. In the USA, under so-called enlightened human rights laws, children are *forced*, solely on account of their skin colour, to sit next to each other in school. They are bussed, sometimes one or two hours each way to and from school, so that black and white children will receive the same education, regardless of its standard or of what they or their parents want.

One of the little-known negative consequences of the racial integration policy has been the destruction of a number of very successful black schools. Thomas Sowell, a prominent North American economist, cites the example of Dunbar High School in Washington DC. This all-black school had an impressive record during its first eighty-five years: the first black general in the US, the first black cabinet member, the first black federal judge, the first black professor at a national university and the discoverer of blood plasma — all were graduates of Dunbar High School. At the turn of the century, its students scored higher on tests than students from any white school in Washington. This school was destroyed in two to three years by forced racial integration; its high academic standards disappeared entirely.[2]

Property rights

Most people agree that the owner of a house has the right to decide who can enter it. If he refuses entry to people with red hair, or demands that all guests remove their shoes, that is his own business: he is king of his castle.

Why should this be any different if he owns a shop, a hotel, a school, a cinema or a club? Anti-discrimination laws cut directly across the right to discriminate on one's own property.

It is sometimes argued that if someone who provides a service refuses to serve certain people, they will have nowhere else to go. However, this problem arises only when there are restrictive licensing laws which limit the number of cafés, taxis, hairdressing salons and so on.

The market is colour blind

Overwhelmingly, people freely choose not to discriminate in business or employment because if they do, their businesses will inevitably suffer. This is why apartheid laws were introduced — to stop people who wanted to do so, from mixing and trading with other races.

If one café-owner chooses not to serve blacks, it won't be long before another trader will see the gap in the market and fill it. The new shop will soon out-compete the other unless the first one has sufficient non-black support to keep going.

If a factory-owner refuses to employ black labour, he will have to pay a higher price for white labour. Provided the market is free, someone will see the opportunity to undercut him by employing black labour and cutting costs. The factory-owner who discriminates will be driven out of the market or forced to employ unskilled labour himself. As black labour becomes scarcer, the demand for it increases and wages rise in response to this demand.

Only where there is a high demand for a segregated facility will it withstand competition from integrated facilities and survive in the marketplace. The entire weight of apartheid has not been sufficient to stop shops, restaurants and theatres from catering to all racial groups in response to economic pressure.

The bittereinders
There are a number of white and black nationalists in South Africa who do not want to mix with members of other races. Some whites will fight to the bitter end for the right to live their lives apart from blacks. Many of them are prepared to buy land and establish white areas through private ownership. This should be recognised as a legitimate way of meeting their needs.

Freedom includes the right to be wrong
A very important aspect of liberty is the right of people to hold views or do things which others find offensive or unacceptable. Smoking and excessive drinking are vices; they are not crimes. Similarly, if someone dislikes people of another ethnic or national group, or regards them as inferior, that may be a vice but it is not a crime.

Provided there is a free press, freedom of speech and freedom of association, anyone who doesn't like what others are doing can try to persuade them to change. If the Aanslag Hotel in Aansluitdorp refuses to serve anyone who is not white, those who disapprove can boycott it. They can prevail on others to do so too. They can picket the hotel, write letters to the newspaper and have the hotel black-listed by the UN. But they should not call upon the government to force the hotel manager to serve blacks against his wishes.

Birds of a feather

Laws are introduced to stop people from doing things which they otherwise might do. If laws are necessary to force people to integrate, it is because there are many people who prefer not to.

Evidence that this is so is found in every heterogeneous country in the world. In New York City, the degree of racial segregation in Harlem is as rigid as anything ever dreamt of in South Africa. Whites are not welcome there, and they don't go there. No amount of affirmative action can change this. Various Chinese communities in American cities are extremely segregated and highly ethnically conscious. There are culturally and ethnically exclusive residential areas all over the world, and this kind of separation usually does not cause offense because it is voluntary.

When apartheid laws were abolished in SWA Namibia and Zimbabwe, there was no 'melting pot' effect. A few blacks moved into white areas and vice versa, but on the whole, people stayed where they were. But racial insult was removed, dignity was restored and hostility reduced.

Conclusion

In a free society, people are not forced together *or* apart. Left alone, people all over the world integrate and segregate spontaneously and to the overwhelming satisfaction of most of them. As soon as governments interfere with the right of individuals to make such choices, they cause serious problems.

In a country like South Africa, with many different groups representing many different value systems, it is particularly important to cultivate a tolerance for diversity.

PART THREE
The solution

The South African government is committed to the democratic ideal, based on universal franchise ... and the establishment of a just and stable society in which the rights, dignity and freedom of all individuals as well as all groups are protected.

Chris Heunis
Minister of Constitutional
Development and Planning

Part Three provides a blueprint for a canton system in South Africa and explains how this would accommodate all the current political parties and pressure groups. The optimum legal order for such a system is discussed, as well as various economic policy options which cantons might pursue. This section ends with a detailed strategy for popularising, achieving and implementing the proposed system.

10 | A free society

*During my lifetime ... I have fought against white
domination, and I have fought against black
domination. I have cherished the ideal of a
democratic and free society in which all
persons live together in harmony and with
equal opportunities. It is an ideal which I hope
to live for and to achieve.
But if needs be it is an ideal for which I am
prepared to die.*

Nelson Mandela, 1964

An ideal society would be one in which there was freedom, peace
and prosperity for all. No society in the world is ideal, but some
political and economic systems create a higher degree of freedom and prosperity than others.

Any solution for South Africa should be based on the political, economic and legal systems which are likely to achieve the best conditions
for the most people. This chapter will consider what they are; the subsequent chapters will examine how they can be applied to our unique
situation.

What is a free society?

In the simplest terms, a free society is one in which all individuals are
free to do as they choose without fear of coercion or the threat of coercion by others. No one may impose their will by force on another.

This principle has been the basis of common law for centuries and, in
recent years, there has been a revival of interest in its application to
political, social and economic analysis.

Perhaps the easiest way to acquire a clear understanding of what a
free society entails is to contrast it with its opposite — a centrally
planned or regulated society. In political terms, a free society is charac-

111

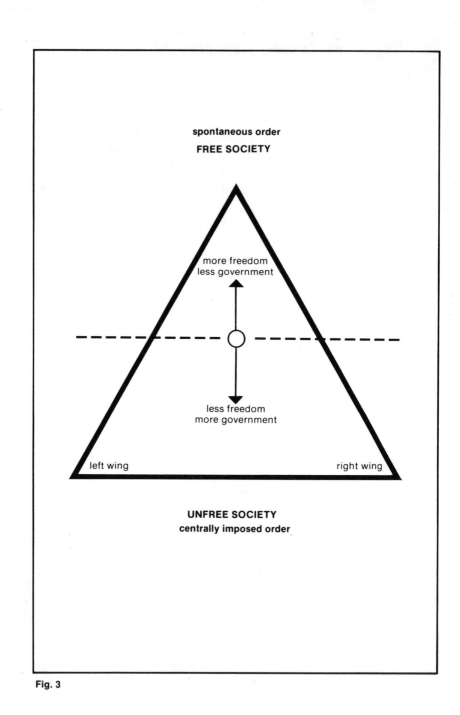

Fig. 3

terised by limited government, decentralisation, devolution of power to local levels, individualism and personal responsibility. Individuals are supreme: the purpose of government is to serve people. In an unfree society, the state is supreme and people serve the state. The political characteristics of an unfree society are powerful central government, collectivism, paternalism, coercion and social engineering.

A free society has a free economy, governed only by market forces. It is characterised by individual planning, entrepreneurial activity, competition and spontaneity. There is rapid wealth creation, and living standards are high. In an unfree society, the economy is centrally planned and people with the ability and resources are compelled by the state to provide the needs of others. Advocates of this type of imposed order generally — though not necessarily — prefer government ownership of the means of production and distribution, and government control of human and non-human resources. Alternatively, they may favour a 'welfare state' in which private enterprise is subject to substantial taxation and other forms of wealth redistribution.

In a free society, social relationships are voluntary and result from free choice and consent. In an unfree society, relationships between people are regulated.

A free society is based on the rule of law and common law, an unfree society on the rule of men and discretionary law.

Economic, social, legal and political freedom are completely interdependent. For instance, voluntary exchange between individuals cannot take place unless there is private ownership of property. Freedom of speech is meaningless if the media are not permitted to publish and disseminate ideas which criticise the existing order. There can be no freedom of assembly if all public meeting places are state-owned.

Fig 3 provides a graphic illustration of the difference between free and unfree societies. The further one moves towards the top or apex of the triangle, the more free the society. The base line represents totalitarianism and is divided into those forms of government generally thought of as 'left' and 'right'.

The myth of the 'golden mean', 'derde weg'

There is no 'golden mean' between a free and an unfree society because the essential concepts which characterise them are opposites; they are mutually incompatible and irreconcilable. The belief that a middle position is possible is the consequence of indecision or a failure to grasp the concepts entailed.

If it is right that government be limited, it cannot at the same time be

113

Social characteristics

FREE SOCIETY	UNFREE SOCIETY
spontaneous order	imposed order
diversity	uniformity
charity	welfare
philanthropy	subsidies
private interest	public interest
self-interest	self-sacrifice
independence	dependence
relevant education	ideological education
free speech/press	censorship
voluntary segregation	apartheid
voluntary integration	affirmative action
social mobility	social rigidity
hope/aspiration	apathy/resignation

Political characteristics

FREE SOCIETY	UNFREE SOCIETY
individualism	collectivism
libertarianism	totalitarianism
personal autonomy	government control
devolution	centralisation
democratic ideal	dictatorship
limited government	omnipotent government
depoliticisation	politicisation
reform	revolution
liberty	statism

Economic characteristics

FREE SOCIETY	UNFREE SOCIETY
voluntarism	coercion
free choice	prescription
active	passive
initiative	obedience
private ownership	government ownership
private planning	central planning
entrepreneurship	bureaucracy
competition	monopoly
free entry	licensure
consumer sovereignty	consumer protectionism
innovation	convention
dynamic	static
exchange	expropriation
risk	security
profit/positive sum	loss/zero sum
price mechanism	price control
integrity	corruption
free trade	protectionism
mutual gain	unilateral gain
mobility	immobility
free movement	influx control
demand	command

right for it to be unlimited. The debate can only be one of degree. For those who believe that the state should serve the individual, there might be discussion as to how limited central government should be, or to what extent power should be devolved. Those who believe the individual should serve the state might debate what, if anything, should be left in private hands.

There are many people in this country who call for a 'middle path'. South Africa should not pursue idealistic extremes, we are told. What we need is the best of both worlds — a realistic, balanced middle path. The rhetorical clichés are many: we need compromise and consensus; interventions that 'improve' or 'preserve' the free market; a caring alternative to capitalism; a just distribution of wealth; and so on.

Those who find it difficult to fault such lofty sentiments should observe what is *really* being said.

First, and most important, there is no *one* third way. There are as many third ways as there are proponents of this mythical 'alternative'. What we have now is one of them. Are these people then saying we need no change? Or are they saying we must shift to some alternative unstable, arbitrary and random mixture of contradictory socio-economic policies — policies based on no guiding principle or paradigm? In truth, each proponent is saying something different, and it is difficult to find any consensus among them.

By dramatic contrast, there is a general consensus at either end, where protagonists have a coherent, fairly consistent and intelligible set of principles, theories and beliefs upon which they base their positions and against which they judge policies. In this sense, both advocates of a free and an unfree society have identifiable positions, whereas those in between have no position, or more accurately, have a meaningless multiplicity of positions.

The free society paradigm is neither unrealistic nor extreme. On the contrary, it takes full account of South African realities and is the *only* system which offers massive and rapid wealth creation, a just distribution of wealth, the kind of 'caring' that works, a real prospect of depoliticising life and reducing inter-group conflict, personal freedom for every individual, and neither imposed segregation nor imposed integration.

The three political prerequisites for a free society are democracy, limited government and decentralisation of government.

Democracy

The word 'democracy' is derived from the Greek words for people (demos) and power (kratos).

The democratic ideal is to vest power in the governed rather than in those who govern them. But however strongly we espouse this ideal, we must recognise the failure of the electoral process to sustain it.

As long as government is unlimited, universal suffrage is no guarantee that people will get what they want. Neither are voting rights any guarantee of personal freedom. Looking around the world, we find that unlimited democracy has led to communism in Chile, national socialism (Nazism) in Germany and welfare statism in many parts of Europe.

In almost every country, the majority of people oppose many of the policies which their elected representatives implement. Numerous studies have shown that most people are against most interventions.

The reason why these interventions come about nonetheless is known as Olson's Law, in honour of the economist Mancur Olson who observed that small powerful groups invariably manipulate government in order to serve their vested interests (see Chapter 4).

Clearly, then, democracy *per se* is not an adequate guarantee of prosperity or freedom. The results of various democratic processes are not consistent with each other or the democratic ideal. A truly free society is one in which the possibility of a democratic accession to power of any form of totalitarian government is precluded; in other words, a limited government democracy, sometimes called minarchy or libertarianism. This, we argue, is the only feasible alternative for South Africa.

One of the first leaders to advocate such a system, Thomas Jefferson, expressed himself thus: 'Bear in mind this sacred principle that, though the will of the majority is in all cases to prevail, that will, to be rightful, must be reasonable; that the minority possess their equal rights, which equal laws must protect, and to violate which would be oppression.'

Principles of good government

Limited government democracy (minarchy) is based above all on two principles, which are essentially two sides of the same coin; the first concerns entrenched constitutional prescriptions of what government may and may not do, and the second the constitutional protection of individual rights. The most popular view of minarchy is that the government should be precluded through constitutional safeguards from revoking or infringing upon the 'natural rights' of the people.

Limitations on government may be general or specific. Specific limitations have been attempted in various constitutions, the most famous of which is the United States Constitution. In South Africa's own history, the constitutions of nineteenth century Voortrekker republics also had entrenched limitations. In these cases, the functions which govern-

116

ment might legitimately undertake, such as national defence, maintenance of law and order, contagious disease control and the judiciary, were prescribed, as well as those which it may not undertake, such as control of religion, press censorship and the invasion of property rights.

Government by law or discretion

Some scholars argue that in order for limitations to be effective, a constitution must declare unambiguously that government has no powers other than those specifically conferred upon it by the constitution. As an adjunct or alternative to such a declaration, the constitution may also incorporate a 'bill of rights' establishing the inviolable rights of individuals. In a free society, there would be a general rule that any government action which would, if performed by an individual, constitute an unlawful act, should likewise be unlawful, excepting only those peacekeeping actions undertaken in terms of the powers specifically conferred on government by the constitution. That which is morally or legally wrong, argue proponents of this general rule, cannot be politically right.

Perhaps the biggest single problem in historical attempts to limit government has been, and remains, the enormous temptation to permit 'exceptional' curtailments of individual rights, and to leave loopholes in the constraints on government 'in case of unforeseen circumstances'.

Once government is granted discretionary powers, there is always the possibility — even the likelihood — that they will be abused, as abundant precedent demonstrates. For one cannot safely assume, as proponents of discretionary government have done, that rulers will be competent and just. Proper constitutional government does not rely on the quality of individual rulers, but on the quality of the laws under which they rule. Thus the basic tenet of limited minarchical government is that government may make general rules of just conduct, equally applicable to all and not permitting of administrative discrimination.

Power Struggle

Apart from the manifest relevance of these principles to any society, they are especially pertinent to South Africa. If government were adequately limited, it would largely depoliticise life and defuse the struggle for power. Axiomatically, the greater the power of government, the greater will be the struggle for power.

117

The necessity for constitutional entrenchment

The relative failure of historical attempts at limited government can be attributed to (a) the overthrowing of governments or suspension of constitutions; (b) constitutional amendment; (c) ambiguous and equivocal drafting of constitutions; and (d) altered circumstances, not envisaged at the time of drafting. Whilst no method of guaranteeing the preservation of good government exists, one can at least provide some safeguards by means of unambiguous constitutional entrenchment. For example, it could be required that the entrenched provisions (defining governmental limitations) may be amended only by a 90% majority in a referendum.

Specific issues

Given the principle of minarchy, the precise degree of limitation still needs to be determined.

Within the limits of a clear conceptual framework the 'legitimate' functions of government might or might not (according to various limited government advocates) be extended beyond policing, judiciary and national defence to include, for example, contagious disease or pestilence control, basic welfare, elementary education, infrastructure or immigration control.

The following are some of the functions and limitations suggested in the standard literature, but not necessarily to be adopted in the South African model:

1. The law-making body of government should not be permitted to perform administrative functions. Examples of administrative functions are making rules and regulations for the implementation of laws, and determining administrative procedures. In this context, remember that laws should not give administrators or rule-makers discretionary powers.
2. Government should not be empowered to run, as legislative monopolies, those functions (especially of a social or entrepreneurial nature) which it is permitted to perform. It should not be permitted to create or grant private monopolies or monopoly privileges or protection from competition.
3. Government functions should preferably be required by the constitution to be put out to tender in order (a) to avoid employment patronage, corruption and bureaucracy, and (b) to give all people equal access at law to the performance of such functions.
4. Common law rights or classical natural rights should be en-

118

trenched (but not codified) with the proviso that the judiciary should be restored to comprising courts not only of law, but also of justice *per se*. (Under present South African law, the operation of justice as a criterion in the judicial process has been abrogated and the judiciary is confined to applying law and legislation irrespective of considerations of justice.)

5. If welfare is to be an authorised government function, it should be clearly defined and circumscribed and the principle should be that government cannot provide welfare directly by, for instance, supplying or running hospitals, orphanages, old-age homes and so on, but may only make payments to welfare recipients who, in turn, will acquire welfare services in a competitive market place.

6. Certain categories of laws proposed by central government should be subject to national referenda and introduced only if they receive the support of the majority. The policy of making decisions by referendum, combined with limited government, provides the best guarantee yet devised that laws will coincide with genuine majority preference and the democratic ideal.

Decentralisation of government

In pursuit of a free society, government functions and powers should be not only limited but also decentralised. The theoretical extreme of decentralised government is to decentralise everything as far as possible, ultimately to the individual; in other words, most powers and functions vest in the people themselves and only those which cannot — or for overwhelming reasons should not — be vested in individuals, may be delegated to highly decentralised government institutions.

Central government should be limited to areas of common concern such as national defence, national finance, foreign relations, trunk roads and contagious disease control. All other functions should be undertaken by regional or local government.

Decentralisation allows for the diversity which characterises a free society. Instead of one law imposed upon all, different regions have their own laws which represent special needs and values. For example, in the USA, laws regarding liquor, gambling, education, licensing, taxation and so on vary from state to state.

Small governments are more flexible and responsive to change than big ones. Changing the course of a mammoth oil tanker takes hours, a small boat minutes, a canoe seconds and a rubber duck in the bath split seconds.

It is far easier to influence a small government, such as a local village

119

council, than a provincial or homeland government, which is, in turn, easier to change than the South African government.

Few of the countries which put pressure on South Africa to become a unitary one-man-one-vote state have such a system themselves. South Africa currently has one of the most centralised government systems in the world. The only other countries which approach our degree of centralisation, such as the Scandinavian countries, are geographically small and have homogeneous populations.

Most democracies have a significant degree of decentralisation, and the more heterogeneous the society, the greater the need for decentralisation.

Conclusion

Throughout the world, countries which are characterised by a high degree of personal freedom, peace and prosperity are those in which the power of government has been effectively curtailed in some way.

However, the model which we propose for South Africa in the chapters which follow does not require that all South Africans share this view. It allows for minarchist and statist societies, and any of the mixed variations in between, to co-exist side by side, proving through practical demonstration which system fulfils the needs of most people.

11 | Cantons: A political solution

The essential feature of the Swiss Commonwealth is that it is a genuine and natural democracy.

Albert Venn Dicey

The Swiss model

In our search for a political system which meets all the disparate and conflicting needs of South Africa's heterogeneous peoples, we can learn much from Switzerland. The Swiss system is so extraordinarily appropriate for South Africa, even more so than for Switzerland itself, that we could take their constitution, almost verbatim, and transplant it into South Africa.

Switzerland is a tiny, mountainous and land-locked territory with no mineral wealth and poor agricultural potential. Indigenous forest, hills, mountains and rocky terrain constitute two-thirds of the total land area. The population is heterogeneous. While approximately two-thirds of the total population is German-speaking, no single population group has a majority in all cantons or communes.

Despite these potential constraints, Switzerland has not only survived but prospered. It is an extremely rich country with one of the highest living standards in Europe, high growth rates, low inflation, low unemployment and low social conflict. Whilst wars have raged around it, Switzerland has remained at peace. What has made this miracle possible?

The answer lies in the country's political system and the economic and social consequences of that system — this is the key to Switzerland's success, and it is from this that we can learn in South Africa.

Why is Switzerland relevant?

South Africa is a unique country with unique problems. Clearly it will have to develop its own solutions based on the needs of its own people.

121

However, we do not need to re-invent the wheel. All we need do is modify it to suit our needs. Fortuitously, Switzerland provides us with a remarkably apt working model in which many of the problems which face South Africa today have been confronted and solved through trial and error over several centuries.

The Swiss system had its origins in the thirteenth century, amongst people very primitive by twentieth century standards. In the course of 700 years, during which there were numerous civil wars, a true democracy was established in which people with many disparate needs and interests live, each according to their own values, in mutual peace and prosperity. This extraordinary testimony to the degree of devolution and democracy attainable in a diverse society demonstrates that South Africa's diversity can become its strength.

The Swiss system

Switzerland, with an area of 41 293 square kilometres, is slightly smaller than Transkei (43 000 square kilometres). It is densely populated with around six-and-a-half million people, which means, if we include uninhabited areas, a density of 250 people per square kilometre.

There are four national languages in Switzerland: German, French, Italian and Rhaeto-Romansh. Sixty-five per cent of the population is German-speaking, eighteen per cent French, ten per cent Italian and one per cent Rhaeto-Romansh, while six per cent, mostly migrant workers, speak other languages. Within the four main language groups there are many local dialects.

The cantons

In 1291, the first mutual assistance pact between three independent cantons was formed. The alliance was based on the principle of complete equality, a principle which remains the basis of the canton system today.

Thus Swiss history has led, not to a centralised state, but to a 'nation by will'. Small communities of varying size, economic strength and cultural tradition live voluntarily and in mutual respect in the same federal state.

The federal state comprises twenty-six autonomous cantons and half cantons. They vary in size from Basle-Town, with an area of 37,2 square kilometres, to Berne, which covers 6 049,4 square kilometres, and in population from as few as 12 800 people in Appenzell to 1 124 200 people in Zurich. Six of the cantons have fewer than 50 000 people, four have between 50 000 and 100 000, ten between 100 000 and 300 000, and five have between 300 000 and 900 000. Each canton has its own constitution and laws. The cantonal legislative authority is a one-chamber parliament which, in most cantons, is elected by proportional representation. The smallest cantonal council has fifty-one members, the largest, two hundred. Each canton parliament has an executive body of five to eight members elected by the citizens of the canton. Nineteen cantons have a majority of German speakers, six French and one Italian.

Five small cantons in Eastern and Central Switzerland have a truly democratic tradition of 'Landsgemeinde' or open-air parliaments. Once a year the electorate assembles in the open air to elect the cantonal government and select members of the Councils of State by a show of hands. They settle many other important matters by public debate and a show of hands.

Each canton organises its administration in its own way but the usual divisions are Interior, Justice and Police, Military, Finance, Economy, Health, Social Care, Education, and Public Buildings and Works. The cantons finance their activities primarily through income and property taxes levied on their own citizens and residents. Because they vary so much in size, economic strength and population, their budgets range from a few millions to thousands of millions of francs.

Cantons are responsible for their own judiciary and have their own courts, police, jails and reformatories.

Communes

Within the cantons there are about 3 000 communities or communes with rights and duties laid down by the cantons. Some regions have a long tradition of communal autonomy, whereas others have always been more centralised. One indication of the degree of autonomy enjoyed by the communes is that they levy their own taxes on their residents.

Like the cantons, communes vary greatly in size, from tiny communities in the mountains with only a few dozen inhabitants to great cities like Zurich, Berne and Geneva. Some of the large communities are bigger than the smallest cantons.

Each commune has a constitution setting out the powers granted it by its canton. People's rights to referenda and 'initiatives' are generally well developed and widely recognised.

In many small communes every adult citizen with the right to vote can participate in the communal assembly. Large communes have a parliament and usually administer canton and federal legislation in addition to their own independent policies.

Examples of areas in which communes typically have autonomy are: schools, energy, refuse collection building regulations, traffic regulations, public parks, bridges, roads, police, fire services, health departments, social care and sports. Communes often form regional associations to deal with matters such as refuse collection, sewage disposal and public works.

The administrative system in the communes allows every citizen maximum participation in public life and in the affairs of his own community.

The Federal Assembly

Between the beginning of the Swiss confederation in 1291 and 1948, many more cantons joined the original three, but their only important common bond was a willingness to hand over the right of making peace and war to the central government. They shared little else, not even the same systems of measurement or a common currency. In 1847, civil war between the cantons frightened them into tightening their links and, in 1848, a new constitution was adopted.

This constitution allowed each canton to retain sovereignty over its domestic affairs, but a few tasks thought to be of common concern were assigned to the Confederation (central government). Article 2 of the Federal Constitution lists three purposes of the Confederation: 'To assert the independence of the Fatherland from the outside world; maintenance of the law and order within; protection of the freedom and rights of the citizens of the Confederation and promotion of their common welfare'. The original intention was to limit federal responsibility to foreign policy, national defence, arbitration of inter-cantonal disputes, and the guarantee of individual rights and freedom of trade and commerce. These areas have grown during the past 130 years to include customs, the mint, the post office, telecommunications and the Federal Railway.

The Swiss parliament or Federal Assembly consists of two houses or chambers which rarely meet in joint session.

The National Council is the direct representative of the people. Its 200 seats are distributed amongst the various cantons on the basis of population but each canton or half canton, even the smallest, has at least one representative. In the general elections, each canton comprises a constituency. The President of the National Council is elected for one year. In terms of protocol, this is the highest official post in the Confederation.

The Council of States

Here the cantons are represented equally, regardless of size. Each canton sends two members and half cantons send one. The cantons decide independently how to elect members and how long they should hold office. Most elect members by ballot for four years.

The National Council and the Council of States hold four regular sessions per year, each lasting three weeks. They have equal status and every parliamentary bill has to be debated and approved in each house. If there are differences of opinion between the Councils, they pass the issue back and forth. Because the 46 members of the Council of States have the same power as the 200 members of the National Council, minority groups in small cantons are protected from being overruled by big cantons.

The two houses meet to form the *Joint Federal Assembly* only in order to pass federal laws, ratify state treaties and elect Federal Councillors and judges.

The legislative decisions of parliament are not, however, final because they are subject to *The Referendum*.

There are two types of Referenda in Switzerland: the Obligatory Referendum, which is used at federal or cantonal level to ensure that all constitutional changes are put to the popular vote, and the Optional Referendum, which enables the public to have its say about any federal policy, legislation or general decree. An Optional Referendum is held if a minimum of 50 000 citizens or eight cantons request it within 90 days of the official publication of a new measure.

The Federal Council

The Federal Executive (cabinet) comprises seven equally ranked ministers who are elected individually for a four-year term by the Joint Federal Assembly. Each is responsible for a department which he represents within the Federal Council. Every year, one of the Federal Councillors is elected by the Federal Assembly to the post of Federal President. The only extra responsibilities this position entails are to chair meetings of the Federal Council and undertake a few protocol duties. Thus the 'prime minister' is essentially no more than the cabinet chairman for one year.

All four main political parties are represented at cabinet level. Theoretically any Swiss citizen may become a Councillor, but no canton may have more than one representative in the cabinet at the same time, and traditionally, at least two of the seven belong to a linguistic minority.

General comments

Over the past seven centuries, Switzerland has developed a political system which recognises the needs and differences of heterogeneous population groups which differ in terms of language, culture, tradition, temperament and, to some extent, ethnicity.

It is a system which may be summarised as one man, many votes. Swiss citizens vote for representatives at community, canton and federal levels. They petition for referenda on specific measures at all three levels. In addition, the Constitution allows for 'Popular Initiatives'. If the signatures of at least 100 000 voters are obtained, an initiative can propose an addition to or a removal from the Federal Constitution. The initiative is discussed by both houses and then put to popular vote.

In recent years, for instance, there have been initiatives in favour of extra air pollution devices in motor vehicles, lawful abortion, the introduction of VAT (value added tax), and grants for universities and research. All of these were rejected. New constitutional articles on equal rights for men and women and consumer protection were accepted.

This means that every individual can play an effective part in the decision-making process, and that new laws are not easily introduced. Indeed, the Swiss boast that 'we never accept anything unless it has been presented to us at least twice', and it is joked that when the Swiss vote on measures proposed by their politicians, they usually vote 'no'.

The Swiss system ensures that there is neither majority nor minority group domination, and that one political party cannot impose its will on the whole country. In this sense, Switzerland probably represents the democratic ideal more closely than any other country.

The Swiss system is open and flexible, permitting changes and developments in response to diverse popular wishes. Some cantons have divided into half cantons, each fully autonomous, while others have merged. Boundaries have shifted and changed. Cantons and communes have formed and dissolved alliances and joint ventures. The laws and policies reflect geographic and community differences (see Appendix II).

Because the powers of the Federal Assembly are severely limited and the Councillors' functions are purely administrative, few people in Switzerland even know who the Federal President is in any given year. There is no incentive for hard-fought winner-takes-all political campaigns at national level because the major political issues are essentially localised. National political life is completely devoluted and fragmented. Great political demonstrations, passionate debates and spectacular confrontations are rare. Because government has few conflict-provoking powers and functions, Swiss society is blissfully depoliticised.

Freedom of movement of goods, capital and people between cantons is entrenched in the Constitution. Consequently, even those cantons in which socialist parties predominate have relatively free economic policies because if they increase taxes and controls unduly, their residents simply vote with their feet and move to another canton. Conversely, free market parties maintain basic welfare programmes. In general, there is a tendency towards minimal government with concomitantly high levels of personal freedom.

Because most government functions are located at the local level, there is a permanent demonstration effect. In other words, there is a continuing visible test of alternative policies within one country, so that society tends towards the optimum policy on any given issue, and there is a spontaneous discipline away from unsuccessful or unproductive policies. Political competition tends to produce benefits in much the same way that economic competition does.

12

A canton system for South Africa

... all history teaches that in small states there tends, other things being equal, to be more personal freedom, more individuality and a higher social vitality than in large. I believe a body of small, highly organised social units self-governing, but uniting together for the furtherance of certain great common aims, to be the highest form of social organisation yet evolved by humanity.

Olive Schreiner, 1908

ny future political dispensation for South Africa must clearly be based on a system which ensures that all her disparate groups can live without fear of domination by any other group. The Swiss system provides many socio-economic alternatives to cater for the conflicting needs of her four main national groups and various sub-groups. In South Africa, there are more social, cultural and ethnic groupings than in Switzerland and, therefore, we have an even greater need for a diversity of political options.

It is for this reason that we propose a canton system for South Africa as the *only* structure through which she can achieve enduring peace and prosperity for all her people: a system in which the country is split into numerous autonomous cantons, linked by a central government whose functions are strictly limited by a constitution which entrenches equality at law for every individual, yet which does not entail the subjugation of minorities or individuals.

Determination of cantons
South Africa currently has 306 magisterial districts, some of which are divided into sub-districts (detached magistrates), with an average

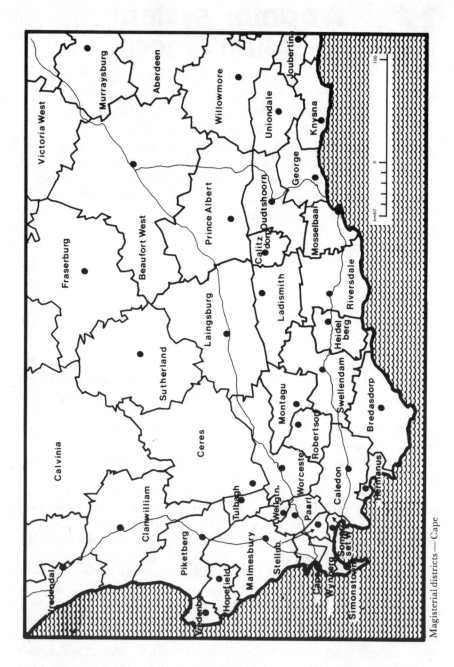

Magisterial districts — Cape

population of 80 000 per district. None is as small as the smallest Swiss cantons. These magisterial districts have existing judicial and administrative infrastructures, and non-ideological boundaries which form sensible *administrative* units. These boundaries are determined by recommendation of the Commission for Administration, an independent statutory body responsible for purely administrative and manpower matters. The functions that usually coincide with magisterial districts include:

- criminal and civil courts
- licensing offices
- receivers of revenue
- public works
- school boards
- labour bureaux
- welfare offices
- population registration
- police districts
- various inspectorates

Many of these and other linkages are not dictated by law but are implemented according to magisterial district for reasons of administrative convenience and co-ordination.

Some magisterial districts have a high correlation with ethnic and/or socio-economic population distribution. This is partly a consequence of past legislation separating races into different areas, but it would occur to some extent in any heterogeneous country, regardless of racial or political policy, simply because people generally choose to live amongst those with whom they identify.

Magisterial districts provide the most logical and least contentious starting point for the creation of cantons. We propose, therefore, that South Africa be divided into cantons corresponding to existing magisterial districts. Of course, in many areas there may be valid geographic, social, linguistic, ethnic, cultural and/or economic reasons for consolidating two or more districts, splitting districts or moving boundaries. There are several feasible ways to finalise canton boundaries; the following proposals are made on the basis that they will be found acceptable by most people.

Canton Judicial Delimitation Commission

In order to defuse and depoliticise the formation of cantons as much as possible, a Judicial Delimitation Commission should be established. It would consist of judges and magistrates, preferably drawn from all the main groupings, who are not identified with any political ideology. Furthermore, they should take an oath committing themselves to the lack of bias which their judicial office requires.

The Commission would receive evidence concerning canton boundaries. It should not be subject to any political control, and its members should have absolute discretion to weigh objectively all the evidence presented to them and to act accordingly.

There would be a rebuttable presumption in favour of existing magisterial districts. In other words, people will have to offer evidence as to why a magisterial district should *not* become a separate canton.

Anyone must be free to present submissions in favour of, or in opposition to, existing magisterial boundaries. For example, arguments could be based on geographic or ethnic features, on the principle of separating urban and rural areas, or simply for reasons of practical administration. Evidence could include anything from public opinion surveys to crime rates, from stages of development to climatic conditions.

Different groups would sometimes lead conflicting evidence. The Johannesburg Central Business District Association might argue convincingly in favour of a 'metropolitan' canton including Soweto, Roodepoort, Dobsonville, Johannesburg, Diepmeadow, Edenvale, Sandton and Randburg. Conversely, a strong case could be made, primarily on ethnic and socio-economic grounds, for maintaining greater Soweto (including Dobsonville and Diepmeadow) as an independent canton.

Purely administrative considerations might lead to calls for consolidating Johannesburg, Sandton and Randburg. Or perhaps it would be argued that each of these fairly large municipalities should become a separate canton which would co-operate with the other two on such issues as, for example, water, electricity and sewage reticulation.

It would probably not be logical to split a village with a few thousand people of various racial groups into two or three cantons based on ethnicity. Geographic or administrative considerations would prevail here. However, this would not preclude a division along ethnic lines should the people concerned vote for it in a referendum initiated (by petition) in order to challenge a ruling of the Delimitation Commission.

We recommend a *judicial* commission because we can think of no other politically acceptable way for the government of the day to win widespread support for these reforms. Although it will always have its critics, the South African judiciary is still regarded by most people of good will as being reasonably independent. It is more likely to make good decisions, to be impartial and to have 'legitimacy' in the eyes of most South Africans than any other institution in or out of the country.

Whilst we have said that all evidence, including that based on ethnicity, should be admissible, we recognise that the idea of political entities based on racial, cultural or linguistic grounds is automatically linked with apartheid and the homelands in South Africa. As such, it tends to have negative and emotive connotations. This is unfortunate. In the course of this chapter, it will be made clear that our proposal is based on the total dismantling of all vestiges of apartheid, and the creation of a genuine democracy, with full equality at law regardless of race, and with more constitutionally entrenched rights and freedoms than, to our knowledge, exist in even the most free societies at present.

In addition, it should be borne in mind that all over the world, countries have been divided according to ethnic and cultural criteria. This is largely the basis on which Europe is divided, for example.

It is not possible to predict where canton boundaries would be drawn or how many cantons would be established in South Africa because these are matters which would be decided by means of a dynamic organic process reflecting as nearly as possible the differences of all the people concerned. Predictably, evidence would be led by Chambers of Commerce, City Councils, public interest groups, political parties, academics, ad hoc lobbies, farmers' associations, trade unions, etc. People would distribute pamphlets, address public meetings and debate through the media. In the early stages, there may be attempts at intimidation, which the judiciary will have to overcome by, for instance, accepting anonymous evidence or evidence in camera. Ultimately, the decisions of the Delimitation Commission would be based to the best of its ability on objective criteria — the most important of these being the results of referenda conducted in the magisterial districts involved in disputes.

Referendum — the final arbiter
If the citizens of two districts wish to merge, or if part of a district wishes to break off and become independent or be incorporated into another area, then referenda must be held in the areas concerned. Those from whom separation is sought, however, would not vote.

Before a referendum concerning canton boundaries is held, a petition signed by 10% of the voters in the area which wishes to change must be presented to the Delimitation Commission.

The freedom of minorities to break away and join other cantons or become independent would be a very important factor encouraging majority groups to consider the wishes of minorities they do not want to lose, and discouraging bad government. If majorities misbehave, minorities will leave or vote for separation.

The Delimitation Commission would be a permanent body, reconvened from time to time as are constitutional conventions in Switzerland and the United States, to consider further boundary changes. The formation of cantons should be a dynamic and on-going process of redefining and re-examining according to the people's wishes.

Homelands and national states

In South Africa the homeland concept is extremely unpopular amongst most people. This is because the homelands have developed hand in hand with apartheid and in particular influx control.

However, in the absence of any coercion or racially discriminatory legislation, there is no reason why the homelands should not be included as ethnic cantons if they so wish. They should have the freedom to decide, preferably by referendum, whether they wish to be completely independent states or autonomous cantons in each case. All of their citizens should automatically have the right to choose South African or homeland citizenship, or both.

Several of the homelands and national states form sensible units as they are. Transkei, for example, has fairly logical boundaries. In the case of Ciskei, however, evidence might be led for the inclusion of the Border Region. The split between Natal and KwaZulu is arbitrary and people in these two regions would have to decide whether they wish to form one canton (the increasingly popular 'Kwa-Natal' idea) or several. Certain parts of Bophuthatswana such as Thaba N'chu could become independent cantons or merge with others. Those homelands which are not contiguous units could still form one independent state or one canton. Many countries, including the USA and the UK, are not made up of one contiguous area.

Whatever the case, the homelands and national states should be free to decide whether to join the canton system or become independent.

Structure and powers of cantons

Political diversity

Each canton would have its own parliament, and possibly its own constitution, as initially determined by referendum. These would probably vary a great deal from one district to another. Different political group-

134

ings would form in different areas with varying proposals. For example, the ANC might propose a form of socialism in terms of the Freedom Charter in areas where it enjoys majority support; and the PFP would probably suggest some kind of social democracy in, for example, Northern Johannesburg, where it has strong support. In other words, a kaleidoscope of opinion and ideologies could and would be accommodated.

Voting

There would be universal suffrage for the *de facto* residents of each canton until a canton parliament is elected. Thereafter, each canton would decide, within constitutional limits, how much say its residents would have on future issues and what method of voting would be adopted — it might choose proportional representation, a Westminster-type system, or a one-party state. Each canton would send representatives to the central government; these would be chosen by plebiscite or canton government decree, again depending on each canton's policy.

The focus of political party action would be at canton level. Some political parties might encompass several or many cantons, while others might be exclusive to one canton. One would expect all the current political pressure groups to be active, and probably others too.

Administrative diversity

The functions of central government would be drastically limited, as the cantons would control all but a few aspects of administration.

Should they so wish, the cantons could devolve power further to local authorities, equivalent to the Swiss communities. Each canton would determine its own degree of devolution. Some, no doubt, would be run entirely by a central body, while others would decentralise almost all aspects of administration to local authorities as proposed by Denis Beckett in *Permanent Peace*. In the case of local authorities representing large areas, or cities, there could be further devolution to groups similar to existing ratepayer associations; these would control all matters of local concern such as shopping hours, street lights, racial policy, zoning and building regulations, and so on. This is what Beckett calls 'maximal democracy'.

Cantons or local authorities would be free to organise themselves into alliances or groupings for administrative purposes. They might wish to share, for example, the administration of policing, transport, water supplies, power, sewage disposal or rubbish collection. Alternatively, they might contract out any or all of these services to private companies which could supply the needs of one or many cantons.

135

Economic diversity

Each canton would determine its own economic policy, its own labour, transport, education, tax, subsidisation, welfare and race policies.

Central government would have no authority to grant monopolies to, for example, the Putco Bus Company, or legislate against 'pirate' taxis. Each canton would decide for itself whether to have an open market in transportation, to license taxis restrictively, to have transport subsidies, or to provide canton government transport.

It is both absurd and cruel to have one set of electrification standards or abattoir standards — or any other standards — for the whole country. Such regulations do not result in the stated intention of high standards for all. Instead they price homes, transport, clothing, food and whatever else is regulated out of reach of the poor. As discussed in Chapter 4, standards regulations usually amount to disguised discrimination against lower socio-economic groups and protection for vested interests parading themselves as advocates of the 'public interest'. One consequence of devolution would be a built-in protection of the public from such abuse of government power.

Racial Policy

Racial policy is discussed at the end of Chapter 14 under the sub-heading 'Racial discrimination'.

Citizenship

Canton governments would have the right to grant or refuse citizenship to newcomers in respect of their own cantons. There are good reasons for this. Although freedom of movement in and out of cantons would be constitutionally entrenched, cantons should be able to restrict citizenship in order to discourage excessive immigration, to maintain their political character, or to raise revenue by selling citizenship as in Switzerland. The more attractive a canton's policies, the more revenue it could raise in this way.

Advantages of diversity

There are two very important advantages to a diversity of economic, political and social policies. The first is that diversity is truly democratic. The greater the diversity, the more real choices people have, and the greater the likelihood that they will be able to live in a way that coincides with their own values.

Secondly, there is a permanent demonstration effect. People can see from day to day which tax policy, which housing policy, which race policy, which subsidy policy produces the best results.

The demonstration effect

The main reason why a system with severe limitations on central government creates enduring peace and prosperity is that political competition occurs between the constituent states or cantons.

Two half cantons in Switzerland, Basle-Town and Basle-Country, provide a striking example of this. Basle-Country decreased taxes and experienced high growth, while Basle-Town increased taxes and stagnated. Between 1970 and 1980, over 13% of Basle-Town's residents moved into the suburbs (Basle-Country); eventually Basle-Town was forced to reduce taxation to bring it more into line with Basle-Country.

Thus the demonstration effect prevents Switzerland's socialist cantons from burdening their economies with excessive regulations and taxes: if they try to do so, they simply lose people and wealth to neighbouring cantons with more attractive policies. Canton governments also lose votes if they cannot maintain levels of growth and welfare comparable to those in other cantons. The result is that even those Swiss cantons with radical socialist governments feature amongst the freest economies in Europe, while on the other hand, even the most laissez-faire cantons maintain basic welfare programmes.

This demonstration effect is apparent to a lesser extent throughout the world. There is a virtually direct correlation between countries with free market policies and prosperity. Countries with a high degree of government intervention typically exhibit low growth and underdevelopment, instability, conflict and oppression. A recent World Bank study found that this correlation generally holds true regardless of the size of a country, its ethnicity, its natural resource endowment, or its level of development. High growth tends to bring with it high life expectancy, low infant mortality rates, low divorce rates, low social problems, and reduced violence and even international peace.

Freedom of movement

Complete freedom of movement for people and wealth is the magic ingredient in our canton formula. The demonstration effect can work properly only if people are able to vote with their feet by moving from one canton to another and taking their wealth and productivity with them.

If AZAPO-ruled cantons introduce full-blooded marxism with disastrous consequences, people will be able simply to move to or seek jobs in cantons with greater wealth and freedom. Conversely, if marxism provides the level of welfare and benefits it promises, marxist cantons will attract more people, and other cantons will follow their example.

Secession

Every canton should have the right to secede. This provides an important safety valve for the system.

Switzerland shows us that socialist and laissez-faire cantons can function comfortably side by side in one country. However, there is still the possibility that radical white or black nationalist cantons might find themselves unable to agree on general principles which the great majority of cantons want entrenched in the constitution. Or they might find central government policy unacceptable as regards defence, foreign trade, or immigration policy.

In order to save the country from being torn apart by civil war, these cantons should have the right to secede if a given percentage of the population of a canton, let us say 75%, votes in favour. For practical reasons this option would seldom, if ever, be exercised, but it should nonetheless be available. Perhaps a number of radical black nationalist cantons would want to form a break-away alliance in an unlimited centralised state. If, in time, the differences which led to secession were ameliorated or seen as less important, the break-away cantons could be re-admitted to the country.

In Switzerland there is a right of secession but it has never been exercised. On the contrary, other areas have wanted to join. A canton system with minimal centralisation reduces conflict and division and leads to harmony and inclusion. There is a good chance that neighbouring territories such as Lesotho and Swaziland would eventually apply for some kind of confederal relationship with South Africa. If they were not included from the start, the four independent homelands would probably seek inclusion, and possibly South West Africa/Namibia as well.

Expulsion

The other side of the right to secede is the possibility of expulsion. If a canton persists in some policy which all the others find unacceptable, there should be a procedure whereby it can be expelled. Expulsion, being a drastic measure, should require a unanimous, or near-unanimous vote in favour by all the cantons other than the one under scrutiny. Alternatively, a referendum could be held in all cantons other than the one in question, with a specified majority necessary in order for expulsion to take place. In the unlikely event of an expulsion, all the citizens of the expelled canton should retain South African citizenship and the right to move freely into an area remaining within South Africa.

13 | Problems arising from a canton system

Life in its own journey, presupposes its own change and movement, and one tries to arrest them at one's eternal peril.

Laurens Van der Post

Unequal wealth

Many people fear that since some cantons will inevitably be wealthier than others, this will lead to friction. However, in all countries these disparities between states occur. Regional differences do not cause conflict as long as there is freedom of movement, so that a person does not *have* to live in a poor canton but may do so through choice. 'Poor' cantons may have other attributes — geography, climate, culture, traditions, economic system, personal freedom, or whatever — which their citizens value more highly than material wealth.

It is important to note that people do not always migrate from rural to urban areas, small to big towns, poor to rich areas. The latest US census, for example, revealed a net migration the other way. There have also been mass migrations from richer to poorer countries, such as occurred from North to South Korea during the 1950s. People most commonly migrate to places where there is more personal freedom and opportunity, or higher growth, than they are currently experiencing.

Is it not possible then that this tendency, combined with freedom of movement, will result in overcrowding of cantons which enjoy high levels of freedom, opportunity and growth? The point to consider here is whether 'over-crowding' is indeed a problem. The population of Hong Kong increased by four million in two decades, thus registering a 600% growth rate. Newcomers, who usually arrive with nothing, move into transitional slums, then quickly move out to better areas as they take advantage of the free economy and begin to produce and prosper.

Hong Kong is a thriving, busy, bustling, exciting and prosperous place. And all the millions who live there do so out of choice — within a half-hour drive of Hong Kong, there are open spaces and beautiful empty beaches.

The very existence of disparities creates choices. People can choose to live in a huge, noisy, crowded metropolis, or in a small quiet dorp, or in a remote part of the countryside. If all places were the same, these options would fall away.

Policies which aim to control the movement of people from one area to another are, in any case, largely ineffectual. Soweto has an official population of 800 000 but estimates place the *de facto* population at somewhere between 1,7 and 2 million. In other words, there are more people living 'illegally' in Soweto than legally. Clearly, influx control is not keeping people out of Soweto, and if it were summarily abolished, chances are that the population of Soweto would not alter very much. Those who move to Soweto, or anywhere else, do so because they are then better off in their own opinion.

In SWA/Namibia influx control and group areas laws were abolished nearly a decade ago. Very little changed. A few black professionals and politicians moved into white areas. A few hundred blacks settled in a squatter camp on the periphery of Katachura (a black township outside Windhoek), but after a year or so this camp returned to its former size. The truth is that barriers to movement are harmful. They cause uncertainty, hostility, resentment and conflict amongst the people they affect, promote abuse and reduce economic efficiency.

Some will argue that even given free movement, it is not fair that some cantons should have rich mineral deposits or agricultural lands whilst others have nothing. We have tried to show in the discussion on redistribution of wealth that transferring wealth through taxation or by any other method does a great deal more harm than good. However, if people remain unconvinced and vote for some form of redistribution, one way of doing this would be to allow the central government to tax profits on natural resources and redistribute this wealth throughout the federation in the form of infrastructure such as roads, or in vouchers for education, medical services, or whatever. This idea is discussed at greater length in Chapter 17 on economic solutions.

Viability

Some people believe that in order for a canton or state to be 'viable' as an autonomous unit, it must be big or rich. This is simply not so. Many sovereign countries, recognised internationally, are tiny in size or population, and many others have negligible per capita incomes or natural resources. Of the 188 countries listed in the 1980 *Book of Rankings,* six have an area of less than 10 square miles and over 30 of less than 1 000 square miles. There are ten countries with fewer than 30 000 citizens and approximately 20 with populations of less than 100 000. Monaco and Liechtenstein each have only 25 000 people, Greenland 51 000, Bermuda 58 000, Seychelles 61 000, Tonga 92 000 and Grenada 108 000. By comparison, the average magisterial district in South Africa has 80 000 people.

Of the 145 countries for which figures are available, fully 30 show an estimated per capita gross national product of *less than $200.* Over half the countries have per capita GNPs estimated at under $1 000. The South African average in 1980 was $1 340. Thus even the most depressed districts in this country are well above the national average in many countries which are considered viable.

What, in fact, makes a country, state, canton, town, suburb, household or individual viable? If viability means the ability of an area to prosper without depending on 'foreign' resources of some kind, then no country, not even the USA or USSR, is viable. If it means the ability to survive and prosper, with foreign trade and investment, then absolutely every unit, no matter how small, is potentially viable — right down to the individual who, given enough economic freedom, can sell his labour, goods or services and be largely self-sufficient. Equally, any two or three individuals are viable, as are 300, 3 000, 30 000 or 30 million. It is not towns, countries, regions or areas which are viable, but the people inhabiting them — provided they are free to produce and exchange.

Does diversity cause confusion?
If many cantons function autonomously, will this lead to a troublesome lack of uniformity in matters of mutual interest such as road rules, railway gauges and electrical voltages? As bylaws change from one municipality to the next, will this create confusion and will there be an unnecessary duplication of services such as garbage disposal, electricity generation, public transportation and higher education?

The answer to these questions is 'no'.

In Switzerland, the federal government may build a trunk road across the country only with the consent of every canton through which it will run. However, this does not stop trunk roads from being built. Also, history shows us that standards tend to emerge wherever they serve people's interests. North America provides a classic illustration of a privately owned and run railway network being standardised through

141

many autonomous states and provinces without any government standards laws. When the railway companies had difficulty in operating through different time zones, they adopted the standardised time zones which still apply in North America today.

Furthermore, South Africa already has relative uniformity in areas such as currency, weights and measures and health laws, although it is interesting that we do not have uniformity in many areas in which one would expect it. For example, traffic regulations vary between provinces and local governments. There are three different government railway gauges in addition to the variety of gauges used by the private sector on mines and factory sites. Pretoria and Johannesburg have different electricity voltages and cycles.

Bylaws regarding swimming pool fences, buildings, cemeteries, outdoor advertising, property taxes and so on already vary from one municipality to the next. The homelands have different tax rates, labour laws, licensing procedures, land tenure regulations and so on. None of these variations create confusion.

Most countries in the world impose uniform standards in some areas and permit diversity in others for no more than random historical reasons. Many diversify where we standardise or centralise where we allow differences.

It is sometimes argued that a uniform economic policy should be imposed by central government on the whole country because if one area deregulates and imposes low taxes it gains an 'unfair advantage' over others. However, in a canton system there is nothing to stop cantons which are 'disadvantaged' in this manner from following suit and achieving equal 'unfair advantages' for themselves! In both the USA and Switzerland there are some states or cantons which have relatively high taxes and others where taxes are very low; obviously, people trade off the advantages of a given economic policy against other factors.

We propose that central government be prevented by the constitution from imposing standards on the whole country because imposed uniformity in a heterogeneous society inevitably leads to inappropriate policies for many groups.

Unregulated markets have a remarkable tendency to provide the best solutions for most people's needs. Spontaneous standardisation occurs where it is in the consumer's interests — even in such seemingly unimportant matters as babies' bottle tops and stone crushers. On the other hand, where standardisation impedes innovation, the market jettisons it. Consumers vote with their Rands for variety or uniformity as it meets their needs. Similarly, in a canton system they would vote through referenda, or 'with their feet', for variety or uniformity in the

142

provision of infrastructure and services. Also, as we have mentioned, wherever it proved convenient, cantons or communities could club together to provide amenities or to contract services out to private enterprise.

Problems resulting from freedom of movement

It is easy to talk about the freedom of people to leave cantons whose political or economic system they do not like and move to more congenial areas, but this will cause considerable disruption, hardship and loss of wealth. A white farmer working and living on land which has been in his family for generations will not be greatly comforted by the knowledge that if he does not like the local policy of racial integration, he can sell his farm and move.

Our answer to this argument is that South Africa is in any case on the verge of great change and change by its very nature will cause disruption.

Black people have never enjoyed any security of tenure and have been evicted from their land and forcibly moved without a second thought on the part of successive governments. The current political unrest and economic recession have already caused great suffering and this will be escalated by any attempt to prolong the status quo. If we do not implement a solution which is acceptable to all the racial groups, a bloody revolution could be followed by a marxist state in which the opportunity to sell one's property and move voluntarily would seem heaven-sent.

Once a canton system is introduced, there would be an inevitable period of readjustment in which boundaries would shift and people would gravitate to congenial areas, but this would create a fraction of the disruption which would result from any of the other alternatives currently facing this country.

Bureaucratisation

One might expect that with a multiplicity of governments there will be a massive increase in bureaucracy. However, in truth, when government is devoluted there are usually fewer rather than more civil servants. In proportion to population, Switzerland has the smallest civil service in Europe, the lowest tax rates and the smallest budget, despite having the greatest proliferation of governments.

The reason for this is both simple and exciting.

When a government is highly centralised, a pyramid of bureaucratic

143

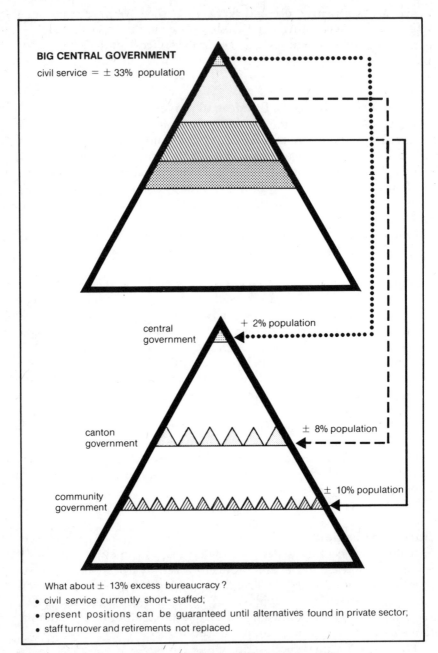

BIG CENTRAL GOVERNMENT

civil service = ± 33% population

central government   + 2% population

canton government   ± 8% population

community government   ± 10% population

What about ± 13% excess bureaucracy ?

- civil service currently short-staffed;
- present positions can be guaranteed until alternatives found in private sector;
- staff turnover and retirements not replaced.

Fig. 4   Relative bureaucracy in a unitary system and a canton system.

management structures is created, with many tiers between central and local government. Every senior official has several others under him, and this occurs all the way down to the lowest level. In a decentralised government, the upper part of the pyramid falls away, leaving only the base. (See Fig. 4).

Does a canton system need a sophisticated population?

It is sometimes suggested that a canton system is suitable only for a society which has reached Switzerland's level of sophistication, and would therefore not work well in South Africa. Remember, however, that the Swiss system originated in the thirteenth century; the first three cantons were 'forest cantons' whose residents were in many senses less sophisticated than South Africa's 'third world' sector.

Secondly, the black tribal authorities in South Africa already function very much as cantons or communities do. There are some 80 tribal authorities in Transkei, over 40 in Ciskei and about 100 in Bophuthatswana. They are small local governments usually made up of traditional rural people who know their own community needs. They debate and discuss issues in the village square, or 'indaba', just as the people in the small Swiss cantons and communities do. If anything, the more simple a community is in structure, the more appropriate a maximally devoluted system becomes. In Chapter 1 we observed the striking similarities between the traditional tribal political system and the one we are proposing now.

In truth a canton system is even more appropriate for South Africa than it is for Switzerland!

145

14 | Central government in a canton system

... apartheid has to go and it has to be replaced with a social and political system which will give both black and white a meaningful stake in the government of their country.

Chief Buthelezi

anton parliaments or assemblies constitute the most important level of government in our proposal and therefore we have discussed them first.

Now let us turn to the central government and consider what its functions should be and how it would relate to the cantons.

The central government should be seen not so much as a governing body but as an agency for the protection of cantons and the basic rights of the citizens of the country. It should assist co-operation between canton governments and be administrative rather than legislative in character.

The central constitution should be based on two main principles: maximum devolution, and strict limitation of power. The implementation of these principles would be assisted by the following provisos:

1. There must be an unambiguous separation of judicial, administrative and legislative functions. The judiciary should have power to override any unconstitutional action by central government.
2. Additional powers and functions that can be effectively devoluted to cantons or communities should not be exercised by central government unless agreed upon by, say, 90% of all the cantons.
3. To avoid domination of minorities, amendments to the constitution should require a 100% endorsement by all cantons at a constitutional convention. (If one obstinate canton keeps vetoing an amendment that all the others support, it can be threatened with expulsion.)

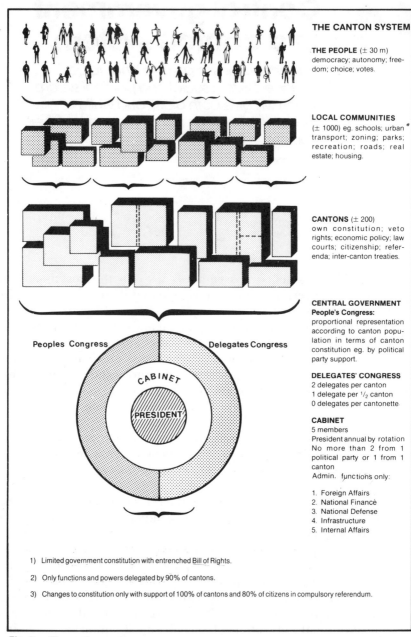

THE CANTON SYSTEM

THE PEOPLE (± 30 m)
democracy; autonomy; freedom; choice; votes.

LOCAL COMMUNITIES
(± 1000) eg. schools; urban transport; zoning; parks; recreation; roads; real estate; housing.

CANTONS (± 200)
own constitution; veto rights; economic policy; law courts; citizenship; referenda; inter-canton treaties.

CENTRAL GOVERNMENT
People's Congress:
proportional representation according to canton population in terms of canton constitution eg. by political party support.

DELEGATES' CONGRESS
2 delegates per canton
1 delegate per ½ canton
0 delegates per cantonette.

CABINET
5 members
President annual by rotation
No more than 2 from 1 political party or 1 from 1 canton
Admin. functions only:

1. Foreign Affairs
2. National Finance
3. National Defense
4. Infrastructure
5. Internal Affairs

Peoples Congress

Delegates Congress

CABINET

PRESIDENT

1) Limited government constitution with entrenched Bill of Rights.

2) Only functions and powers delegated by 90% of cantons.

3) Changes to constitution only with support of 100% of cantons and 80% of citizens in compulsory referendum.

Fig. 5   The canton system

148

4. Central government must balance its budget — its spending must not exceed its income, and limitations should be prescribed on its ability to borrow or to inflate the money supply. This would keep the country solvent and free of inflation.
5. Central government must not be able to subsidise cantons. Throughout the world, unions, federations and confederations have used their ability to subsidise constituent units in order to centralise power. States, provinces or districts are bribed by central government into accepting certain regulations in exchange for grants. In the USA, many states have unwillingly accepted national standards regulations for this reason.

Structure
As in Switzerland, the USA and elsewhere, the central government should consist of two houses of equal status and a cabinet. These would be constituted as far as possible to avoid the potential for bad government regardless of who governs.

People's Congress
With the proviso that there should be at least one representative from each canton, representation in the first house would be on the basis of population. It would be the direct representative of the people by proportional representation.

South Africans are used to the Westminster system inherited from Britain. Under this system, candidates run as independents or for political parties in constituencies or wards. It is hypothetically possible that a single party could receive 51% of the votes in every constituency. It would thus win 100% of the seats in parliament despite having only a fractional majority of supporters. It is not uncommon under the Westminster system for a party to win a majority of constituencies even though it has received a minority of votes. This is the present situation in Malta, for instance. It usually happens when urban constituencies are loaded so that rural votes carry more weight.

The Westminster system is unusual. More commonly, countries have opted for proportional representation. Political parties or geographic units are represented in government in proportion to the number of voters. If there are, say, three parties that win votes in the ratio of 60:30:10, they will have representatives in roughly that ratio.

Proportional representation can take various forms but tends to fall into two main categories. One option is for representation to be based

149

on population density. In the canton system, this would mean that a canton with a million voters would have twice as many representatives as one with 500 000, ten times as many as a canton with 100 000 voters, and so on. The second option is for each political party to have proportional representation based on the number of votes cast in its favour nationwide.

We suggest the former system for a number of reasons. In order to depoliticise central government and reduce inter-group hostility, it is important that party politics be primarily a canton affair. There may be a handful of parties that are represented in all cantons but technically, although they have central bodies and the same name and policies, they should be separate canton parties which constitute a national movement. The whole object of devolving power to autonomous geographic units is to ensure that minorities are not swamped. Representation based on national political parties would probably lead to entire populations having no representation in the People's Congress.

On the other hand, representation based on canton population is likely to reflect party proportionality. Cantons would be free to elect their representatives on any basis, including that of proportions based on party support.

It is likely that some very small cantons would not qualify for representation on the basis of population. We therefore suggest that each canton, regardless of size, be entitled to one representative in the People's Congress.

A Delegates' Congress

The second house would comprise two delegates from each canton regardless of size. Should a canton split into two parts, each would send one delegate. If further splintering occurred and part cantons or 'cantonettes' were formed, they would enjoy the same autonomy as other cantons but would forfeit their right to representation in the Delegates' Congress. They would still be represented in the People's Congress. Since cantons would be unable to increase their initial representation, this would prevent pseudo-cantons from forming merely in order to dominate the Delegates' Congress.

This formula of one house with proportional representation and another based on equal representation avoids the risk of group domination and works very well in other countries where the case for it is less compelling than in South Africa.

So long as ethnic consciousness and identification survive, both houses may be expected to have black majorities in this country. The

150

People's Congress will probably reflect the numerical relationship between the major population groups: ie ±72% black, 16% white, 9% coloured and 3% Asian. The various black groups (Zulus, Xhosas, Sothos, etc) may also be represented on a roughly proportional basis, depending on how people ultimately vote.

Until the initial delimitation procedure has taken place, we have no way of knowing how many cantons would have black majorities, but it is certainly likely that most will. Thus the Delegates' Congress would probably also have a black majority. In every sense South Africa would have 'black majority government' and 'one man one vote' — or, more precisely, 'one adult many votes'. But there would be an adequate set of checks and balances to prevent 'black majority dictatorship' or 'one man one vote once'.

The smaller rural cantons would have a majority in the Delegates' Congress, and they would tend to be 'moderate' or 'conservative' regardless of race. The major metropolitan cantons, which would have a majority in the People's Congress, would probably be more 'radical'. The two would balance each other, much as the House of Representatives and Senate do in the USA.

Moderate minorities would rely on the Delegates to preserve their values and interests, to the extent that they are not already protected by the Bill of Rights, the degree of local community autonomy and inter-canton autonomy and all the other factors we have mentioned. (See Chapter 16)

The cabinet and central government departments

To ensure the maximum depoliticisation of central government, we propose that the central government be responsible for only five areas of central administration, each with one presiding minister. The five ministers would constitute the cabinet. They would be elected by both houses sitting together in the *Joint National Congress*. The cabinet ministers could be chosen from any canton and any political party provided that each minister is from a different canton and not more than two belong to the same political party.

The Joint National Congress would elect one of the ministers each year, and for one year only, to chair cabinet meetings. He would be the National President and his functions would be purely administrative, and include matters of protocol.

The five central government departments would have the usual responsibilities as follows:

151

1. Foreign Affairs: international relations, immigration, diplomatic corps.
2. Finance: central budget, import and excise duties, currency, mint, foreign exchange, reserve bank.
3. Defence: protection against foreign invasion and civil war, emergency relief.
4. Infrastructure: national roads, railways, power supplies, pipelines. (This department may run infrastructure, for example roads and railways, only through cantons that give their consent — as in Switzerland.)
5. Internal Affairs: registration of births, marriages, deaths and population distribution, national statistical services, appeal court, environment, functions delegated by cantons.

Treaty functions of central government

In addition to the five primary functions, the central government would have 'secondary' or 'treaty' functions delegated to it by cantons, in much the same way that the ex-protectorates and homelands have arranged for the RSA government to do certain things for them. These might range from administering a customs and monetary union to providing transport services and registrars of financial institutions.

Initially, many cantons and communities would be unprepared to take on various responsibilities. They could arrange for the central government to perform these functions for them until they are ready — or indefinitely. As a rule, delegated functions would go to the Department of Internal Affairs and Regional Services Councils. Alternatively, arrangements could be made between cantons, or communities, or with private companies. Every situation will suggest an appropriate solution, and provided one starts from a position of maximum devolution, the optimal amount of centralisation will come about spontaneously and organically.

Citizenship

Everyone will have dual or treble citizenship, as each individual will be a citizen of the country, of a canton and possibly of a community as well. National citizenship will be automatic and immediate for present South Africans and homeland citizens. Citizenship of cantons or communities will be subject to canton policy and procedures.

Voting

In most cantons there will be 'one man many votes'. People will vote in their communities on community issues, in cantons on canton issues, and in national referenda on national issues. It is possible that some cantons might have authoritarian governments which make unilateral decisions without involving the citizens. The citizens of such a canton would have the constitutional right to call a referendum on an unpopular measure, to oust the canton government or to amend its constitution as outlined in our discussion on the 'Bill of Rights'.

Depoliticisation
With maximum devolution to canton level, there would be very little contact between citizens and central government. Citizens would not vote directly for the central government, nor would they be directly taxed by it. Any contact would be purely administrative and limited to matters which do not provoke conflict. For example, you might deal with a central customs officer, or register your child's birth or your marriage at a central agency, but this would not provide any basis for dispute or hostility between groups.

The majority of people in the central government would certainly be black, but this would not mean that Indians, coloureds, whites, Chinese, Japanese, Jews, Moslems, Hindus, or Buddhists would be ruled by blacks, because the central government would not have the power to impose its policies or values on anyone.

Defence
Some people fear that if central government controls defence and blacks constitute a majority in central government, they will use the army to seize power and create a black one-party state.

This fear is based on the assumption that the majority of cantons would be dominated by the same political party and that this party would want to dominate the entire country. There is no evidence to support this assumption. Opinion surveys indicate that black support is split among a number of different groups, none of which attains anything approaching a majority. Cantonisation would probably result in the formation of even more political groups representing local interests. Surveys also indicate that the majority of blacks are moderate. They want economic freedom and political representation but few nurse a desire for revenge or retribution. We have discussed this in greater depth in Chapter 16. Even the relatively 'radical' groups with strong support, the ANC and UDF, are in favour of minority rights and 'power-sharing'.

The fear of a black military coup is also based on the assumption that blacks will not be happy with the way things are. In a canton system they would have both freedom and the power to control their own lives.

There would be no incentive to risk civil war in order to remove rights of whites, coloureds and Indians which don't infringe on their own rights, and to risk chasing away white capital, investment and expertise. The black political groups which propose controlling the entire country and nationalising all wealth have such a small following that they pose no real threat.

There would be citizens of all the cantons in the armed forces, and the canton governments would decide together whether servicemen should be volunteers or conscripts. Alternatively the cantons might decide on a system whereby each runs its own army and contributes to a National Defence Alliance as do the European countries to NATO. Under such a system if war broke out between two or more cantons the Defence Alliance of the remaining cantons could still be called in to restore peace.

Racial discrimination

Whether people should or should not be allowed to discriminate — or, indeed, should be *forced* to discriminate — on racial grounds is a highly emotionally charged and conflict-provoking issue.

We suggest two alternatives:

Our first preference would be a constitutionally entrenched prohibition on discrimination by government at all levels. In other words, government would be colour-blind — entirely nonracial. Any law that results in any form of compulsory integration or segregation would be unconstitutional. But if someone wanted to establish a trade union with black members only, or a school open to Jews only, or a swimming pool reserved for women only, or a theatre open to all — all of these options would be legal, provided they are voluntarily and privately financed.

Thus all citizens would have the right to integrate or to segregate voluntarily at their own expense, but it would be unconstitutional for any level of government to enforce integration or segregation, or to practise discrimination itself, for example, in its employment practices or the provision of public facilities.

The general constitutional prohibition on discrimination would be supported by a number of entrenched clauses in the Bill of Rights regarding equality at law, freedom of movement, freedom of association and disassociation, and property rights.

If this position were adopted, South Africa would be the only country in the world that recognises true personal liberty and human rights with respect to race policy.

The second option would be to include a 'sunset clause' in the constitution allowing local communities or cantons to maintain racial laws

154

for ten years. This alternative would mean that the thorough protection of individual rights which our system offers would become fully effective only when the sunset clause lapsed. Prior to that date, cantons and communities could maintain existing race laws, relax them, or abolish them *in toto*.

We offer this alternative because significant numbers of South Africans, mostly white Afrikaners, but also members of other population groups, are determined to maintain racial segregation.

This approach would give cantons or communities controlled by white nationalists breathing space in which to buy up land so that when the sunset clause lapses, they could exclude unwanted people from their areas by exercising their property rights. 'Whites only' cantons could be created in a number of ways. Racial separatists could make representations to the Delimitation Commission for the creation of an adequate number of cantons in which there already are, or could relatively easily be, a majority of whites. To the extent they did not succeed at the delimitation stage, they could organise a popular initiative and create white majority cantons through referenda. These could be consolidated by purchasing land.

In order to refuse entry to blacks in 'whites-only' cantons, they would have to buy *all the land* in their cantons or communities. They would not, however, be able to prevent people who are not white from using national roads.

They would be taking the risk that such an extreme degree of voluntary discrimination might be so offensive to the majority of cantons that the expulsion procedure might be implemented or threatened against them. It might simply be unacceptable to blacks, who will constitute a majority in by far the most cantons, if a neighbouring canton or town is characterised by such signs as 'no blacks allowed' or 'net blankes'. Nonetheless, we believe that the system we have proposed gives white nationalists the only realistic prospect of indulging their racial preference indefinitely into the future in a manner that should gain international and local acceptance even though frowned upon. Conversely, there is no realistic prospect that statutory apartheid can be sustained in the long term.

However, if racial separatists are not convinced, our system still leaves them with the option of secession. If separatist cantons secede, they will become sovereign countries, free to do as they choose. They would be taking it upon themselves to face the wrath of the world without, at the same time, forcing the rest of the country to suffer from international condemnation.

The sunset clause would also allow black nationalist governments in areas such as Soweto to refuse entry to white businesses in order to give black businessmen a chance to make up for historical disadvantages. The influential black chamber of commerce movement, NAFCOC, favours a policy along these lines.

The canton system would produce its own dynamic, spontaneous order and process, the results of which cannot be forecast with accuracy. But our guess is that there will be such a massive de-escalation of racial tensions and conflict that even those groups which now feel seemingly boundless racial hostility will be moderated.

For this country to have any prospect of enduring peace and prosperity all the major groupings need to see light at the end of the tunnel in terms of their own perspective. It is highly unlikely that any of them will attain their presently stated goals on a national scale. The best they can hope for is to do so in the limited spheres of influence permitted by a canton system.

Bill of rights

The law shall guarantee all their right to speak,
to organise, to meet together, to publish, to
preach, to worship and to educate their
children.

Freedom Charter

We have suggested a canton system with a limited government constitution as the political solution for South Africa.

In the preceding chapters we have discussed various provisions which should be included in the constitution, notably a bill of rights. The Bill of Rights which we propose would be an entrenched provision listing certain fundamental and inviolable rights of citizens and cantons. Amendments would require unanimous agreement by all canton governments and an 80% majority of voters in a compulsory national referendum.

We have suggested that a sunset clause might be included in the constitution to the effect that should some cantons not want to abolish discriminatory legislation immediately, they would be entitled to a twilight period of ten years in which to phase it out. This clause would override Articles I, III, V, VI(iii), VII and X of the Bill of Rights until sunset date, after which every canton would have to comply with all the articles.

Since most cantons would have a black majority, it is unlikely that more than a handful of them would make use of the sunset clause.

The Bill of Rights outlined here is written in lay rather than legal language. A definitive Bill of Rights would of course be carefully worded by legal experts.

There are explanatory notes at the end of the Bill of Rights for each clause designated by an asterisk.

157

BILL OF RIGHTS

PERSONAL RIGHTS

Article I   Equality

No law, practice or policy of government at any level shall discriminate on the grounds of race, ethnicity, colour, creed, gender or religion, provided that all existing discriminatory laws, practices or policies shall continue until relaxed or repealed, or until the Sunset Date, whichever is the earlier.

Article II   Citizenship*

All people will be citizens who presently qualify for South African citizenship under the terms of the Citizenship Act, including those who did so prior to homeland independence, and those who would have qualified had the homelands not become independent. Every citizen is entitled to the citizenship of the canton and community of their birth, or of their permanent residence at the time of delimitation.

Article III   Universal Franchise

Every person of voting age shall be entitled to vote in all national referenda (and elections if any), and in all elections and referenda of the canton or community of which he or she is a citizen.

Article IV   Referenda*

(i)   Popular initiatives

Every citizen will have the right to launch a popular initiative calling for a referendum on any law, practice or policy, or calling for a general election, subject to the following conditions:
— at the national level, there being a petition by not fewer than 100 000 citizens entitled to vote;
— at the canton level, there being a petition by 100 000 or 20% of the citizens of that canton entitled to vote, whichever is the lesser;
— at the community level, there being a petition by 50 000 or 20% of the citizens of that community entitled to vote, whichever is the lesser.

158

(ii) Compulsory referenda

— Changes to ordinary provisions in the constitution require the approval of a majority of the electorate in a national referendum; changes to entrenched provisions require the approval of an 80% majority of the electorate in a national referendum.

— No canton boundary may be changed, including splitting from or amalgamating with another canton, unless approved by a majority of all the registered voters directly affected thereby; provided that if a part of a canton wishes to split from an existing canton, the citizens in the remainder shall not have a vote in the referendum, but if that part is to amalgamate with or be incorporated into another canton, all the citizens of the latter shall be entitled to vote in a separate referendum.

Article V   Freedom of movement

All citizens of South Africa may move freely from, into or through all parts of the country upon public thoroughfares and in public places.

Article VI   Property rights

(i)   Basic property rights*

All citizens of South Africa may own, acquire, use and dispose of movable and immovable property.

(ii)   Expropriation*

It shall be unlawful for government at any level to confiscate, commandeer or expropriate any private property (movable or immovable) except for bona fide infrastructural purposes or national defence and security where there is no reasonable alternative, under due process of law, or for the purposes of settling a binding debt to the state.

(iii)   Right of admission*

The proprietor or lawful possessor of any movable or immovable property may exclude or refuse admission to any other person.

(iv)   Nominative boundaries*

Any landowner or group of landowners whose land is on a boundary between cantons may opt at any time for the boundary to be adjusted so as to place such land under the jurisdiction of a neighbouring canton subject to the agreement of that canton.

159

Article VII   Freedom of association and disassociation*

Any person may associate or transact with any other person or refuse to associate or transact with any other person for any reason.

Article VIII   Civil liberties

There shall be freedom of speech and freedom of the press, subject only to considerations of public decency and safety according to the norms of the canton or community concerned.

Article IX   The right to trial and due process*

No person shall be convicted, sentenced or imprisoned without due process of law, including the right to trial and habeas corpus, and there shall be no detention without trial.

Article X   The right of appeal

In respect of every judgment of the highest court in a canton or group of cantons, there shall be a right of appeal to the ultimate court of appeal; provided that in a civil action parties may agree in advance that there should be no right of appeal.

Article XI   Minority victimisation*

Every minority group of people shall be protected from victimisation by government at any level; and what constitutes a 'minority' or 'victimisation' shall be determined by the court according to the circumstances of each case.

Article XII   Intimidation*

Every person and every group of people shall be protected from politically motivated intimidation by any other person or group, and upon conviction on an intimidation charge, the court may impose the severest penalty permitted at law, and in any event, the accused shall be sentenced to a term of imprisonment without the option of a fine.

CANTON RIGHTS

Article XIII   People's Congress

Every canton or part canton shall be entitled to proportional representation based on the number of registered voters in it, in the People's Congress.

Article XIV   Delegates' Congress*

All cantons shall be entitled to representation by an equal number of delegates in the Delegates' Congress regardless of their size or population, and all semi-cantons shall be entitled to be represented by half that many delegates.

Article XV   Canton veto

Each canton has the right to veto any proposed amendment of any entrenched clause in the constitution, and any proposed delegation of any power or function to the central government which is not already conferred by the constitution.

Article XVI   Secession

Every canton has the right to secede from the country upon a declaration of secession being approved by not less than 80% of its registered voters, whereupon it shall become a sovereign independent state in accordance with international law.

Article XVII   Boundary changes

Every canton and every part of a canton may by referendum, as provided in the constitution, break away from or amalgamate with any other canton.

Article XVIII   Constitutions and bills of rights*

Every canton may adopt its own constitution or bill of rights entrenched in such manner as the canton may determine, provided any additional rights conferred upon its inhabitants do not conflict with the central constitution.

Article XIX   Alliances

All cantons or communities are free to enter into alliances, agreements or arrangements to their own satisfaction with other cantons or communities.

Article XX   Citizenship

Every canton may adopt its own citizenship policy subject to Article II and provided that no canton may grant citizenship to someone who is not a citizen of South Africa.

161

EXPLANATORY NOTES

II Citizenship

South African citizens would have to choose citizenship of either the canton of their birth or the canton of their permanent residence at the time of initial delimitation. The cantons may not refuse them, or strip them of citizenship for which they qualify at this time. After initial delimitation, canton governments may stipulate citizenship requirements for future citizens. Canton governments may offer to buy citizenship rights back from citizens who qualified at the time of initial delimitation.

IV Referenda

In Chapter 10 we observed that universal suffrage is no guarantee that all laws which are introduced by elected representatives are supported by the majority. By granting citizens the right to call for referenda and ensuring that changes to the constitution are subject to referenda, the Bill of Rights helps to guarantee basic democratic rights.

It is difficult to get 50 000 or 100 000 signatures on a petition, so the right to launch popular initiatives would not result in an excessive number of referenda as some people fear. Also, Swiss experience shows that the administrative cost of referenda is very low. We would suggest that this be contracted out to private enterprise.

VI (i) Basic property rights

In its literal sense, this clause would make all government intervention unconstitutional. This is not our intention. The clause is intended to protect every citizen's fundamental property rights according to reasonable definition, and in a final bill of rights the wording would need to be carefully worked out by legal experts.

VI (ii) Expropriation

Many of the worst injustices in South African history have resulted from the expropriation of private land by government. We have shown how the land rights of blacks were progressively eroded so that today they scarcely exist at all. We have discussed the extent to which coloureds, Indians and whites have also suffered loss of land, homes and businesses as a result of expropriations by government.

To ensure that these injustices never recur, we propose this unambiguous anti-expropriation clause. This would prevent expropriation for other than 'genuine' purposes, and in such cases proper compensation based on market value, sentimental value and subsequent losses would have to be made.

If government at any level wanted land or other assets for any other reason such as the provision of schools, housing, parks, or whatever, it would have to buy it by voluntary agreement, like anyone else.

VI (iii) Right of admission

In South Africa, proprietary discretion has been violated by various acts, particularly the Separate Amenities Act, which dictate with whom people may or may not transact on their own property. In the USA and other countries, various measures dictate whom people must serve on their own property. By entrenching right of admission, South Africa would become the first country in the world with properly protected property rights.

VI (iv) Nominative boundaries

This novel clause is proposed so that landowners on boundaries between cantons will be free to nominate which canton they wish to join. Unpopular governments would lose citizens to neighbouring cantons and find their boundaries closing in on them if they didn't change their ways!

VII Freedom of association and disassociation

In Chapter 9, we argued that the right of people to mix with or separate from others as they choose is fundamental to a free society. Apartheid laws interfere with the right to associate; affirmative action laws with the right to disassociate.

This clause ensures that any individual or group of individuals acting in a private and voluntary capacity may discriminate in favour of or against any other person or group of people on the grounds of race, gender, religion or otherwise for any reason and in any manner that does not entail a transgression of common law rights.

This includes the right of companies to determine their own employment policies, and the right of private schools, clubs and other organisations to refuse or admit members as they choose.

IX The right to trial and due process

Whilst we do not condone it, if South Africans decide that there is to be detention without trial, it should be subject to authorisation by a supreme court judge. Authorisation would be granted only if there is evidence beyond reasonable doubt that such detention is necessary for the safety of the state. In any such case, the following conditions should be met:

— The detainee must be maintained at all times in comfortable 'civilian' conditions.
— The detainee must have liberal access to friends, relatives, physicians and legal counsel.
— Such detention should not exceed three months provided that detention for further periods of three months may be ordered upon the case for detention being re-established *de novo*.
— The detainee should retain all rights which are not in conflict with the basic objective of detention, including unlimited access to materials and literature.

X Minority victimisation

Most white South Africans, and many coloureds and Indians, fear that with universal suffrage the black majority will impose a system which does not recognise minority interests or which aims specifically to plunder non-black wealth.

The principle has long been established in company law that victimised minorities have protection. We advocate that this be entrenched in the bill of rights so that any minority is free to bring a court action to show that a given government measure, at any level of government, amounts to the abuse of majority power so as to victimise the minority.

XI Intimidation

Many people are afraid that although the majority of South Africans are moderate and reasonable, when elections are held many may be intimidated by a handful of radicals into staying away from the polls or voting for political groups which they would otherwise not support.

In order to discourage intimidation, we propose that it be a serious offence. In a final bill of rights, 'intimidation' would need to be very carefully defined.

XIII Delegates' Congress

Further subdivisions of cantons (cantonettes) will not be entitled to representation in the Delegates' Congress.

XVII   Constitutions and bills of rights

Here are examples of the additional rights cantons might introduce in their constitutions. This list is not exhaustive, and some of these rights are mutually exclusive:

— freedom of contract — the right to conclude any mutually volitional agreement amongst any consenting adults whether commercial or social;
— the right to work — the right of anyone to obtain employment, regardless of occupational licensing, minimum wage or closed shop union provisions;
— conditions of employment — the right to minimum conditions of employment such as annual leave, pregnancy leave, rate for the job, occupational safety, etc;
— welfare rights — the right to a pension, unemployment benefits, medical aid, etc;
— freedom of speech and press — ie, going further than the central government bill of rights, under which cantons or communities could impose restrictions in regard to public safety or indecency;
— academic freedom — the right of educational institutions to determine their own admission criteria, course content, staff appointments, student rights, etc.
— property rights — ie, the protection of property rights beyond that provided in the central government bill of rights.

16 | Protection of minorities

The Afrikaner people will have to become physically the undisputed majority of the inhabitants in the geographical area which it sees as its own fatherland.

Hendrik Frensch Verwoerd
(son of late Prime Minister H F Verwoerd)

pproximately 72% of South Africans are black, 16% white, 9% coloured, and 3% Asian.

The large black majority causes most whites, and many Indians and coloureds, to fear a winner-takes-all political system with universal suffrage. They are afraid that blacks will impose a system which does not recognise minority interests, or that there will be 'one man one vote *once*'. Only a canton system such as we have outlined in the preceding chapters allows for universal suffrage and complete equality of every individual before the law within a structure which protects minority rights in many different ways.

What are minority rights?

Minorities are individuals with common interests or values which are not shared by the majority. Examples of minorities include not only whites, Indians and coloureds, but also Xhosas, Afrikaners, Jews, South Sothos and Muslims, as well as old people, the unemployed, foreigners, homosexuals, the handicapped and lefthanded people. Minority rights may be defined as the right of these groups of people to live according to their common values, provided they don't interfere coercively with the equal right of others to do likewise.

Ultimately every individual has a unique set of interests and values and is therefore a minority. Stated differently, there are not 'minorities' or 'majorities', but only individuals with some interests that they share with a few or many other individuals. Thus if individual rights are ad-

167

SOUTH AFRICA'S MINORITIES

Blacks:		Total	72%	Whites:	Total	16%
Zulu	21%	Ndebele	2%	Afrikaans-speaking		10%
Xhosa	19%	Swazi	2%	English-speaking		6%
Sotho	13%	Venda	2%			
Tswana	9%	Others	1%	**Coloureds:**		**9%**
Tsonga	3%			**Indians:**		**3%**

equately protected, so will the rights of minorities and majorities be protected.

We have seen that in the course of South Africa's history white minority rights were not only protected but were artificially advanced by gross violations of blacks', coloureds' and Indians' rights. Laws were passed, not just to protect white rights, but to safeguard white privilege. The time has now come when most whites, including the present government, are prepared to phase out the vast body of discriminatory laws and policies which have been built up over the last 330 years. But the fear of black domination — the 'swart gevaar' — remains the major stumbling block.

The 'Swart Gevaar'

What most whites fear is that, given unlimited and centralised political power of the kind that whites have held and abused, blacks will evict whites from their homes, nationalise their businesses and loot their property in an orgy of redistribution and revenge. But there is a good deal of evidence to suggest that this fear is more imagined than real.

True, there are many articulate political leaders who speak openly about the day of reckoning when AZAPO would restore the land to its 'original owners', and the ANC to 'those who work it' in terms of the Freedom Charter. A handful would like to see a fully-fledged marxist dictatorship with no private property at all. But the majority of blacks seem to want no more than the removal of all barriers to black advancement and enfranchisement.

Many people point to the rest of Africa to illustrate their fear of black domination. They describe the socialist dictatorships and one-party states such as Zaire, Tanzania, Ethiopia and Angola, and argue that there, but for white control, go they — into an abyss of poverty and mismanagement.

To be fair, we should observe that this is not universally true. Botswana is a real multi-party democracy; in Swaziland white farmers own well over half the land and enjoy full property rights under black government; the Ivory Coast is a capitalist economic success story; Kenya has heterogeneous harmony, and increasingly black African countries have turned to the West for advice and support. Even in communist countries like Angola and Mozambique there are popular resistance groups fighting for freedom and democracy.

In addition, South African blacks are more sophisticated, better educated and have higher living standards than the vast majority in the rest of Africa.

Evidence suggests that the assumption that voting would be along ethnic, linguistic and cultural lines may be mistaken. There may be stronger ideological alignments.

Various surveys have been undertaken to assess the relative followings of different political groups. While findings vary, it seems that many people who are not Zulus nonetheless support Inkatha, and many people other than Xhosas support the ANC; one survey even indicated a large following for President P W Botha amongst blacks. It seems that the majority of blacks would support some kind of moderate alliance (see Appendix I).

None of the four independent homelands have adopted the policies whites most fear. They have all repealed all race laws, but none have espoused Marxism. Bophuthatswana and Ciskei have recently taken major steps to free their economies. All four have been more financially responsible than the South African government.

In his book *Permanent Peace*, which we highly recommend, Denis Beckett describes the type of black leaders which might be expected to emerge in a typical small rural town, serving a population of around 50 000 of which over 90% are black. He points out that the whites are barely aware of the existence of the people who enjoy distinction in the eyes of the local black community.

> Foremost of these is the principal chief in the area, one Kelly Molete.
>
> Chief Molete is a middle-aged man, a committed Christian and university graduate of considerable sophistication, well endowed with charm and old-world courtesy.
>
> There is also a prominent businessman Khumalo, a man of Zulu stock who lived in the area for years with his Zuluness never an issue until recently, when the rise of Tswana ethnicity induced by the creation of Bophuthatswana has tended to accentuate his outside origins. His farming activities and brickworks nonetheless

make him the major black work-provider in the district and he is generally well thought of.

There is a lawyer named Absolom Motleleng, who is the nominal Azapo presence in the area. He is about thirty years old and after some time in Johannesburg recently returned to his home district to set up a practice there. His maroon BMW is well known to the people of the townships. There is also one Phaka, a one-time farm-worker from Ventersdorp who lost both home and job when his employer decided he was a trouble-maker. He was dispatched to a resettlement camp which borders on and overlaps with Chief Molete's land. There he has by force of personality, and with the backup of a crew of henchmen who are according to viewpoint, either the sustainers of local order or a gang of toughs, established a position of dominance.

Beckett points out that these are real people, known to him and representative of typical black community leaders. He has, however, changed names and places for the usual reasons.

When these black leaders approach the local white town council to discuss a new dispensation they do so en bloc because they are bound by common interests. However, Khumalo is dedicated to free enterprise, Molete is not very interested in economics but wants to do his best for his tribe, and Motleleng, while theoretically committed to socialism, is in practice concerned about peace and stability and improving the quality of life of blacks. Phaka is right out of the delegation:

> In the first place, he will have none of this parleying with the boere. He has his fiefdom, and he perceives black power as on the horizon with the declared constitutional changes. He'll wait and he'll make his run a little further anong the road, when he can see the opening to power that counts, not just petty Sannieshof power. In the second place, there is no way that Chief Molete is going to have Phaka sitting on any delegation that he leads. Phaka is a thorn in his flesh. He considers him an upstart and a nuisance, and the organisation which Phaka runs in the squatter township is a major disruption to Molete's tribe.

Beckett continues:

> The traditional white idea of the black bogeyman waiting to take over the country ... a red-hot Africanist and a communist and an anarchist all at the same time ... does not actually exist in any single person, least of all one with leadership pretensions. The Africanists and the communists tend to be quite drastically at log-

gerheads with one another, with the Africanists such as they are being also thoroughly divided among themselves over their attitude to the rights of whites, and the only true anarchists are a few white middleclass intellectual mavericks. The teenage township stone-throwers who are alleged to be anarchists are really the resentful flotsam which a hopeless political structure such as ours inevitably throws up.

Even if all the evidence we have presented is invalid, and if most blacks do indeed nurture in their hearts a desire for revenge or an urge to plunder, the system we propose offers many effective protections for minorities.

Entrenched minority protection

All the safeguards listed here are discussed in detail elsewhere. We repeat them only in order to highlight the extent of protection they afford to minorities.

The proposed Bill of Rights includes the following entrenched provisions which are specifically intended to protect individual and thus minority rights:

1. *Freedom of movement:* This would enable people to leave cantons whose policies did not concur with their own values and move to more congenial ones.
2. *Property rights:* The fundamental right of all people to own and acquire property is supplemented by an anti-expropriation clause, a proprietal rights clause and a nominative boundary clause. The anti-expropriation clause would prevent government from expropriating land for any reason other than the provision of infrastructure, and it would ensure that there is proper compensation in such cases. The proprietal rights clause would protect the right of a property owner or proprietor to admit or exclude anyone, regardless of his reason, to or from his property. The nominative boundary clause would enable property owners living on canton boundaries to apply for inclusion in whichever canton they prefer. This would be particularly useful for farmers.
3. *The right to associate and disassociate:* This ensures the freedom of individuals to fraternise with or separate from whomever they wish and would render compulsory integration (affirmative action) unconstitutional.
4. *The right to call for referenda:* When government officials abuse their office, people could launch popular initiatives through which they

171

could call for a new election, request inclusion in another canton, or have any unpopular measure withdrawn. Within black majority cantons, spheres of white, Indian or coloured majority influence could be created by establishing semi-cantons or cantonettes and by negotiating for maximal autonomy in local, predominantly white, coloured or Indian communities or towns.

5. *Victimisation of minorities:* Any minority would be able to bring a court action against a government measure which amounts to the abuse of majority power in order to victimise the minority.
6. *Intimidation:* Intimidation would be a 'Schedule I offence' so that the moderate majority would have effective protection and be free to pursue their interests without fear.

In addition to these specific clauses in the Bill of Rights, the entire structure of the canton system is based on the idea of returning decision-making to the people concerned. We have discussed how political competition between cantons and the 'demonstration effect' discipline canton governments to act in the interests of their residents.

On the other hand, any system with a powerful centralised government automatically and inevitably results in the violation of minority rights and often, as we see in South Africa, majority rights as well.

Ultimately the only way to avoid group domination is by allowing people self-government. Given self-government, even without all the constitutional safeguards we have included, we can safely rely on the most meaningful protection of all: the goodwill of most South Africans — black, white, Indian and coloured alike.

17 | Socio-economic solutions

All people shall have equal rights to trade where they choose, to manufacture and to enter all trades, crafts and professions.

Freedom Charter

hroughout this book we have put the case for a free society, a society with maximum individual autonomy and responsibility and minimum government intervention.

We have suggested that the primary prerequisites for a free society are limited government, decentralisation, privatisation and deregulation; that central government should be limited to five areas of control: foreign affairs, finance, defence, infrastructure and internal affairs; and that canton governments should control all other aspects of government in their own areas.

In this chapter, we recapitulate the advantages of economic freedom and consider some of the socio-economic functions of central, canton and community government in more detail. We also suggest ways in which education and welfare might be provided more satisfactorily and list economic measures which the present government should undertake immediately in order to de-escalate conflict.

Canton powers

Most economic policy decisions would be made at canton and community government levels. Provided they comply with the Bill of Rights, cantons would be free to pursue any economic policy. They would have, for example, their own company laws and deeds registry laws, and their own policies regarding tax, welfare, housing, agriculture, licensing, standards, health, education etc.

South Africa's political groups have divergent views on economic policy, at present the competition between them is confined to largely theoretical, acrimonious and abstract attacks on one another.

In a canton system, there would be a visible and lively contest between their differing views of the optimum world. We would see through practical demonstration which policies produce the best results.

The purpose of what follows is not, then, to suggest that the policies we advocate be forced on canton governments, but rather to persuade people that 'government can do more by doing less'. [1]

Advantages of a free market: recapitulation

A free market economy is based on freedom of movement, private ownership of property, freedom of exchange, freedom of contract, freedom of association and disassociation and freedom of entry. These freedoms ensure that any individual or group of individuals can enter into any transaction or exchange with any other person or persons, provided the terms of the exchange are mutually agreed and volitional.

The interventions which typically interfere with these rights, and hence with the market mechanism, are: minimum standard laws, health laws, occupational and professional licensing laws, apprenticeship laws, labour regulations, transport regulations, state-protected monopolies, state monopolies, tariff protection, import and export controls, subsidies, influx control, price fixing and many more. Many of the ill-effects of these regulations have been discussed in previous chapters, particularly Chapters 4 and 5. The following 'laws of intervention' provide a summary of these ill-effects.

Louw's eleven laws of government intervention

1. All interventions are instituted for the benefit of a few at the expense of many.
2. All interventions are declared to be in the public interest.
3. All interventions are easier to introduce than to repeal.
4. All interventions reduce liberty.
5. All interventions produce side-effects contrary to their stated intention.
6. All interventions are rationalised by reference to their supposed benefits and omission of their inevitable costs.
7. All interventions produce an apparent need for more interventions, which have the same effect as the former *ad infinitum*: interventions beget interventions.
8. All interventions increase bureaucracy, red tape, government

174

spending, taxes, corruption, and lobbies for more interventions exponentially.
9. All interventions tend to come from politicians who promised less intervention.
10. All interventions are supported by business people who oppose government interventions except those which they support, which, it turns out, support them.
11. All interventions would be crimes if performed by civilians: thus all interventions are legalised crime.

Throughout the world there is a powerful correlation between economic success or failure and the degree of central planning.

Free markets result in cheap and efficient methods of production and distribution, and innovative technology and product development. They provide the best products at the lowest prices. This is why Hong Kong and Japan provide cheap, high-quality cars, radios, watches and sound systems for export, and the People's Republic of China doesn't. It is why the USA exports tons of food and the USSR doesn't. It is why Kenya and the Ivory Coast feed their people, and Ethiopia and Tanzania don't.

Free markets focus effort on productivity. When governments intervene, an enormous amount of time and effort is wasted on unproductive methods of making profits. Economists call this 'rent seeking'. Rent seeking is the process whereby interest groups lobby for the government to introduce transport permits, import permits, licenses, tax deductions, subsidies and so on which benefit themselves but do not produce wealth for society.

Deregulation decriminalises society by drastically reducing the number of laws which can be broken. In a highly regulated economy like ours, it is a crime to sell soap after 6 pm or to employ a gardener who doesn't have a permit. Countless 'victimless crimes' of this nature fall away in a free society, along with the cost of administering them which is borne by the tax payer.

Free economies are characterised by charity, philanthropy, corporate social responsibility and social caring. A great deal of anti-free market sentiment revolves around the myth promoted by enemies of a free society that free enterprise creates selfishness, greed, poverty and exploitation in a dog-eat-dog society.

There is essentially no difference in the welfare objectives of most people, regardless of their station in life. People want better housing, education, health, love and comfort. They want a TV set, a flush toilet, a fridge and insect repellent; less work, more pay, and freedom of choice, movement, speech, association and disassociation. All these things are provided more effectively and generously by a free economy than by any other economic system.

Taxation in a canton system
In the system proposed in this book, central government would have no power to tax citizens directly, nor would it be empowered to redistribute wealth or subsidise cantons.

The relatively small amount of revenue required to finance its own administrative functions should come primarily from foreign trade in the form of customs duties, export earnings, excise duties or tariffs as agreed by the cantons. It would also derive income from user charges such as tolls on national roads and court fees for supreme and appeal courts.

With the unanimous agreement of the cantons, revenue might be raised for central government through an annual canton tax based on population. For example, each canton might pay to central government R100 per citizen for the next budget year. Cantons could finance this in their own way.

Each canton would have its own taxation policy and it would soon become evident which policies achieved the best results.

Economic theory shows that when taxes are raised higher than about 25% of GNP, the effect on the economy is so counterproductive that revenue collected is less than it would have been if taxes had been kept down.

This has been demonstrated in Ciskei where a flat tax rate of 15% has been introduced with the first R8 000 of income being tax free. Some 90% of Ciskeians in the lower income bracket no longer pay tax, but early evidence suggests that as a result of an influx of industries and capital, Ciskei will gather more revenue than it did previously under the South African tax structure. Ciskei also held sales tax at 10% instead of raising it to 12% along with South Africa, and monthly returns show an increase of more than 50% in revenue from sales tax. Ciskei is currently experiencing an annual growth rate of around 8% compared to South Africa's 2%.

Prior to this century, in most countries of the world, there were no income or corporate taxes and governments got along very well without them. They were introduced mainly during the first world war as a temporary war measure and, unfortunately, they remain with us.

Personal income tax was not introduced in South Africa until 1914 and company tax (apart from a very low tax of about 5% on gold and diamond mining activities) not until 1925.

Transport

All South Africa's transport services — sea, road, rail and air — were started by private enterprise under free market conditions. For various reasons, under different governments, and at different times, all of these have been nationalised or heavily regulated. Unaware of this many people now subscribe to the myth that the state had to undertake these activities because 'the private sector could or would not.'

One of the primary reasons for transport regulations has been to keep blacks, Indians and coloureds out of the transportation sector.

During the nineteenth century, blacks discovered, as they do today, that one of the easiest entry points to the economy was through transportation. 'I can well call to mind the time when, with only one or two exceptions, there were no wagons in Kaffraria but those belonging to Europeans; now, however, native wagons are so plentiful as to be quite a nuisance.' (Evidence to Native Affairs Commission, 1865)

In the late 1800s most 'transport riders' responsible for conveying people and goods thousands of miles across Southern Africa were blacks. Today there is apparently not a single black licensed road haulier operating in South Africa. The handful of blacks who do have road haulage permits are not using them because there is no demand on the routes for which they are authorised. The effect of restrictive transport licensing has been to ensure that virtually all licences have gone to government-owned or private white-owned transport monopolies.

Perhaps no other area demonstrates as unambiguously as transport that government interference with the market is conflict-provoking (and politicising). Visitors who ask how good the transport service is in Soweto, are likely to be told that 'It is very good — a bus is only a stone's throw away!'

The deregulation of transport in general, and of black urban transport in particular, would not only help defuse unrest in the townships but would also provide thousands of job opportunities for blacks. Men and women can become taxi-drivers with little education and training, and no more money than is needed to pay for a driver's licence and a deposit on a vehicle.

The government is currently pouring hundreds of millions of rands into ill-conceived job creation and small business development programmes, at great net cost to the economy as a whole. It could achieve a great deal more by the simple expedient of drawing a line through the

177

road transportation act.

South Africa is one of the few countries outside the communist bloc that has a totally centralised and uniform transport policy. In most countries, urban transport policy is devoluted to local governments and regional transport to states or provinces, while central government controls only national transport. Whether or not South Africa is cantonised a policy of this kind should be pursued.

In the canton system we propose that central government has no power to regulate transport. Each canton would have its own transport policy and many would probably deregulate transport or devolute transport policy to communities. This would prevent the following kind of incident from occurring.

In 1979 a company called City Mini Cabs applied to the transportation board for a permit to run 100 cruising taxis in Johannesburg. South African cities have possibly the worst taxi services in the world. There are very few taxis in proportion to population and they are hard to identify. They may not cruise, nor may they be hailed in the streets; they must wait at taxi ranks for clients to come to them or call for them by telephone. The situation is so bad that at one time the American trade consul felt constrained to produce a pamphlet explaining to visiting Americans why they would have difficulty finding taxis in South Africa.

City Mini Cabs seemed to have an open-and-shut case. Their permit application was argued at great cost by experienced lawyers and supported by the Johannesburg Municipality, the Central Business District Association, the Free Market Foundation and the Chamber of Commerce. It was turned down by the transportation board.

If Johannesburg controlled its own urban transport, City Mini Cabs' application would have been granted, along with many others. The same applies to cities and towns all over the country.

Transport specialist Terry Markman estimates that the full cost to the South African economy of transport regulation exceeds R1 billion per annum. Deregulation and privatisation would make the country R1 billion richer, provide small business opportunities for many thousands of blacks, depoliticise one of the most conflict-ridden areas of the economy, provide greatly improved services to the community, and reduce traffic congestion because more people would use urban transport instead of private cars.

Agriculture
Several important changes should be made in South Africa's agricultural sector which, like transport, would be controlled at the canton

level in our system.

The rigid agricultural controls and socialisation which handicap farmers should be phased out and all attempts to keep sub-economic farmers on the land should be discontinued. This would mean that large tracts of under-utilised and over-utilised farm land would come onto the market at about the same time that legislation preventing blacks from buying land is abolished. Blacks with insufficient capital to purchase land could initially become tenant farmers. The few successful black commercial farmers who have emerged in recent years are mostly farmers in the homelands who have leased farms from tribal authorities, the homeland development corporations or the Development Trust (the single biggest land holder in South Africa).

Since blacks have been denied experience in real estate markets, many do not realise that very little up-front capital is required to purchase land. Usually loans can be raised for the deposit and the balance may be paid off in instalments generated from farming profits.

Restrictions on the sub-division of farm land should also be removed. Their effect is to prevent those who can only afford small units from becoming farmers. The theory behind restrictions is that the government should prevent the creation of non-viable units. But non-viable units would not survive if they were not propped up by various government policies designed to 'keep white farmers on the land'. There need be no concern about excessive sub-division. Given a free market system in which all farmers would stand or fall on merit, farmers on small portions which proved uneconomic would either sell them to others who would consolidate them, or lease them to farmers who would utilise economies of scale on many small portions nominally owned by others. In all countries with a successful agricultural sector and efficient land use the trend has been for less and less of the population to farm and for each farmer to feed increasing numbers of people through increased productivity and efficiency.

Mineral wealth

Nearly all of South Africa's mineral wealth — the diamond fields, gold fields, platinum mines, coal deposits and iron mines — are concentrated in the north-east Cape, the southern and western Transvaal, parts of Bophuthatswana and the north-west Free State. Together these areas comprise less than 20% of South Africa's surface area. Is it fair that a few cantons should control all this wealth?

There are a number of answers to this question. First of all, nearly half of the country's population is already concentrated in these areas. Secondly, the wealth of one district does not impoverish another. On the contrary, as long as there is free trade, the wealth of any part of the country benefits all other parts. This was demonstrated very clearly in the past when gold and diamonds were discovered and the entire country boomed.

Another point, and perhaps the most important, is that mineral wealth plays a minor role in determining the prosperity of a society. As discussed in Chapter 4, many countries with abundant natural resources are poverty-stricken, whereas others with negligible resources are 'economic miracles'. It is economic policy which determines whether countries, cantons or communities prosper or starve.

To those who believe the mines should be nationalised, we point out that they already fall under the Mineral Rights and Mining Titles Acts. Mines are contracted out to the private sector through mining leases and the government gets its return from taxes on profits, volumes, wages and salaries. This arrangement is more profitable for the government than running the mines itself; this would be true for any government. We advocate that mining policy be decided at canton level and we would urge canton governments to privatise all minerals and apply the same regulations to mines as to any other business venture. Whatever policies are chosen, given the demonstration effect, the optimum solution will soon become apparent.

If the architects of South Africa's future constitution decide that mineral wealth should remain under the control of central government in order that profits can be redistributed, we suggest that this be done in the form of welfare vouchers or cash grants, which are the only means of ensuring that the money reaches the intended beneficiaries.

Welfare vouchers
A number of things in South Africa such as bread, bus fares, housing and education are subsidised in order to help the poor.

Most people assume that subsidies do result in lower prices and do, in fact, help the needy. Unfortunately, they are mistaken. Subsidies actually increase prices; and instead of helping the poor, they benefit suppliers and manufacturers.

Studies show that subsidised bread is more expensive than unsubsidised bread currently being sold in the informal sector. This is in spite of the fact that informal sector bakers have to purchase their materials at retail prices, can't advertise and distribute openly and often have to pay bribes or fines.

Similarly, unsubsidised bus fares are cheaper than those which are subsidised. In fact, the higher the subsidy, the higher the fares tend to be. When bus fares were investigated by the Free Market Foundation a few years ago, the most expensive bus fares in South Africa were those charged by white buses serving the richest suburbs of Johannesburg and Pretoria. They received the biggest subsidy, up to 65%. The cheapest bus fares were charged on the Indian buses in Durban, which were not only unsubsidised, but in some cases paid taxes. Studies in America reveal a similar pattern.

The idea that subsidies actually increase prices is certainly surprising. How can it be explained? A clue to the answer lies in the fact that the most vociferous advocates of subsidies are the people who provide the product or service concerned. Bus operators spend hundreds of thousands of rands employing top public relations people to represent them in the media, lobbying the government and undertaking research to establish a case for bus subsidies. The same is true of bakers who want bread subsidies, or builders who want housing subsidies or anyone else who wants a subsidy.

If the true beneficiary were the consumer, it would be immaterial to the producer or supplier whether there were subsidies or not.

The reason so much time and money is spent in this way is that subsidies are in effect based on a percentage of production costs. For example, if the cost of a product or service is ten million rands, the supplier might be subsidised by 10% or one million rands. He is supposed to pass this on to the consumer in the form of lower prices. Clearly, his incentive is to maximise his cost: 10% of a high cost is more money than 10% of a low cost. Therefore, it is in the self-interest of a supplier to maximise inefficiency and waste, to avoid innovation and risk-taking, to use accounting methods that overstate real cost and to decrease productivity. Higher costs mean higher prices.

Not only do subsidies result in higher prices, but such benefits as do get passed on to consumers seldom, if ever, reach the lowest income group. Millions of poor blacks in South Africa never buy bread in the formal sector, ride a subsidised bus or train, or live in a subsidised house. Their children do not get subsidised education. The people who do 'benefit' are the ones who paid the taxes with which the subsidies were financed in the first place — the middle and higher income groups.

Subsidising manufacturers, distributors, suppliers or administrators does not help the poor, it penalises them. If the poor are to be helped, they must be subsidised directly. The only way to do this is by giving them cash grants or welfare vouchers. Cash grants are preferable because each individual knows best what his own personal hierarchy of needs is. However, the fact that some might spend the money on gambling or liquor makes this an unpopular option. The alternative is welfare vouchers, which may be used by the recipient only for certain purposes. For example, poor people might be given transport vouchers, education vouchers or food stamps. The vouchers must be freely usable in the market place.

Education

One of the great tragedies of present-day South Africa is the popular belief that the quality of education is a function of the quantity of money spent on it by government, and that therefore the problem of inadequate black education can be solved through 'free and compulsory' state schools with the same per capita budget as white schools. On the contrary, evidence both here and abroad shows a correlation between increased state spending and declining education standards.

It is said that per capita spending on white education in South Africa is the highest in the world. Yet few would regard the quality of education as being anywhere near the top. In recent years, there has been a disproportionate increase in education expenditure by government, averaging over 18% per annum. The 1984/85 budget proposed a 23% increase (R3,4 billion in one year). For blacks the budgeted increase was 26,3%. The amount budgeted for black education has increased by a staggering 2648% since the 1972/1973 financial year. These increases have not been matched by increases in quality, especially not in the perception of discontented black school students, and a simple calculation shows that if the government spends the same on black, coloured and Indian students as it currently does on whites, it will soon be bankrupt.

There are several much more effective ways in which the quality and availability of education can be rapidly improved.

First, and most important, the government must encourage private education. Until recently it was doing just the opposite. Consider two examples:

During the 1960s, some concerned farmers in the Colesberg/Norvals Pont area built a farm school on Andries Louw's farm, Eenzaamheid, at their own cost. They arranged transportation to and from the school for the children of farm labourers, hired a teacher and provided the necessary equipment and learning materials. The school was closed by Education Department inspectors. It did not comply with building or health regulations, it was not registered with the Education Department, it did not have an approved syllabus or the requisite number of pupils, and the teacher was not properly qualified. So black children who were getting reasonable and relevant education, however imperfect it may have been, at no cost or inconvenience to taxpayers or the state, were deprived of schooling. This case, however, was different from countless others in that the farmers fought back with the determination that characterised their voortrekker ancestors; after a prolonged battle, in which even the Minister became involved, the school was allowed to reopen.

The second example is a school which is owned and run by Mr Monna in the Winterveld squatter settlement. There are no desks and the teachers are not 'qualified'. The children sit on long benches with their books on the floor. But three hundred children receive a basic education there which costs their parents approximately R20 per year. Government inspectors have waged a long campaign against Mr Monna, as they have against 20 or so other informal sector schools in Winterveld. Again, at no cost or inconvenience to the state or the taxpayer, these children who would otherwise be wholly uneducated are receiving some education. According to the headmaster, the children who go on to higher education from this primary school do better on average than those who have been to government schools.

Even if the state partially finances education, it need not provide it. Let the private sector provide schools while the government finances the students through education vouchers.

Under a voucher system, each child of school-going age, regardless of race, would be entitled to an education voucher. These vouchers could be used at either private or government schools, and schools would compete with each other to attract students.

Government schools need not be privatised, but neither should they be subsidised. They should compete on an equal basis with private schools.

A voucher system would encourage greater school autonomy over curricula and teaching methods. Education would be more relevant, and would cater for a kaleidoscope of different needs and preferences.

A voucher system would avoid the distortions created by subsidies which we discussed in the previous section. Vouchers could be of equal face value or they could be graded according to the ability of the parents to pay for schooling. High income parents could supplement the vouchers to send their children to more expensive schools.

In addition to a voucher system, or as an alternative, there could be a tax-credit system. Parents who send their children to private schools would receive a tax-credit in the form of an income-tax deduction. This would put an end to the present inequitable situation whereby parents pay twice for their children's education, once to the state and once to the private school; and this in turn would encourage more people to use private schools. The credit could be limited to the per capita annual expenditure in state schools.

At present, childless adults and small families subsidise education for large families. The tax-credit system would also stop this from happening.

If all South Aricans are to receive at least sufficient education to be numerate and literate, some government spending will have to be diverted from higher to lower education. The present scale of government spending on higher education favours people in the higher socio-economic bracket at the expense of those in the lower bracket as most people who pursue a higher education come from upper income groups. A voucher system would ensure that children receive the education they need, and would automatically shift the emphasis to primary education which is in greatest demand. Also, students who want to pursue higher education could be offered a government loan, to be repaid when they enter employment.

The devolution of control over schooling to canton and community government levels would go a long way towards solving the problem of race and education. Central government would no longer dictate whether schools should be segregated or multiracial: each canton would establish its own policy in this regard. Moreover, a canton could decide to devolve control even further, to local communities, municipalities or school boards.

Privatisation and/or a voucher system would ensure that schools provide what people want in terms of cost, quality, content and racial mix. Schools which did not meet people's needs would go out of business.

Private schools — with or without subsidies, vouchers or tax-credits — would bring to education all the advantages of enterprise, motivation, innovation and cost-effectiveness which flow from healthy competition.

Education has been a focal point of political unrest and boycotts because it is provided by central government. Decentralisation and deregulation would not only improve the quality and quantity of education, they would depoliticise it.

Labour relations and trade unions

In the system which we have proposed, Article VII in the Bill of Rights entrenches freedom of association and disassociation. This includes the right of employees and employers to join or refrain from joining trade unions and employers' associations respectively.

Trade unions would be free to organise nationally, cantonally or within specific enterprises. Most of them would probably continue to function much as they do now, subject to complying with the Bill of Rights. Many would have a good chance of persuading one or more canton governments to adopt the policies they prefer. They would probably continue to operate through existing branches, and would deal with diversity in labour legislation in the same way as their counterparts in the many countries where labour laws are not uniform.

Some cantons might encourage different forms of labour organisation such as the 'enterprise unions' found in the Far East. There unions are organised by company staff so that instead of a boilermakers' union there would be, for example, a Barlow Rand union. Employees in enterprise unions see themselves as part of a team which includes managers and employers.

In some cantons government would not regulate labour at all and labour relations would be subject to freedom of contract. Employers would decide whether or not to recognise unions, and nonparticipating employers and employees would not be bound by industrial agreements signed by others, as they are now. Disputes would be settled in civil courts under laws of contract.

The canton system allows for all labour policies to be tried and tested except those which contravene the Bill of Rights. Employees, guided by labour activists, would seek employment only in cantons with satisfactory labour policies, and would flock to those which promoted their interests most successfully.

Privatisation

The present government is already committed to privatisation and a high-powered Privatisation Committee under the chairmanship of Minister Eli Louw has been appointed. Dr Wim de Villiers, the prominent industrialist who recently conducted an investigation into the privatisation of transport services, is now also a member of the Privatisation Committee. There is also a committee investigating the privatisation of government forests, and a programme for the privatisation of most government low-income group housing ($\pm 500\,000$ units). The government has announced a scheme for the progressive and genuine privatisation of land in black areas. Private television has been allowed (albeit in the form of a monopoly granted to newspaper companies for some reason that defies comprehension). In some areas refuse removal and other urban services have been privatised by local government. Various municipalities have organised a conference to explore practical strategies for privatisation of their services. These are all big steps in the right direction, but it is very important that privatisation is done in such a way as to avoid certain common pitfalls.

State monopolies must not become private monopolies. Privatisation should occur only under conditions of free competition, and wherever possible it should be accomplished through public auction or open tender rather than private negotiation.

It should be implemented in a way that creates opportunities for small business, especially for blacks. For instance, if refuse removal in KwaMashu is to be privatised, contracts should be offered for small areas in order to give small contractors a chance to compete for them. Similarly, park or road maintenance could be privatised so that individual contractors are able to bid for the jobs. It is possible that one large contractor may quote the best price on all contracts and get all or most of the work anyway, but at least the public will know that the best price has been obtained and that small business has been given a fair opportunity.

Although subcontracting is a popular way of transferring government monopolies to the private sector, there is no reason why most government 'enterprises' should not be privatised completely. Virtually every function undertaken by government, especially local government, has been successfully privatised somewhere in the world. There are now private courts, police, water suppliers, and prisons elsewhere in the world.

A source of resistance to privatisation is often the officials who perceive their status and jobs to be at risk. There is no need for this. Privatisation can and should be implemented so as to offer new opportunities (such as a shareholding), greater job security and higher incomes to existing employees who would then find themselves in the private rather than the government sector. There are many ways of achieving these objectives.

Whether or not a canton system is introduced in South Africa, the central government should divest itself of state corporations, parastatals and state-protected monopolies through devolution, or better still, through privatisation.

In a canton system, decisions regarding privatisation would be in the hands of canton governments and the demonstration effect would enable the public to see and experience for themselves which approach they prefer.

Urgent reforms
There are a number of economic measures which the present government should undertake as a matter of utmost urgency in order to rap-

idly reduce political unrest and prepare for the successful introduction of a new order.

Racial Equivalence
First and foremost, a Racial Equivalence Act should be passed which would sweep aside all laws governing blacks in black areas which differ from those governing whites in white areas. One of the major sources of frustration for blacks is the bureaucratic interventionism and official discretion which they face from day to day. No consultation is required in order to introduce equivalence, and white nationalists would not object since it would take place within existing black group areas and homelands.

Inversion
At the same time the principle of inversion should be introduced through a Regulatory Inversion Act. At present the onus generally rests on people who want to enter the market to prove that in doing so they are not acting against the public interest. Instead, the onus should rest with anyone who opposes the opening of a business or the granting of a licence to prove that such a move would be against the public interest. In other words, there would be a rebuttable presumption in favour of business people. This would make an enormous difference to the speed and facility with which people (blacks in particular) could enter business.

Small business deregulation
A Small Business Deregulation Act should be passed exempting all businesses employing fewer than 20 people from most or all regulations. This is by far the most effective way of encouraging small business. Such an Act has been introduced in Ciskei with excellent results.

During the first year of deregulation literally thousands of new small businesses sprang up throughout Ciskei — with no government subsidies to help them. Unemployment is falling. Consumers are getting better services and products at lower prices. Everyone is better off, except those who used to have monopony protection.

Free enterprise zones
In recent years, hundreds of free trade zones have been created around the world in order to encourage the development of new businesses and additional employment opportunities.

Free enterprise zones are currently being developed in Natal (Zero Based Regulation Areas or ZEBRA zones) and Natal's example should be followed throughout the country.

The main objection to free trade zones is that by their nature they bring about economic and social distortion by causing an artificial movement of investment and people from one place to another.

However, the advantages of free trade zones would far outweigh the disadvantages. They would give blacks a chance to enter and participate in the market economy before they are enfranchised. Free trade zones also create a demonstration effect. When the evils which regulations are supposed to protect us from do not occur on a significant scale, governments are encouraged to extend deregulation on a wider basis.

The power to expedite urgent reform

In President Botha's Rubicon speech on the 15th August 1985 he said, 'I am of the opinion that there are too many rules and regulations ... Even if I as State President have to take power during the next session of Parliament so as to enable me to deregulate in the interests of the country, I will do so!'

The Temporary Removal of Restrictions on Economic Activities Bill was passed in the middle of 1986, granting President Botha these powers. The government has lost a lot of credibility because their words speak louder than their actions, and now it is essential that they move fast. We therefore advocate that the State President make use of the power he now has to deregulate: to exempt any kind of enterprise from statutory law; to exempt defined areas (Free Zones) from specified measures regardless of the size of businesses there; and to repeal all laws that discriminate on the grounds of race. This is the only way to ensure that civil servants, some of whom may oppose change, do not either deliberately or inadvertently sabotage socio-economic reform.

18 | The legal order

Law is often but the tyrant's will, and always so when it violates the rights of an individual.

Thomas Jefferson

A free society is characterised by the rule of law and common law, and an unfree society by the rule of man, statutory law and discretionary law. In South Africa at present we have a mixture of both. To achieve true justice we must reduce the rule of man and increase the rule of law.

Common law

Over the centuries, common law systems have developed in societies throughout the world on the basis of what the 'average reasonable man' thinks is just and unjust. Despite regional differences, almost all systems of common law protect fundamental individual freedoms such as we have listed in the proposed Bill of Rights, and prohibit basic violations of person and property such as theft, arson, fraud, assault and murder. The application of common law varies from one society to another, even from one community to another, but the substance remains the same whether one is in the Amazon jungle, Outer Mongolia or New York City.

In South Africa common law is consistently and unambiguously embodied in the Roman-Dutch common law system.

Statutory law

Statutory law is the body of laws built up through government legislation and regulations. The purpose of legislation is to change common law to bring it in line with the way governments believe society should be run.

The extent to which any country or society depends on common law

189

is in inverse proportion to the amount of legislation its governments enact. A totalitarian state has almost no common law, while a minarchy relies almost entirely on a common law system. In this country we have both.

Discretionary law

If laws, be they common laws or statutory laws, are applied according to specifically stated criteria, we have objective law. If, on the other hand, officials have the power to apply the law according to their own subjective opinions, then we have discretionary law or the rule of man.

In Chapter 5 we showed that perhaps the greatest disadvantage experienced by blacks in South Africa is that they live in a world of discretionary law. They have no way of knowing, when they apply for a licence or almost anything else, whether or not they will be successful because their success does not depend on compliance with objective criteria, but on the whim of the officials in charge.

Discretionary law is bad law, and should have no part in any just legal system. For example, if a trader must be licensed and comply with certain standards, the law should set forth the required standards clearly and unambiguously, so that any individual who complies with these requirements will be entitled, as of right, to a licence. There should be no application procedure whereby, in the name of so-called public interest, administrative officials or boards may grant licenses to preferred people or refuse them to those, who, for some reason, are out of favour.

All evidence regarding eligibility under various regulations should be led in public hearings, and written evidence should be freely available to the public. Deliberations of official bodies should be open to the public, and these bodies should be required to give reasons for all their decisions.

At present countless official decisions, especially those regarding blacks, are made behind closed doors, and there is no accountability to the public.

Limiting legislation

Justice in a free society is based mainly on common law. The judiciary is independent of the legislature and all individuals are equal before the law.

We have advocated a strictly limited central government because we believe this is the best way to avoid the submergence of common law rights under a deluge of legislation. We have suggested further that central government be allowed to enact or administer laws only in those areas of authority specifically delegated to it by the cantons.

Five main areas of administration which might be assigned to central government have been outlined. However, as the relationship between the cantons and central government would be essentially contractual, groups of cantons might choose to delegate further functions of mutual interest. For example, the coastal cantons might delegate control over the beaches. Whatever the case, the more limited the functions of central government, the less likelihood there is that common law will be swamped.

The importance of independent judiciaries
If a limited government constitution and bill of rights are to be effective, they must have the protection of an independent judiciary. In other words, the judiciary must be free from any influence or pressure by the government or any other lobby. True independence means much more than a mere policy declaration to that effect; the judiciary must be equal to the government and, like it, subject only to the constitution.

Since the judiciary is a branch of the government, true independence is problematic. However, a number of devices have been developed to protect judicial independence. One is security of tenure for judges: once a judge is appointed, he may not be dismissed, except under the most extreme conditions such as insanity or the conviction of a serious crime, regardless of how offensive the government finds his judgments.

Another method is to leave the appointment of judicial officers largely in the hands of the legal fraternity. This is based on the assumption that the legal fraternity is incorruptible, which unfortunately is not necessarily valid. In the USA, many public officials such as judges, attorneys-general and police chiefs are elected by the citizens. This may be a better way of ensuring their independence.

In many western countries there is a popular view that the jury system guarantees judicial independence. However, there are serious problems with this such as the susceptibility of the jurors to the influence of popular and media opinion.

Some people maintain that the judiciary will be truly independent only if courts are privately owned and run. Courts would compete with one another and litigants would agree to the jurisdiction of a court or group of courts which had established a reputation for being efficient, objective and just. Once considered highly unorthodox, this idea is gaining in popularity and there are now private courts in the USA. The increasingly popular system of arbitration in South Africa has similarities to a private court system.

Some countries, for example the UK, have a system of 'lay magistrates'. Whereas South African magistrates are full-time civil servants, lay magistrates are respected citizens in the local community such as headmasters and doctors. They evaluate the evidence and determine the court's ruling with the aid of advice from the clerk of the court on questions of law.

There are interesting similarities between lay magistrates and the traditional courts of black chiefs and headmen in South Africa. Under the conditions of judicial devolution which we propose for the canton system, we would expect most of these different methods of administering the law and appointing officials to be used in various forms and combinations. The demonstration effect would help to bring about the best judicial system.

South African courts — the status quo
In South Africa at present we have civil and criminal law, and civil and criminal courts.

Civil law concerns problems which arise between private citizens such as breach of contract, divorce, motor car accidents and conflict concerning deceased estates. Such cases are tried in civil courts and judgment is usually based on common law and government regulations. A breach of civil law, or a civil wrong, is called a 'delict' in this country and a 'tort' in North America.

Criminal law is primarily concerned with differences which arise between individuals and the state. All infractions of statutes, that is victimless crimes, are tried in criminal courts. However, certain violations of the common law which occur between private citizens are also tried in the criminal courts. These are called common crimes, and include murder, rape, robbery, theft, arson and fraud.

There are three tiers of courts in this country. Magistrates' courts are the 'inferior courts' and make up the lowest tier. They have a limited jurisdiction and deal with petty infractions in civil and criminal cases. Black chiefs and headmen try cases which involve breaches of tribal common law (customary law) at this level, and the recently introduced small claims courts, which only hear civil actions, are also inferior courts.

Above the magistrates' courts are the supreme courts. There are supreme courts in each province and they have limitless jurisdiction. People whose cases have been tried in magistrates' courts have the right of appeal to supreme courts, and serious civil and criminal cases are automatically tried there.

Those who are not happy with the judgment of the supreme court have the right of appeal to the highest court in the country, the appeal court in Bloemfontein.

Canton courts

We have suggested that South Africa be divided into cantons based on magisterial districts. Thus, while canton boundaries in their final form will not conform exactly to existing magisterial districts, it is likely that every canton will have an established magistrate's court within its area of authority. Courts at this level would vary a good deal from canton to canton in accordance with customary law (the common law of different cultural groups) and local administrative systems.

Supreme courts would also be controlled by canton governments. The existing infrastructure could be retained virtually as is, with present supreme courts falling under the joint administration of surrounding cantons. Some cantons might prefer to establish their own second-tier court as has happened in some homelands, but this should not interfere with the right of appeal to the appeal court. This would remain under central government, as will be discussed later.

Recognition of customary law

A major advantage of a system of independent canton courts is likely to be a substantially increased respect for, and recognition of, customary law. When the judiciary is centrally controlled, the legal system of one group is inevitably imposed on others. This is a serious problem in a heterogeneous country. At present, South African law does recognise African customary law, but no formal account is taken of the differences between black tribes, nor is the customary law of other groups such as Hindus and Moslems recognised.

Differences in customary law arise mainly in regard to 'the law of persons', in other words laws relating to matrimony, divorce, children and inheritance. Given the dynamic nature of the canton system, it is likely that cantons with many Indian citizens would make provision for differences between Indian and European law. Similarly, areas with significant numbers of, say, Sothos or Xhosas would probably make corresponding provision.

To ensure that customary law does not violate constitutionally entrenched individual rights, we propose that all people be free to elect the legal system of their choice. This already occurs to some extent in

193

South Africa: the judge or magistrate may determine, at the instance of the parties involved, whether Roman-Dutch law or tribal law applies in a particular case. In other parts of Africa too there is a limited application of different common law systems to different individuals by choice.

Some cantons might introduce the concept of class action. This, unfortunately, is alien to our current system but is presently being introduced in Ciskei. In the case of class action or public interest action, an action can be brought to court in the public interest against someone who is committing fraud or selling contaminated food, for example. Public interest actions largely circumvent the need for health and safety legislation and all its attendant ill-effects.

One of the greatest problems with our current judicial system is that law is effectively accessible only to poor people who qualify for legal aid and the well-to-do. It is likely that with a variety of systems and with small claims courts and customary courts, access to law would become quicker and cheaper.

Conflict of laws

Clearly, if laws differ from one canton to the next, some of them will conflict. This is not a new problem. It occurs in Switzerland and the USA and all other federal systems in which different constituent units have different laws. It also occurs between countries, and to a limited extent between the provinces in this country.

We do not need to re-invent the wheel; an entire body of law has been built up over time to settle disputes which result from conflicting laws. In cases regarding contracts, for instance, the law of the place in which a contract was concluded is usually invoked.

In some cases, there may be conflict between cantons or communities. For example, some areas might want to control rabies through compulsory inoculations while others might not. If such matters are not settled in the supreme court, they can be settled by the central government appeal court which would act, in the canton system, as an international court does in disputes between countries.

Legal precedent

The system of judicial precedent applies currently in South Africa. In other words, when there is a legal dispute the court settles the point by referring to previous judgments on similar cases. If a higher court has made a decision regarding a point of law, its decision is binding on all lower courts and virtually binding on equal courts throughout the

194

country. At present, with regard to homelands, decisions in South African courts have persuasive value. In other words, homeland courts attach a lot of importance to such decisions and tend to favour them.

In the system we propose, appeal court decisions would be binding on every court throughout the country to ensure that individual rights are protected. However, each canton would be free to adopt its own policy with regard to decisions made in the courts of other cantons. Some might pass a law to the effect that judgments made in other cantons would have the same force in their own courts. What is more likely is that groups of cantons, and conceivably all cantons, would enter into judicial treaties regarding such questions as legal precedent, reciprocal enforcement of judgments and procedures for serving court documents across canton boundaries. These questions would probably be resolved in much the same way as they presently are. Some cantons may adopt an entirely different legal system, but this seems highly unlikely.

Central court of appeal

In order to protect individual and canton rights laid down in the central constitution, we advocate an independent central appeal court which would supersede canton courts.

An independent court of appeal helps to avoid the possibility of local ethnic or cultural domination or miscarriage of justice. In any legal system it is essential to be able to take certain matters beyond local jurisdiction to a court in which there is some guarantee of an objective trial. All citizens would have an entrenched right of appeal, first to the highest court in the canton, and then to the central appeal court.

The appeal court would apply the law of the canton in which the case originates. There is a lot of precedent for this as many ultimate appeal courts have had to apply different systems of law. Citizens of commonwealth countries, for example, have the right of appeal to the Privy Council in London.

The present South African appeal court in Bloemfontein handles appeals that must be judged according to laws that differ from province to province. It is also the ultimate appeal court for three of the four independent homelands, which have increasingly different legal systems. For instance, all four have repealed all racially discriminatory legislation and changed their tax rates, labour laws and licensing laws. Two of them have a Bill of Rights. The Bloemfontein appeal court is the ultimate court for cases based on both African customary law and Roman-Dutch common law.

If all the cantons are to have confidence in the central government judiciary, special care must be taken to ensure its independence. In addition to the precautions already proposed, there might be provisos to the effect that there may not be more than one judge from any one canton; that a certain number of cantons may veto the appointment of a judge; and that the state attorney be elected or nominated by cantonal rotation.

Certain conventions would probably evolve, as they have done in the USA and Switzerland, to take account of ethnicity and socio-economic factors. A recent U S supreme court judgment ruled that unless ethnicity is accommodated in the selection of jurors, proceedings may be set aside. It found that a black accused of murder was entitled to insist upon blacks being included in the jury.

South Africa's judiciary has a reputation, even amongst the current government's most bitter enemies, for a reasonable degree of courage and independence. The lower courts have sometimes been suspected of ethnic bias, but there have been many higher court judgments against the state on sensitive matters, especially in recent times. For example, in the Ngwavuma case, a government attempt to cede land to Swaziland was set aside; in the Komani and Rikoto cases, judgments were made against government policy regarding influx control; and recently members of the UDF were released on bail against an order by the attorney-general. The government accepted the court rulings in all of these cases.

There is no perfect judicial system, but there is no reason why South Africa should not have a judicial system as good as the best in the world.

Interpretation of the Bill of Rights

According to present South African law, when there is a dispute as to the meaning or interpretation of a law, the courts have to establish the supposed intention of the law-maker.

The need to interpret the law arises because, regardless of how careful legal draftsmen are, language is seldom entirely precise and unambiguous. Additional problems are created when the version originally drafted and approved by politicians is translated into a second or third official language and the translated version becomes binding. Translations can never be precise. Apart from the difficulties presented by minor variations in punctuation, words have different shades of meaning which vary from person to person and from time to time, and according to context.

We have recommended methods of entrenching the Bill of Rights. It is equally important to protect it from misinterpretation. The courts should be obliged to interpret the Bill of Rights according to the true objectives of the people and their representatives.

This is a serious problem throughout the world. The USA has an admirable bill of rights, but many of its key provisions have been interpreted in such a way as to legitimise gross infringements of the rights they were intended to preserve. The interpretation of the bill of rights is now at such great variance with the intentions of the founding fathers that they must be turning over in their graves.

Conclusion

We propose that each canton choose its own legal system, and we have offered arguments in favour of an objective system based primarily on common law.

It is conceivable that some or many of the cantons would reject these ideas and that South Africa will end up with a majority of totalitarian states. But we think this is extremely unlikely because all available experience shows that when power is devolved societies tend to move towards greater personal freedom. As long as people are free to move, they will move to where there is freedom and justice.

In a canton system, there would be competition among legal systems and those which provided the most objective, just law would act as models for the others.

FREE SOCIETY	UNFREE SOCIETY
Legal Characteristics	
voluntarism	dirigism/coercion
rule of law	rule of men
natural law	positive law
common law	statute law/legislation
objective law	discriminatory law
due process/habeus corpus	arbitrary process
open society	closed society
freedom of contract	non-contractual/regulation of contract
consent	compulsion
non-aggression axiom	state aggression axiom
legal relevance	legal uniformity
protection of rights	proscription of rights
freedom	regulation

19 | **Strategy**

*... change does not roll in on the wheels of
inevitability. It comes through the tireless efforts
and hard work of those who are willing to take
the risk of fighting for freedom, democracy,
and human dignity.*

Allan Boesak, 1983

I n the course of this book we have considered the political and economic realities and dynamics of the current South African scene, as
well as some of the historical factors which led up to them. We have
provided a detailed description of a system which we believe would
meet the needs of all South Africans and achieve lasting peace, prosperity and freedom.

We have discussed where we have come from and where we want to
go. The question remains — how do we get there?

In answering this question, this chapter will consider the current climate of opinion and whether it is conducive to radical change in the
direction of greater individual freedom and responsibility; the steps
which the present government must take in order to achieve maximum
support for major reform; the specific procedures by which a change
from the current system to a canton system would be implemented; and
ways in which ordinary South Africans could contribute on an immediate and personal level.

Fertile soil
Throughout the world there is a clearly detectable trend away from
paternalism and statism towards individualism and personal responsibility. Denationalisation and privatisation are taking place not only in
the UK and the USA but also in communist countries. The socialist
government in Italy is privatising the telephone system. China is making significant free market reforms to the extent that it now has some

privately-owned profit-making roads! India under Rajiv Gandhi is following suit.

Since World War One, there has been a massive growth in government throughout the world. Now the pendulum is swinging the other way. The public rebellion against bureaucracy and excessive government manifests itself everywhere.

The myth that the state can produce wealth or justice or equality is dying. Few academic economists today continue to defend central planning or Keynesianism. In a survey of American economists in 1978 about 85% agreed on basic free market propositions. This trend amongst economists, which is visible in South Africa as well, is part of a general swing back to free markets, classical liberalism and libertarianism.

South Africans are ready for change. Those who aren't recognise that nonetheless it is inevitable. But political groups in South Africa are characterised by their inability to agree with one another. None represents anything approaching a majority of South Africans and none has come up with a plan which is attractive to all.

The strength of the solution outlined in this book lies in the fact that it offers an option which can meet the needs of all South Africans — except for the ultra-left and right-wing radicals who will oppose any peaceful and equitable resolution of our problems. Community consciousness is in such ferment now that we believe it can and will adjust to something new very quickly.

The present government's role

The Nationalist Government has an electoral mandate to bring about real reform and that is what it must do. President Botha has stated the government's objectives, which are to bring about genuine democracy, universal suffrage and equality at law within a system which protects minority rights. The time has come for it to proceed with a system which embodies these objectives and to prove to South Africa and the world that apartheid is indeed 'outdated'.

Many political groups have called for a national convention at which representatives of all South Africans can negotiate a solution. However, there are several difficulties with this idea, the greatest of which is the 'Catch 22' regarding representation of blacks. Many black leaders are not prepared to negotiate until the government has spelt out a plan to dismantle apartheid, in other words until the government has found a solution. At the same time they insist that a solution cannot be found without negotiation.

200

Even if black leaders could be persuaded to attend a national convention it would be difficult to ascertain who are the 'real' representatives of the people. So many organisations and parties currently claim to represent most blacks that the total of the alleged followings of all these groups is equivalent to several times the present population. Public opinion surveys are of little help as they produce conflicting results which tend to reflect the ideological predispositions of the researchers (see Appendix I).

Another serious drawback of the national convention idea is that those groups which did eventually attend would almost certainly not be able to reach agreement; the differences between them run too deep. Rather than bringing together a group of people with axes to grind and ideological positions to defend, therefore, the government should decide on a workable solution and call for negotiation and discussion around the basic idea.

The purpose of a convention would be to develop a solution and to decide how power is to be 'shared'. If the government decided to implement a canton system, half of the convention's task would be done. The question of power-sharing would become a non-issue since central government in a canton system would be so limited that there would be almost no power to share.

The government should appoint experts to draw up a draft constitution and detailed proposals and simultaneously employ a top public relations company, as it has done for the current reforms, to 'sell' the solution both domestically and internationally; and a diplomatic initiative should be launched to gain the support of as many foreign countries as possible. Foreign governments should be informed that South Africa is to have a multi-party democracy with universal franchise and the abolition of all statutory discrimination. They should be asked to terminate sanctions and boycotts and to stop supporting guerilla movements as a gesture of encouragement and goodwill.

It should be pointed out that apartheid is a cancer which can be destroyed in one of two ways. Either the patient can be clubbed to death, through war and disinvestment, or the cancer can be removed through careful surgery and the patient nursed back to health.

In order to de-escalate political unrest and violence, the government should immediately, during the current parliamentary session, lift the State of Emergency and introduce racial equivalence, meaningful small business deregulation, free enterprise zones and the principle of inversion, all of which were discussed in Chapter 17.

It is unlikely that any of the major political groups would object to these measures and they would make a significant contribution to decreasing political unrest.

Next, all political prisoners — including Nelson Mandela — should be released and all banning orders on people and organisations — including the ANC — should be lifted.

Consultation and negotiation should take the form of informal contact with key people, and the submission of evidence to the present Special Cabinet Committee on Constitutional Affairs, or a specially appointed Constitutional Commission.

In the model we have proposed there are numerous aspects which must be considered and resolved. Many of them, such as the sunset clause and the use of magisterial districts as a departure point, lend themselves to negotiation. These negotiations should start as soon as the government opts for the canton model.

There is no logical reason why the various political groups should reject a solution which fulfils their requirements simply because it is being implemented by the current government. Most parties are calling for the eradication of statutory discrimination, for universal franchise, the recognition of minority rights, and genuine control of people over their own lives. If the government is openly committed to a plan which meets all these requirements, then it should receive the full support of all the other groups.

When a draft constitution has been finalised to the government's satisfaction, the public should be given the opportunity to study and debate its contents thoroughly. It should then be put to a national referendum in which all adult South Africans would vote.

The Nationalist Government was elected by whites and is answerable to them; this precludes a national multiracial election without their permission, but it does not preclude a national referendum. Some will argue that a new constitution should first be put to the white electorate, but it would be an important sign of good faith to begin the new era with the first genuine universal plebiscite in South Africa's history.

As a compromise, whites might vote on a separate roll and the adoption of the constitution could be made conditional on receiving their support. However, we believe that if the canton system is properly understood, a majority of all the ethnic groups will support it.

Implementation of a canton system
Once cantonisation has been accepted in principle the Judicial Delimitation Commission will go into action.

Delimitation Commission courts will sit in all the provinces simultaneously to receive evidence regarding canton boundaries. As there will not be enough judges to staff them, they should be supplemented by politically 'neutral' black, coloured and Indian academics, head-masters, professionals and businessmen.

Maps showing the boundaries of magisterial districts will be printed in local papers and the courts will hear evidence as to whether these boundaries should become canton boundaries or should be altered. The delimitation courts will not only consider submitted evidence but will also undertake their own enquiries into local public opinion. There will be a presumption in favour of magisterial districts and the onus will fall on those who do not want the current magisterial district bound-aries to prove that other boundaries would be better.

Once a canton boundary ruling has been made by the court it must be put to a referendum of all the people living in the area concerned. Delimitation decisions will be made with varying speed depending on the amount of unanimity or dissension among residents of the area in-volved. If a court decision is rejected in a referendum, the court will have to go back to the drawing board.

From the time the court starts receiving evidence regarding the boundaries of a proposed canton, it will have two years within which to make a ruling. At the end of that period, failing a decision to the con-trary, magisterial districts and sub-districts will automatically become cantons.

As soon as a canton's boundaries have been approved by the major-ity of its citizens, it will be issued with a charter at a suitable ceremony and will become fully independent subject to holding an election within six months.

When a canton government has been elected, it can decide whether or not to draw up a constitution for the canton, and its independence will be subject only to the national constitution.

Canton laws will be those inherited from the present system until these have been changed by the canton or community government. This is the normal procedure when devolution takes place.

The administrative infrastructure will also remain until changed by the canton government.

Decentralisation and devolution

One of the few blessings of the homeland system and the constitutional and infrastructural changes that have occurred in South Africa in re-cent years is that we now probably have more experts on the mechanics of restructuring and decentralising government than any other country in the world. Degrees of devolution under the homelands system have varied from the transfer of four or five areas of concern to local government, to full independence in the national states. Each case has been different, and so it would be with cantonisation.

During the decentralisation process all existing local administrations would essentially continue as they are. Most administrative structures between them and central government would fall away, and the civil servants who head them would be elected locally and would hold office locally rather than in Pretoria or Cape Town. They would be the most senior officials at local (eg magisterial district) level and would be directly answerable to local politicians.

At least initially, in many cases, local people would not have the required expertise or experience to assume high levels of responsibility. In such cases, officials in the central government structure could be seconded to local government, as occurred with homelands and decolonisation. Areas which do not already have local administrative structures could continue to make use of, for example, the Regional Development Boards or Regional Services Councils, which they would then control. Cantons which so desired could subsequently form local boards or contract out local administrative functions to private enterprise.

To show more precisely how devolution would occur, we will discuss one example, education, in more depth.

Currently, apart from homeland education, all black education is administered by a central Department, but every school has a parent-teacher committee and a governing body. The administration of white education is somewhat different and varies from province to province. In general there is a local school board in each magisterial district. For each school there is usually a school committee and in the Cape Province, for example, parents have a considerable degree of control. However, Transvaal school committees have very little say.

Above the school boards are regional inspectorates and provincial education departments. Above them is the Department of National Education, which has very little direct control.

The strategy for implementing devolution in white areas would be simply to sever the little control that central government presently has over the provinces. Next, each canton would take over its own existing school board or boards. Cantons without school boards could establish them. Provincial education department officials could be seconded to local levels or taken over permanently through a gradual process differing from canton to canton. Groups of cantons with a harmony of interests might form Education Co-ordination Committees, or Regional Education Councils. At present there is a network of 'multilateral' and

204

'bilateral' committees and working groups between the homelands and RSA. These could be phased out or continued, according to canton choice.

Within each canton control over education could, as it is in the USA, Switzerland, West Germany and Belgium, be devolved further to local communities. Control of education by local school committees would ensure that schools meet the requirements of local parents and teachers.

Although every black school has its own governing body and parent-teacher committee, these organisations have almost no autonomy. They have no budget and no control over teachers or syllabi and are not permitted to make decisions even on issues which are unrelated to education policy.

A black school committee in the Transvaal recently decided their school should be supplied with electric power. They informed the Department of their intention and when no objection was forthcoming they collected R10 from the parents of every child to pay for electrification. On the day that the electrician was to start work, they received an urgent memo from the Department forbidding them to make any changes to the school building pending a departmental investigation of the matter. Months later, nothing has happened.

The frustration experienced by black school committees is immense. They are desperate for autonomy. All that needs to be done is to cut the links with the central department and let them run their own affairs. There are already committees for chairmen of school governing bodies; these could continue to liaise should they wish to do so.

In the course of cantonisation, many black and white schools would fall into the same cantons. They could all be administered by a canton school board, or retain local autonomy and liaise with each other as they wished. They would also be integrated or segregated according to local school board or canton policy.

Some people think there should be a central governing body which sets minimum standards and approves syllabi. This belief can be explained by the fact that South Africans have become accustomed to centralisation and uniformity of standards.

The notion that uniform educational standards are possible is mistaken, since schools inevitably vary, both in the quality of their teachers and in the quality of the education they offer. When employers evaluate the qualifications of a job candidate, they assess his ability through interviews and tests; they also consider the reputation of the school, technikon or university he attended. This is true throughout the world: universities — and more specifically, individual faculties within

205

universities — acquire international reputations for the excellence or inferiority of their graduates.

Currently AZAPO is instituting a system of private education as an alternative to government schools, and is soliciting recognition of its qualifications directly from the business community. One can safely predict that employers will be objective. All they are concerned about is the *de facto* quality of the person they employ.

Cantons that adopt the voucher or tax credit system discussed in Chapter 17 will have the fewest problems with education, as under this system the standard of education will be left to market forces to determine. Parents and students will pursue the best and most relevant education that their vouchers can buy and schools will compete for their custom.

Further devolution to local communities will be decided on by canton governments and as a consequence of popular initiatives. Communities might be based on electoral wards, local authority areas or ratepayers' associations.

In the period prior to the chartering of cantons, unbanned political groups will have time to establish themselves, multiracial parties will be formed, and all political groups will campaign, and probably offer evidence to the Delimitation Courts regarding boundaries. Whites, blacks, Indians and coloureds in racially mixed magisterial districts will have time to negotiate with one another, and what Beckett calls the horse-trading of a market-place democracy will occur.

A popular movement
If a canton system is to be accepted and implemented, it must first receive popular support. How can you, the reader who responds positively to these ideas and who would like to see them realised in South Africa, help?

The first priority is to disseminate these ideas as widely as possible. Talk to friends and family, offer them this book to read. Write to newspapers and magazines: letters pages have a very high readership. Speak to people who are influential in business, academic, social or political circles. Few people realise how accessible opinion-makers and policy-makers are.

When you explain the system be specific. We hear too many foggy clichés and vague generalisations about social justice and equality for them to make any impression.

The existing government must make the necessary moves to set South Africa on the right course. It is much more likely to make these moves if there is a visible groundswell of support for a canton system amongst ordinary South Africans (see p. 238).

Once the government has introduced the canton system, an evolutionary process will take over. Legal, economic and social factors will change to reflect the new order, unpopular institutions will disappear and unacceptable laws will be repealed.

Competition between different political, economic, legal and social policies will bring the best to the fore, and the involvement of all South Africans in all decisions affecting their own lives will bring prosperity and peace to this divided and unhappy land.

PART FOUR
The future

Don't imagine that you will encounter a perfect world ... Here on earth there is no perfection: but the closest approach to perfection is the progress achieved by the continual striving for that unreachable perfection.

Langenhoven

Part Four is a light-hearted glimpse into the future to illustrate the kinds of developments that might occur in a cantonised South Africa. Some names and places and a few details are drawn from reality, but most of the events, attitudes and characters are purely imaginary.

20 | From communism to laissez faire in one country

Cover-story **International Tribune**
December 28 1999

O
n this, the eve of the 21st century, the media world-wide are focussing on the major developments of the last hundred years. Undoubtedly one of the greatest success stories of the century has been the transformation of South Africa from a conflict-ridden and divided country to one of the world's most prosperous nations.

Many people have forgotten how insurmountable South Africa's problems seemed in the mid-1980s. Would there be a military coup? A full-scale violent revolution? Big power involvement? Few were optimistic despite President Botha's assurances that a peaceful solution would be found.

The new constitution was approved by a healthy majority in the first truly national multiracial referendum in December 1987. However, few were convinced that it could accommodate political policies which seemed wholly irreconcilable, or that it would achieve enduring peace. They voted for it because it seemed the best of the various options being suggested. Now South Africa is a model nation which offers irrefutable proof of the ability of an extremely diverse society to prosper and grow in peace and harmony.

Before we take a look at the four cantons which have attracted most international attention — Workers' Paradise, Witwaterberg (which may change its name to Blankeberg depending on the outcome of a canton referendum next week) H-Q and Cisbo, we will briefly describe a few of the more conventional cantons.

During the two years following adoption of the new constitution, delimitation referenda resulted in a total of 108 cantons, with 27 part-cantons and 13 cantonettes forming within the next five years. Today there

211

are a few unusual cantons and one or two rather strange communities, but the average canton is much like any other democratic country.

KwaNatal

After three years of shadow boxing, Zulu, white and Indian moderates formed the Moderate Alliance Party, which surprised everyone by winning a landslide victory in the first election it contested. More government proposals have been accepted by the voters in referenda in KwaNatal than in any other canton.

KwaNatal has average tax rates, typical welfare programmes and basic civil liberties. The economy is fundamentally capitalist with social democrat elements, such as modest consumer protection laws, state-owned utilities, trade licensing, and free and compulsory education. Official languages are Zulu and English. Buthelezi is still President and his following extends well beyond KwaNatal.

Apart from racial integration, the most conspicuous change has been the return of Durban's colourful rickshaws. 'Just like the good old days', senior citizens say, recollecting the time before the rickshaw clampdown in the 1950s after which only a token number were allowed for tourists.

Along with rickshaw deregulation has come taxi deregulation, so that now, just like most other places in the world, KwaNatal's cities have an efficient taxi service. Indians play an important role in the canton's life. Because they are a minority in all but one area, special measures have been introduced to ensure that they have reasonable representation in government. There is also official recognition of customary Hindu and Muslim law for those who prefer it.

In sympathy with world-wide trends there has been steady but modest privatisation, deregulation, and relaxation of censorship and liquor laws. 'Zebras' (zero base regulation areas), which are KwaNatal's version of enterprise zones, are now common throughout the country.

Cape Flats canton

Cape Flats canton is much like KwaNatal, except that the Presidency rotates for the time being between the two Reverends, Allan Hendrikse and Allan Boesak, and the official languages are Afrikaans, Xhosa and English. Cape Flats is regarded as a 'low tax, low intervention area' and gambling has been authorised in two casinos.

The only observers who view Cape Flats with any real interest are political analysts. This is because, contrary to general expectation, the differences between Afrikaners and Cape coloureds have evaporated, and the RANC-UDF (Cape) Party and the Labour Party work together in a way once thought inconceivable.

WPICHIER

Apart from occasional reminders of the past, there is such a prevailing atmosphere of normality that the most newsworthy events this year have been the disqualification of the first three runners in the Kuilsrivier Marathon and the burglary at Elseby's Pannekoek Paleis. Occasionally demonstrations are organised by members of a radical Trotskyist movement, most of whom are coloured students and factory workers.

Four categories

The governments of most of the other cantons fall into one of four basic categories. Many are ruled by a moderate multiracial alliance, often including members of the old NP, NRP, PFP, Inkatha, UDF and Sofasonke parties as well as members of the new Liberal and Reformed ANC (RANC) parties. The NP, Inkatha and RANC are the only parties represented in all cantons.

In a second group of cantons, predominantly black parties or alliances have adopted socialist policies which have precluded any chance of a significant non-black following. Despite fears to the contrary, Indians, coloureds and whites in these cantons are adequately protected by the constitution.

In a surprisingly large number of cantons the major parties are no longer characterised by race. Most of these have a two-party system, and candidates and officials are generally appointed on merit, regardless of race. As it happens, most politicians are black, many of the senior officials under them are white, and the balance of the civil service has much the same ethnic mix as the private sector.

There is also a fourth group of cantons with black nationalist governments. Until the Sunset Clause lapsed these governments practised discrimination in favour of blacks. They still preach voluntary affirmative action, but most are beginning to moderate their policies as fewer and fewer blacks feel any need for special programmes to assist them.

Now let us turn to the cantons which have been the subject of special interest and study amongst political scientists, sociologists, economists and jurists, not to mention the general public, all around the world.

These cantons have shown South Africa and the world that one country can contain political, economic and social systems which differ from one another in almost every respect.

Workers' Paradise

Workers' Paradise canton is situated on the Vaal Triangle and has a population of about a million. Soon after chartering, the Marxist Alliance came to power. This was a coalition of the largely black Azapo Youth Party, the coloured Trotsky Party, Die Radikale Werkersparty (mostly Afrikaans unskilled and semi-skilled labourers) and the Communist Party (a small multiracial party led by academics). Even though these parties participated in what they denounced as 'the system', the Security Police revealed that some of them had connections with the external wing of the Pan African Congress, which continued fighting for a few years because it maintained that the new constitution and Bill of Rights entrenched 'bourgeois values'.

The Marxist Alliance soon discovered that the only constraints it faced were the entrenched 'freedom of movement' and 'property rights' clauses in the Bill of Rights. These prevented the Alliance from freely expropriating land and businesses, and it was not able to create a 'Haak en Steek Curtain', which some members would have liked. Also, because the entire country is a common customs and monetary area, it could not prevent people from taking their assets and leaving. Some people did leave, but many others, especially members of the emergent radical union movement, relocated there.

The Marxist Alliance lost no time in introducing pure communism. Surprisingly, this proved easier for the Alliance than for its counterparts in the eastern block, who have the COMECON customs union to contend with and are hamstrung by a conservative old guard which won't give real freedom to worker co-operatives and communes.

Sweeping reforms stunned observers. The canton adopted the name of 'Workers Paradise', and the main towns became Maoville and Machelstad. Everyone was issued with a copy of Mao's little red book. Many black citizens donated their redistribution compensation cheques to a government fund; this money was added to revenue gained from heavy taxes and used to buy out all private enterprise. Factories were handed over to worker co-operatives and farms were communalised. Civil servants took over the shops. Advertisements, billboards and neon signs were ripped down, and all publications other than those issued or approved by the party propaganda office were banned.

When the Alliance was formed some hard bargains had to be driven. At the insistence of Azapo Youth and the Radikale Werkers, there had to be some segregated facilities, such as public toilets, because they refused to mix with each other socially. Since the constitution specifies that governments must be colour-blind, the problem was solved by turning segregated facilities over to the Public Workers Co-operative

which is controlled by COWPU, the Council of Workers' Paradise Unions, to which all unions must affiliate. The critics are dumbfounded. How could such blatant vestiges of apartheid survive in a marxist canton!

'This is quite different,' explained the Quality of Equality Commissar. 'This is a "people's policy", it is not imposed by white fascists. As far back as the early 1980s many of us in Azapo and Cosas would have nothing to do with whites.'

The government of Workers' Paradise has found that the canton system offers a unique benefit: there are no dissidents, counter-revolutionaries or reactionaries. They have all left. That is why Workers' Paradise has become what it claims is the purest example of communism in the world.

It boasts of a completely egalitarian wealth distribution. The President never fails to claim that there is no unemployment, that class has been eliminated, and that nowhere else are workers so thoroughly in control of their own destiny.

Encouraged by this, all the revolutionary socialists who had left South Africa, except for a handful of die-hards, have returned. Only two small terrorist groups continue to cause trouble from time to time: the all-white Herstigte Blanke Weermag (HBW), which wants the restoration of classical Verwoerdian apartheid throughout South Africa, and Black Mamba, a regrouping of black guerilla movements which decided to carry on fighting for an unconditional handover of all of South Africa and SWA-Namibia.

Perhaps the most remarkable thing about Workers' Paradise is that the state is showing signs of 'withering away' since devolution of power to workers *in situ* has been accompanied by a reduction of civil servants directly employed by the canton government.

The canton is the subject of interminable debate amongst academics. Critics point to low growth, the underground economy and corruption. Others ask, what does it matter? Everyone is happy and no one has to live there. In fact the National Happiness Index (NHI) for the whole of South Africa, compiled by the Quality of Life Research Council (Qualrec) is at an all-time high and rising in Workers' Paradise.

Witwaterberg

Predictably, the process of reform produced a radical white racist reaction, the HBW military wing. In the late '80s it had about one million followers, half of whom wanted to live in a white supremacist canton. The remainder were willing to live in multiracial conservative cantons with strict censorship, Christian national schools and private 'whites only' clubs and social amenities in their communities.

All of them contributed generously to the Wit Volk Fonds (WVF), a nation-wide body that raised funds to finance segregated facilities. One of its major projects is to buy all the land in certain cantons and then to use private property rights to exclude blacks. Everyone was surprised how many blacks contributed to the WVF.

Witwaterberg is South Africa's notorious radical white separatist canton. When the new constitution was introduced, Witwaterberg had a small black majority, but the WVF undertook a successful campaign to persuade most white employers and landowners to replace many of their black employees with whites, and to increase mechanisation.

Farmers bought mechanised milking machines. Fast food outlets introduced disposable utensils so that they no longer needed black staff to do the washing. Manufacturers replaced many black labourers with machines operated by highly skilled white workers. White bus drivers and cash till operators were employed. Black tenants, such as attorney Gabriel Makopondo, who had become an accepted member of the local fraternity, were given notice on their leases. All leases in the black 'lokasie' were terminated.

One of the most controversial developments in Witwaterberg was the mass dismissal of black workers. Most households had had a black gardener and a maid who lived, often with their families, in 'servants' quarters' adjoining their employers' houses. After considerable social pressure all 'domestics' were laid off.

This measure sparked a curious debate in labour circles. The Domestic Employees' Rights Association (DERA), with the active support of the emergent union movement, had been a vociferous campaigner against the 'exploitation' of domestic workers since the early 1980s. Many abuses had been exposed by its dedicated President, Ethel van der Merwitz. DERA stood for a national minimum wage and improved working conditions. No one was opposed to the idea of higher wages and good conditions, but some people argued that they might increase unemployment and thought that 'a low wage was better than no wage'.

Prior to the lay-off of black workers in Witwaterberg, Ms Van der Merwitz exposed Witwaterberg whites on national TV as archetypal bigots, exploiters and racists. Black workers there had the worst working conditions, the poorest housing and the lowest wages. She cited one family that paid its maid only R40 a month, an amount which she showed was less than the family spent on one meal at Graaf's Boere Brunch every Thursday on the 'maid's night off'. When the Witwaterberg lay-off campaign began, DERA's Council was irreparably split down the middle. The black lay-off campaign was succeeding, and might spread to other areas. Thousands of blacks could lose their jobs. How should DERA react? Should it call for all these blacks to be kept on under the intolerable working conditions which it had condemned? Should it demand that black employees not only be kept on but also paid much more?

Witwaterberg's President, Mr Staal Noordhuis, announced triumphantly that DERA should rejoice, since Witwaterberg would 'no longer exploit blacks'.

Witwaterberg, unlike the few other white majority cantons, had no desire to reach an accommodation with its people of colour. 'The Bible is clear,' insisted President Noordhuis, 'we were created differently for a reason. Whites were destined to be the custodians of blacks, just as parents are of children, and blacks are to be the drawers of water and hewers of wood.' He was stoically self-righteous in the face of lampooning and criticism, and became a folk hero in his little canton which claimed to be the only place ever to achieve true apartheid.

By December 1997, when the sunset clause in the constitution lapsed, all the public and private facilities, all the land and all the houses in Witwaterberg were owned by whites. Now the only blacks to be found in the canton are daily commuters who are prepared to put up with

racism because they are so highly paid.

The blacks who were laid off soon found jobs in the rapidly expanding industrial sectors of other cantons.

'Servants' quarters' have become garden flats for whites who moved into Witwaterberg. The old 'black locations' have been converted into quaint 'Chelsified' white lower-income areas.

Occasionally even to this day there are unpleasant incidents, such as when 'Bullfight' Nokokosi, as he was known to his friends, insisted upon being served at Graaf's Boere Brunch. Or when President Noordhuis' nephew, nicknamed 'Donderstorm' in recognition of his fearsome tactics on the rugby field, took after his gardener with a sjambok for pulling out his treasured waterblommetjies instead of khakibos weeds.

But most of Witwaterberg's critics concede that it has become a peaceful, quite harmless canton with a rustic character all its own. The few unfortunate incidents that occur are only newsworthy because they take place in Witwaterberg. One sociologist has observed that there are far fewer racial incidents in Witwaterberg than in Washington DC.

Harrismith — QwaQwa (H-Q)

No one could have predicted the incredible events that unfolded in Harrismith-QwaQwa, culminating in a happy ending with a unique twist.

In H-Q blacks outnumber whites by 10:1. Most blacks live in the area that used to be the Basotho-QwaQwa homeland in the southeast corner of the old Free State province, where H-Q borders on Lesotho and KwaNatal.

After delimitation, Paramount Chief Mopedi was elected canton President in a landslide victory. White and black 'radical' candidates were routed: support for traditional chiefs was much more widespread than modernists had bargained for.

Black radicals were enraged and a mood of despair descended on white nationalists. Farmers started neglecting their fields, businesses were 'for sale' and property values plummeted. 'Women wept quietly in the kitchens and men worked silently in the fields; parliament was in session and they feared that no man's property was safe.' Township unrest increased.

But Chief Mopedi had no malicious ambitions. He wanted no more than official recognition of his tribal laws and customs and freedom and independence for all blacks.

Even though his people had suffered centuries of discrimination, he harboured no desire for revenge. The first thing Chief Mopedi did after becoming president was to call a canton convention at his tribal head-quarters. His charisma and statesmanlike qualities were admired by onlookers everywhere. At the convention he announced his new policy of 'parallelism', and explained that there would be no interference by his government with the local affairs of whites or urban blacks. The erstwhile QwaQwa homeland would become the QwaQwa tribal cantonette in which tribal law would apply.

In the black townships each person could choose whether to fall under the tribal system or the European system. In white areas there would be no 'Africanisation' policy. Whites who wanted separate private facilities would not be discouraged, nor would blacks be deprived of their blacks-only football league.

The political system he introduced was similar in many respects to that which had operated in the 'tri-cameral parliamentary system' between 1985 and cantonisation. In his own party, he appointed a White Affairs Sub-committee, whose main task was to ensure that the whites' traditional way of life would not be unduly disturbed under black rule. Almost overnight property values soared above their pre-referendum levels. Harrismith-QwaQwa is now booming again. One filling station still has segregated toilets, and the Harrismith Jukskei Club admits only whites. No 'colonial era' names have been changed, except that the canton has come to be known as 'H-Q'.

Today H-Q seems like a strange anachronism. To all outward appearances not a great deal has changed since the 1980s — yet there is one very big difference: there is harmony and prosperity in H-Q and the segregation that survives offends almost no one.

Cisbo

The last of South Africa's four most unusual cantons, the free market Ciskei-Border canton, now called Cisbo, has become a *cause célèbre* for libertarians worldwide. During his Ciskei independence speech in 1981, President Sebe, now retired, announced that Ciskei was to become the 'Hong Kong of Africa'. He sometimes referred to Ciskei as the 'Switzerland of Africa in the making'. He could not then have had any idea that Ciskei and the Border Region would one day combine to form a canton much like those in Switzerland. On the contrary, independence was working so well for Ciskei that Sebe's government steadfastly resisted all efforts to reincorporate during cantonisation.

Between 1984 and 1987, Ciskei's free market reforms were introduced in earnest. They included sweeping deregulation, the privatisation of tribal land, and low taxes which encouraged the establishment of many new businesses and industries. By 1990 Ciskei was booming. A respected American business journal called it 'Africa's first economic miracle' — a far cry indeed from the gloom and doom depicted in the celebrated 1980 BBC documentary 'Last Grave at Dimbaza'.

Meanwhile, whites in the Border Region (between Ciskei and Transkei) had lobbied since the late 1970s to become a 'free trade zone' or 'co-prosperity zone'. Soon after the five cantons in the Border Region had received their Charters, they formed a joint Co-prosperity Zone Authority (COZA), and became known as the COZA (pronounced 'Xhosa') group of cantons. They had learnt much from their close proximity to Ciskei, and adopted similar laissez-faire policies. The serious 'black spot problem' which they had experienced prior to cantonisation was solved automatically when blacks in these settlements had freedom of movement and freehold title, and the right to go into business.

Inevitably there were moves for a closer alliance with Ciskei. However, Ciskei was still an independent country, although not recognised by the UN. Since the cantons had no power regarding foreign affairs, it was unconstitutional for the COZA cantons to negotiate with Ciskei. This led to a series of court actions and top-level debates called the Frontier Cases.

221

Most cantons, having black governments committed to the eradication of all vestiges of apartheid, wanted to force Ciskei to reincorporate. The COZA cantons tried to secede but could not get a sufficient majority in the referendum.

Time passed and emotions subsided and then, when it was satisfied that it had nothing to lose, Ciskei proposed formal amalgamation with South Africa, subject to the creation of one large canton, the Cisbo canton, covering the entire area between the Great Fish River and Transkei.

At the formal signing ceremony President Sebe announced his retirement. He said that he had always advocated the restoration of all his people's traditional territory to them and that he had always wanted a confederation of states, which was what the new arrangement amounted to. He had fulfilled his dreams of freedom, independence, democracy and equality for his people, and high growth, development and enduring peace.

Cisbo flourished, and became a libertarian mecca. Not only did its economy become the freest on earth, but other radical deregulations occurred. As in some US states and Swiss cantons, dagga (marijuana), pornography, prostitution and homosexuality were decriminalised. The coastal resort of Pleasure Bay grew into a mini-Monaco, with over

twenty independent casinos, two privately owned deep-sea yacht basins and several film production houses. It boasts deep-sea fishing, parachuting, water skiing, oriental pleasure palaces, countless 'extravaganzas', stuntmen, boxing championships, golf and much more. An incredible 50 000 new jobs have been created there alone. Cisbo's Pleasure Bay is now the world's most popular playground.

As always, success attracts criticism. Conservatives and socialists alike charge that Cisbo is causing unemployment elsewhere by attracting a disproportionate amount of investment. They have also accused it of moral decadence. On this one issue several otherwise irreconcilable groups are united. Cisbo's numbered bank accounts are suspected of being a haven for 'laundered' money.

We must remind you that Workers' Paradise, Witwaterberg, H-Q and Cisbo are so atypical that there is constant talk of threatening them with expulsion. Many people feel that there is a point at which a canton becomes so deviant as to be intolerable. There is growing support within Cisbo for secession on the grounds that membership of the South African customs and monetary area is inconsistent with the otherwise laissez-faire policy. Even so, as we go to press, we are pleased to say that this is all still just talk. There will never be a time when everyone is satisfied.

What is certain, though, is that 'South Africa's problems', as they used to be called around the world, have been solved. All sanctions were lifted by 1990; South African athletes won 13 gold medals at the '96 Lusaka Olympics; and Mandela, Botha, Van Zyl Slabbert, Buthelezi, Treurnicht, Tambo, Motlana and Terreblanche have all become Presidents — of their own cantons.

Perhaps the last word should go to UN Secretary-General Artofon Glalkis. When he reported to the General Assembly after his second fact-finding mission to South Africa last April, he made this historic statement:

> 'The mistake we all made was to believe that a single political system would solve South Africa's problems. But the solution proved to be many different systems working simultaneously. We thought there should be one popular leader, but now there are many popular leaders working side by side.
>
> 'We thought a demagogue would preside over central government. Now a relatively unknown person does so. We demanded one-man-one-vote in a unitary state. South Africa chose one-man-many-votes in a cantonised state.
>
> 'We wanted single citizenship for all South Africans. Now they

each have three citizenships — of their country, their canton and their community.

'My predecessor said it took us too long to suspend South Africa from the General Assembly. I say it has taken us too long to readmit her.

'With her new-found diversity added to her heterogeneity, resources, beauty and history, South Africa has truly become "the world within one country".'

Notes

Terminology

In a country which is characterised by racial dissension words describing racial groups and government institutions quickly develop different connotations for different people. Consequently, it is almost impossible to avoid offending someone no matter what terminology is used. We have used the words which are most commonly used in South Africa and which we judged as least likely to cause confusion, and acceptable to most people.

1. BLACK SOUTH AFRICANS : THEIR RISE AND FALL

In this chapter we have drawn a great deal of information from Colin Bundy's book *The Rise & Fall of the South African Peasantry*. This meticulously researched work provides a fascinating account of nineteenth century black farming and we recommend it highly.

1. Wilson, Monica and Leonard Thompson, Eds. *A History of South Africa to 1870* (Cape Town: David Philip, 1982) p 123.
2. Bundy, Colin. *The Rise & Fall of the South African Peasantry* (London: Heinemann, 1979) p 33.
3. *ibid*, p 52.
   There is no precise way of calculating the present-day equivalent of currencies at various times in history. During the nineteenth century the value of the pound did not fluctuate a great deal. A conservative rule of thumb estimate is that £1 in the nineteenth century is equal to approximately R20 in 1986. We have provided rough estimates of present-day equivalents for the convenience of lay readers.
4. *ibid*, p 54.
5. *ibid*, p 71.
6. Houghton, D Hobart & Jenifer Dagut. *Source Material on the South African Economy*, Vol. One, 1860-1870 (Cape Town: Oxford University Press) pp 201-219.

7. Bundy, *op cit*, p 75.
8. *ibid*, p 77.
9. *ibid*, p 161.
10. *ibid*, p 141.
11. *ibid*, p 114.
12. *ibid*, p 136.
13. *ibid*, p 139.
14. *ibid*, p 116.
15. *ibid*, p 174.
16. *ibid*, p 192.

2. THE RISE OF AFRIKANERDOM
1. Wilson and Thompson, *op cit*, p 187.
2. *ibid*, p 195.
3. Muller, C F J. *500 Years : A History of South Africa*. (Cape Town: Academica, 1981) p 99.
4. Walker, Eric. *A History of Southern Africa*. (London: Longmans, Green, 1959) p 199.
5. Muller, *op cit*, p 158.
6. De Klerk, W A. *The Puritans in Africa*. (Middlesex: Pelican, 1976) p 23.
7. Wilson and Thompson, *op cit*, p 365.

3. THE RISE OF APARTHEID
1. Böeseken, A J. *Slaves and Free Blacks at the Cape 1658-1700*. (Cape Town: Tafelberg, 1977) pp 45, 46.
2. Muller, *op cit*, p 361.
3. *ibid*, p 361.
4. O'Brien, Terence H. *Milner* (London: Constable, 1979).
5. Hutt, W H. *The Economics of the Colour Bar*. (London: André Deutsch, 1964) pp 62, 63.
6. Muller, *op cit*, p 415.
7. Houghton & Dagut, *op cit*, p 84.
8. Hutt, *op cit*, p 80.

8. THE REDISTRIBUTION OF WEALTH
1. McGrath, M D. *Racial Income Distribution in South Africa*. Natal University, 1977, and Nattrass, Jill. *Narrowing Wage Differentials and Income Distribution in South Africa*, 1977.

2. Adams, K A H. *Political Engineering*. Transactions of the SA Institute of Electrical Engineers, June 1979.
3. Tullock, Gordon. *Economics of Income Redistribution*. (Boston: Kluwer-Nijhoff Publishing, 1983) p 94.

9. AFFIRMATIVE ACTION : FASHIONABLE RACISM

1. *The Fairmont Papers*. Black Alternatives Conference, Dec 1980.

17. SOCIO-ECONOMIC SOLUTIONS

1. Friedrich Hayek, in a speech made during visit to South Africa in 1978.

APPENDIX I

Opinion surveys

Schlemmer's findings

In 1984 Lawrence Schlemmer of the Centre for Applied Social Sciences at the University of Natal conducted research into 'black industrial worker attitudes' towards political options, capitalism and investment.

His research team interviewed 551 black production workers ranging from 16 to 50+ years old, in Johannesburg, Durban-Pinetown, Port Elizabeth, East Rand, West Rand, Pretoria and the Vaal Triangle. Some 65% were lower semi-skilled and unskilled and 35% were higher semi-skilled and skilled.

Regarding political support his question was:

> 'Here is a list of organisations. Which one of these organisations do people like yourself support most?/Which other one do people like you support?'

The results were:

	Witwatersrand and Port Elizabeth 1st Choice	*Durban 1st Choice*
	%	%
ANC/Nelson Mandela	27	11
UDF	11	23
AZASO	1	1
AZAPO	5	1
Inkatha/Buthelezi	14	54
Sofasonke	15	6
Other — diverse	5	4
None	22	—

If these results are re-grouped according to how radical the groups represented are, the following picture emerges:

	PWV/PE	*DURBAN*
	%	%
Moderate (Ink/But/Sof/none/other)	56	64
Fairly radical (ANC/Mandela/UDF)	38	34
Radical (AZASO/AZAPO)	6	2

228

We have included 'none' and 'other' as moderate because most 'other' groups and community leaders are moderate, and Schlemmer assumes that there is no 'none' in Durban because they are absorbed into Inkatha, and that their counterparts elsewhere are probably moderates in a 'political vacuum'.

The 'resources of the greatest value' to blacks were regarded as:

	%
Skills training for job advancement	43
The franchise	19
A better education	16
Strong black leadership	10
Strong trade union	9
Strong political organisation	3

Only 3% saw the role of trade unions as 'working for political rights'; the vast majority saw them as a means of improving wages and working conditions.

Free enterprise vs socialism

Schlemmer's respondents were asked who should own factories and shops in a black-ruled country: 1) the government 2) black businessmen or 3) anyone who can be successful in business, not only black people. The third option was chosen by 60%.

Proportions in the sub-samples indicated that trade union members, 'radical' workers with high-school education and workers with experience in multinational corporations were substantially more likely to favour private enterprise. Groups least likely to see benefits in it were those in areas or companies with severe racial discrimination, those who were least skilled, and, to a lesser extent, those who had recently left school.

Schlemmer found that when various factors were taken into account, there was 'virtually no support among black workers' for total disinvestment.

Orkin's findings (1985)

Mark Orkin of the Community Agency for Social Enquiry conducted a survey into black attitudes to disinvestment which apparently differs dramatically from Schlemmer's in its results. However, if the results are interpreted according to the same criteria as Schlemmer's, they are very similar.

Orkin's survey had 800 respondents in ten major metropolitan areas.

229

Unfortunately, some of the questions are so misleading that the answers are not an accurate indication of anything.

According to the published 'overview' of the findings, 'more than three-quarters of respondents favour socialism over capitalism.' The question on which this conclusion is based (Question 9) asks:

> 'Suppose South Africa had the government of your choice. There are two main patterns how it should organise people's work, and the ownership of factories and businesses. Which view do you most support?
> — the capitalist pattern in which businesses are owned and run by private businessmen, for their own profit.   22%
> — the socialist pattern, in which workers have a say in the running of businesses, and share in the ownership and profits.
>   77%'

This question is phrased in such a way that the only surprise lies in how many respondents chose the 'capitalist' option! The definition of 'socialism' corresponds more to the West German capitalistic 'social market' economy than any dictionary definition of socialism.

The disinvestment question is inordinately long (225+ words) which frustrates the prospect of reliable responses. Also it links the three options offered with people and groups — for instance Bishop Tutu is listed as being in favour of restricted investment and Buthelezi, Oppenheimer, the government and other homeland leaders are lumped together to represent the pro-investment position. The ANC, PAC, UDF, AZAPO and some trade unions are listed as wanting no investment because it 'only help(s) to keep apartheid alive and exploit Blacks.'

Despite the lack of objectivity in the phraseology of the questions, the results were strikingly similar to Schlemmer's if properly interpreted.

They were as follows:

	Orkin %	Schlemmer %
Pro-investment	26 ⎫	75
	⎬ 75	
Conditionally pro-investment	49 ⎭	
Anti-investment	24	25
Don't know	1	—

Orkin adds the 49% who were conditionally against investment to the 24% who were definitely against and comes up with 73% against investment. However, the section which 49% of the respondents ticked says that 'foreign firms should not be allowed to invest here unless they actively pressure the government to end apartheid, and recognise the trade unions chosen by the workers.' Since virtually all foreign firms do meet with these requirements, we have put the 49% with the 26% in favour of investment.

The overview of Orkin's survey observes that 80% of respondents were in favour of 'one central government' but the only alternative offered to 'a unitary arrangement in which all *blacks* and whites together vote for their leaders' was 'a federal arrangement in which *Africans* are partly governed by homeland leaders, but also have some representation in central government' (our emphasis). Non-racial devolution, the most common form of democracy, was not offered.

When Orkin asked, 'Which leader or organisation would you most like to represent you in solving problems or grievances?,' the response was as follows:
Mandela and the ANC 31%; Buthelezi and Inkatha 8%; Bishop Tutu 16%; UDF 8%; 'other anti-investment organisations' 6%; P W Botha and government 5%; 'other pro-investment groups' 3%; other 3%: none 13%; don't know 8%.

Other surveys
Further conflicting results come from other surveys, presumably conducted among different groups of people and also affected by the attitudes of the researchers and the analysis of the results.

The December 6, 1985 issue of the *Financial Mail* cited a survey in which 7,5% of blacks chose P W Botha as their preferred leader.

The referenda which have been held amongst homeland blacks have indicated overwhelmingly moderate attitudes. For instance, the Ciskei referendum on independence was carried by a 90% + majority in a ±90% turnout. (Critics alleged that the results were rigged.) Most of the homelands have had high turnouts at the polls and landslide victories for the ruling party.

In 1983 the Louw Commission undertook black opinion surveys (not yet published) in Ciskei and the Border Region.

Questions were aimed at avoiding confusion, and care was taken to minimise the 'lie factor'.

For example, there was a multiple choice question regarding who should be allowed to do business in Ciskei. Respondents could answer 'Yes' or 'No' to any of the alternatives: Nobody, Ciskeians, Transkeians, Other Blacks, Afrikaners, English, Indians, Coloureds, Everybody. 'Nobody' was rejected by 99%, so they were all in favour of some private enterprise. 'Everybody' was endorsed by 78,2%.

Like these, many other answers reflected an overwhelming endorsement of the free market position on *specific* policy, even though the same people did not necessarily endorse *generalised* propositions regarding 'free enterprise'.

For instance, although 22% said they favoured socialism, and 7% marxism:

77% opposed wage control
71% supported private urban land ownership
85% supported private rural land ownership
97% supported the right to go into business
84% supported the right to form trade unions.

There was a great deal of further evidence to show that specific questions get 'moderate' answers, while general or ideological questions elicit a good number of (though not a majority of) radical answers.

Schlemmer's and Orkin's studies reveal a minority of radicalised blacks and they were conducted among urban blacks. Rural and small town blacks are generally considered to be 'traditional' in their attitudes in that they have strong tribal loyalty.

Many observers nonetheless believe that Mandela has become such a folk hero, and the ANC so much a symbol of 'the black liberation struggle', that they would win an overwhelming majority in, at least, a first election. It may well be true that they would receive more support than opinion polls indicate. However, 28% of the national population is non-black, which means (assuming that not many non-blacks would vote for them) that the ANC would need to win 70% of the black vote in order to gain 50% of the national vote, which seems highly unlikely by any analysis. It should also be remembered that most blacks, especially rural blacks, have a strong ethnic consciousness. Neither Zulus, Sothos, Xhosas nor any of the other main black groups are likely to vote in substantial numbers for a leader from a group other than their own. This is not a fashionable view, but it is nonetheless true.

Add to this the fact that 4-6 million blacks are followers of the Zion Christian Church which has a moderate policy and leader, and we are led inexorably to the conclusion that most blacks would support moderate leaders, and that no single group has a chance of a clear majority.

Without referenda there is the risk and likelihood, which we have discussed, that politicians will act contrary to their voters' wishes. However, given referenda, regardless of who is elected, all the evidence indicates that the vast majority of blacks will support freehold title, free trade and free competition. The system we recommend is not dependent on the outcome of one election but many elections and referenda, regarding many policies, candidates, parties and presidents.

All things considered, it seems clear that most South African blacks prefer free market economic policies and peaceful reform. A large number of blacks in the 'radicalised' urban areas support fairly radical leaders and organisations, but espouse moderate policies.

White attitudes
The results of white opinion polls indicate that most whites accept that 'power-sharing with blacks is inevitable'.

	All whites %	Afrikaners %	English %
Yes	67,3	59,1	81,6
Neutral	17,8	20,4	13,4
No	14,9	20,5	5,0

(*Rapport*, November 1985)

APPENDIX II

Switzerland's newest canton, Jura, is a particularly good example of how minority domination can be avoided in a canton system.

For nine centuries Jura was an autonomous unit of the Holy Roman Empire, but in the course of the nineteenth century it was split between France and the Swiss canton of Bern.

The official language of Swiss cantons and communities is traditionally the language spoken by the majority of the population. Occasionally there are two official languages, but this was not the case in German-dominated Bern. For various reasons an increasingly strong French-Juran separatist movement emerged.

The Bern government always protested that it spent more on each Juran (Jurans constituted 7% of the Bern population) than on any other citizen, and that they were better off than the average French-Swiss citizen. However, 'what was really at stake was the identity and self-respect of the Jura.'

The separatists did not want handouts, they wanted 'the power to transform their economy so that it needed no subsidy' by adopting a liberal constitution and liberal economic and social policies. The Bern government considered the idea 'unthinkable', but by Swiss law, the matter could be decided by the Jurans alone.

Amongst the Jurans there was also a unionist movement that wanted to stay with Bern. To the ultra-democratic Swiss, this meant there should not be a simple majority referendum, but various referenda: one for Jura as a whole, one for each border community, and one for each district in which 20% of the electorate petitioned for it. Thus even within Jura, there could be no majority domination. If the separatists were a minority in Jura as a whole, they could still get a new canton in those parts of Jura where they were the majority.

To gain support for unionism, the Bern government held its own referendum in which an overwhelming majority voted in favour of granting Jura 'self-determination', but not independence. However, in 1974, the separatists gained a small majority (54,2%) in one of the highest polls in Swiss history (91,8%) thus achieving their goal.

In 1975, three French border districts voted to opt out of Jura, but in subsequent community referenda, eight border communities voted for the new canton and one for Bern.

Jura was to become independent but this did not mean that it would automatically become a member of the Swiss confederation. In 1978 there was a national referendum in which the majority of Swiss citizens voted to admit Jura as an additional Swiss canton.

Bibliography

Adams, K A H. *Political Engineering*. Transactions of the S A Institute of Electrical Engineers, June 1979.

Ashworth, Georgina, Ed. *World Minorities in the Eighties*. Middlesex: Quartermaine House, 1980.

100 Basiese dokumente by die studie van die Suid-Afrikaanse geskiedenis 1648-1961. Johannesburg: Nasou Beperk, 1980.

Bauer, P T. *Equality, the Third World and Economic Delusion*. London: Weidenfeld and Nicolson, 1981.

Becker, Gary S. *The Economics of Discrimination*. Chicago & London: University of Chicago Press, 1971.

Beckett, Denis. *Permanent Peace*. Johannesburg: Saga Press, 1985.

Berman, Harold J. *Justice in the USSR*. Cambridge, Massachusetts: Harvard University Press, 1963.

Böeseken, A J. *Slaves and Free Blacks at the Cape 1658-1700*. Cape Town: Tafelberg, 1977.

Bundy, Colin. *The Rise & Fall of the South African Peasantry*. London: Heinemann, 1979.

Bulletin of Statistics, June 1975. Pretoria: Department of Statistics.

Buthelezi, M Gatsha. *Power is Ours*. New York: Books in Focus, 1979.

Cranston, M. *What are Human Rights*. London: Bodley, 1973.

Davenport, T R H. *South Africa: A Modern History*. Johannesburg: Macmillan S A, 1978.

Davenport, T R H and Hunt, K S. *The Right to the Land*. Cape Town: David Phillip, 1974.

De Klerk, W A. *The Puritans in Africa*. Middlesex: Pelican, 1976.

Depoliticising South Africa. Papers and proceedings of 1984 Free Market Foundation Congress. Pretoria.

Elphick, Richard and Hermann Giliomee, Ed. *The Shaping of South African Society, 1652-1820*. Cape Town: Longman, 1979.

Faith, Nicholas. *Safety in Numbers*. London: Hamish Hamilton, 1984.

The Fairmont Papers. Black Alternatives Conference, December 1980. San Francisco: Institute for Contemporary Studies, 1981.

Friedman, David. *The Machinery of Freedom*. New York: Arlington House, 1978.

The Hammond Almanac, 1980. Maplewood: Hammond Almanac Inc.

Hayek, Friedrich A. *The Constitution of Liberty.* Chicago: Henry Regnery, 1972.

Hayek, Friedrich A. *Law, Legislation and Liberty.* Chicago: University of Chicago Press, 1973.

Heldman, D C, Bennett, J T and Johnson, M H. *Deregulating Labour Relations.* Dallas: Fisher, 1981.

Hollyer, Beatrice. *Targets of Contrast. Frontline:* Vol 5 No 5, April 1985.

Houghton, D Hobart & Jenifer Dagut. *Source Material on the South African Economy,* Vols I-III. Cape Town: Oxford University Press 1972/3.

Hutt, W H. *The Economics of the Colour Bar.* London: André Deutsch, 1964.

Indicator South Africa. Vol 3 No 1. Winter, 1985. Centre for Applied Social Sciences, University of Natal.

Innes, Duncan. *The Real World of the Left. Frontline:* Vol 5 No 8, August 1985.

Kantor, B and Rees, D. *South African Economic Issues.* Johannesburg: Juta, 1982.

Malherbe, E G. *Education in South Africa, 1652-1922.* Cape Town: Juta, 1925.

Markman, T. *Transport Policy.* Johannesburg: Free Market Foundation, 1984.

McGrath, M D. *Racial Income Distribution in South Africa.* Interim Research Report No 2, Dept of Economics, Natal University, 1977.

Mises, Ludwig von. *Human Action: A Treatise on Economics.* Chicago: Contemporary Books, Inc. 3rd Revised Edition, 1966.

Mises, Ludwig von. *Planning for Freedom.* Illinois: Libertarian Press, 1980.

Muller, C F J. Ed. *500 Years: A History of South Africa.* Cape Town: Academica, 1981.

Nattrass, Jill: *Narrowing Wage Differentials and Income Distribution in South Africa. S A Journal of Economics,* Vol 45(4) 1977.

Noble, John. *The Cape and South Africa Official Handbook.* Cape Town: Juta, 1878.

Nozzik, Robert. *Anarchy, State and Utopia.* New York: Basic Books, 1974.

O'Brien, Terence H. *Milner.* London: Constable, 1979.

Occupational Licensing and the Supply of Non-Professional Labour. Manpower Monograph No 11. Washington, D C: Department of Labour, 1969.

Orkin, Mark. *Black Attitudes to Disinvestment: The Real Story.* Opinion Survey in conjunction with the Institute for Black Research.

Rabushka, Alvin. *A Theory of Racial Harmony.* South Carolina: University of South Carolina Press, 1974.

Race Relations Survey, Vol 38 1984. Johannesburg: S A Institute of Race Relations, 1985.

Rothbard, Murray. *Conceived in Liberty, Vols I-IV,* New Rochelle: Arlington House, 1975.

Rothbard, Murray. *The Ethics of Liberty.* Atlantic Highlands: Humanities Press, 1982.

Rothbard, Murray. *Man, Economy & State.* Los Angeles: Nash Publishing, 1970.

S A Reserve Bank Quarterly Bulletin, Sept 1975.

Schlemmer, Lawrence. *Black Worker Attitudes.* Indicator Project, Centre for Applied Social Sciences, Durban, 1984.

Smith, Edward Conrad. *The Constitution of the United States.* New York: Barnes & Noble, 1979.

The South African Society: Realities and Future Prospects. Pretoria: HSRC, 1985.

Sowell, Thomas, *Race and Economics.* New York: David McKay, 1975.

Swart, Prof N J, Chairman. *Report of the Commission of Inquiry into the Economic Development of the Republic of Ciskei.* Ciskei: Office of the Presidency, 1983.

Templeton, Kenneth S, Ed. *The Politicization of Society.* Indianapolis: Liberty Press, 1979.

Thomas, Wolfgang H. *Labour Perspectives on South Africa.* Cape Town: David Philip, 1974.

Trade Union Directory, 1983-84. Johannesburg: TUCSA.

Tullock, Gordon. *Economics of Income Redistribution.* Boston: Kluwer-Nijhoff Publishing, 1983.

Walker, Eric. *A History of Southern Africa.* London: Longmans, Green, 3rd Edition, 1959.

Whittington, G W and J B McI Daniel. *Problems of Land Tenure and Ownership in Swaziland.* (Reprinted from *Environment and Land Use in Africa*) London: Methuen & Co Ltd.

Wilson, Monica & Leonard Thompson, Ed. *A History of South Africa to 1870.* Cape Town: David Philip, 1982.

Williams, Walter E. *The State against Blacks.* New York: McGraw-Hill, 1982.

Williams, Walter E. *America: A Minority Viewpoint.* Stanford: Hoover Institution Press, 1982.

Groundswell

There is one thing stronger than all the armies in the world: And that is an idea whose time has come — VICTOR HUGO.

If you believe, like thousands of South Africans, that a canton system of government deserves further study and public attention, there is something you can do.

Arising out of the same sense of frustration that spawned this book, a movement dedicated to 'successful' change has been formed... GROUNDSWELL. Its aim is to create a climate in which 'THE SOLUTION' can become reality.

GROUNDSWELL is non-party political, non-racial, and run on non-profit lines, by people who have a vested interest in the dynamic future of the country.

If you are interested in being part of 'successful' change, write to: GROUNDSWELL, P. O. Box 70076, BRYANSTON 2021.